Facing Evil

Nashville
Public Library
Foundation

*This book
made possible
through generous gifts
to the
Nashville Public Library
Foundation Book Fund*

FACING EVIL

John Kekes

PRINCETON UNIVERSITY PRESS

PRINCETON, NEW JERSEY

Library of Congress-in-Publication Data

Kekes, John.
Facing evil / John Kekes.
Includes bibliographical references.
1. Good and evil. 2 Character. I. Title.
BJ1401.K43   1991   170—dc20   90-32001

ISBN 0-691-07370-8
ISBN 0-691-02095-7 (pbk.)

This book has been composed in Linotron Baskerville

Princeton University books Press are printed on acid-free paper
and meet the guidelines for permanence and durability of the
Committee on Production Guidelines for Book Longevity of the
Council on Library Resources

Printed in the United States of America

10   9   8   7   6   5   4   3   2

For J.Y.K.

Contents

Acknowledgments

MORALITY has a good-approximating and an evil-avoiding aspect. In this book, I consider its evil-avoiding aspect. In two previous books, *The Examined Life* and *Moral Tradition and Individuality*, I concentrated on the good-approximating aspect. Each of these books aims to present a self-contained view, but since the two aspects of morality are not sharply separable, I had to cover again some ground here that was first covered in the previous two books. In chapters 1, 5, and 10 I use some ideas from chapters 10, 2, and 5, respectively, of *Moral Tradition and Individuality*, and in chapter 11 I use some ideas from chapters 6 and 1 of *The Examined Life*.

I also draw on articles I published in various journals: in chapter 1, "What Makes Lives Good?" *Philosophy and Phenomenological Research* 48 (1988): 655–68; in chapter 6, "Human Worth and Moral Merit," *Public Affairs Quarterly* 2 (1988): 53–68; in chapter 7, "Understanding Evil," *American Philosophical Quarterly* 25 (1988): 13–24; and in chapter 9, "Moral Intuition," *American Philosophical Quarterly* 23 (1986): 83–93. I am grateful to the editors and publishers of these journals for allowing me to use parts of these articles in the present book.

Joel Kupperman, Robert Louden, David Norton, and Evan Simpson read the entire manuscript and gave me the benefit of their extremely helpful criticisms; I have also been helped by Josiah Gould, Wallace Matson, and Nicholas Rescher in conversation and correspondence. I gratefully acknowledge their help.

It would have taken much longer to complete this work if Francine Frank, dean of the College of Humanities and Fine Arts of my university, the State University of New York at Albany, had not helped with arranging for me several leaves so that I could concentrate on research. I am grateful for her support.

It is a lamentable fact that authors often have just cause to complain about their publishers. I am especially grateful, therefore, to Princeton University Press for handling the publication of this book, and of the previous one, in a way that I could not improve. I want to thank two of my editors in particular: Frank Hunt, whose efficiency, tact, and helpfulness were all that an author could wish for, and Beth Gianfagna who has by now seen three of my books through the many stages of production. It has been a pleasure to work with her, and I thank her for the scrupulous attention to detail and good humor that made the process of transforming the manuscript into a book so much less onerous.

I dedicate this book, as all the others, to my wife, Jean Y. Kekes, whose philosophical, literary, and private help were essential to its completion.

Facing Evil

Introduction

THIS BOOK is about a fundamental problem, and it proposes a response to it. The problem is evil, and it is a problem because it jeopardizes our aspirations to live good lives. The response to it is a particular conception of morality, which I call *character-morality*. Unlike other currently available conceptions, character-morality is centrally concerned with how we should respond to evil. My aim is to develop character-morality and to show some of the far-reaching implications it has for our moral sensibility and conduct.

Evil is not an inviting subject. Its contemplation tends to evoke pity, anger, fear, and the suspicion that our interest in it may be motivated by pleasure in the misfortune of others, search for titillation, or a detached, clinical, inhumane curiosity. Yet the unpleasantness of the emotions evil provokes and the possibility that unworthy motives may lead us to focus on it should not deter us. For evil is a formidable obstacle to human well-being, and if we care about humanity, we must face evil.

Widespread evil is a sad fact of life. We see it in the reigns of Stalin and Hitler; in the countless people tortured in many countries throughout the world; in the massacres of Armenians, Cambodians, Gypsies, Indonesians, Jews, and kulaks; in violent crime involving murder, rape, and battery; in the killing and maiming of soldiers and civilians in many wars we have waged; and in millions being brutalized by poverty, disease, and starvation.

However, we must not allow our horror of all this to cloud our judgment. For suffering may actually be preferred if it is the best way to avoid even greater suffering. Furthermore, people may suffer because they live foolish, risky, or vicious lives and the consequences catch up with them. The problem is that much suffering is undeserved. Pain, accident, injustice, crime, war, and persecution often claim innocent victims. And it also happens that even when there is some culpability, the consequent suffering is disproportionately great, revealing a marked discrepancy between what people deserve and what they get. Nor is the problem exhausted by undeserved suffering, because people are often harmed, although they do not suffer. They may feel anger, cynicism, or resignation, not pain; or they may not realize that they have been harmed, because they are ignorant, brutalized, or deceived. Thus, the problem is not merely undeserved suffering but a broader one of undeserved harm.

I shall take evil to be undeserved harm inflicted on human beings. Much more needs to be said to make this idea precise, but the formula—*evil as undeserved harm*—will serve as a beginning. The problem, then, is the prevalence of evil. It cries out for an explanation, outrages our sense of justice, makes us wonder about the prospects for humanity, causes us to fear for ourselves and for those we love, and naturally compels us to seek a remedy or at least amelioration.

Evil has long preoccupied Christian theologians and their critics: if God has the perfections attributed to him, how then can evil exist? But the Christian formulation of the problem is only a special case of the more general metaphysical question about the apparent inconsistency between the scheme of things being good and the lamentable fact that human beings often suffer undeserved harm.[1] There are a number of long-standing answers, but it is not my purpose to explore this well-trodden territory, because I do not accept the underlying assumption that the scheme of things is good. It is not that I suppose instead that it is evil or a mixture of good and evil parts. Rather, reality, or the cosmos, or whatever we want to call it, has moral qualities only insofar as it actually or potentially affects human beings, or, possibly, sentient beings. Thus, I shall be concerned not with the traditional religious or metaphysical problem of evil but with the *secular problem of evil*.[2]

It has become fashionable to talk about the banality of evil.[3] It is generally meant by this phrase that a lot of undeserved harm is caused by an almost casual, unthinking, low-grade human meanness. This move toward deromanticizing evil is certainly a step in the right direction. Milton's Satan, one ancestor of perfervid existentialist heroes, grandiosely declaring, "Evil, be thou my good," and Goethe's nihilistic Mephistopheles are insufficiently horrible figures to attribute authorship to them for the vast amount of sordid and humiliating misery that informs human lives.

But banality and romanticism are not the only options in characterizing evil. An older, deeper, and, to my mind, more profound approach to evil is through tragedy. In it we find "the terrible side of life. The unspeakable pain, the wretchedness and misery of mankind, the triumph of wickedness, the scornful mastery of chance, and the irretrievable fall of the just and innocent . . . and here is to be found

---

[1] For an exploration of this theme in the history of ideas, see Lovejoy, *The Great Chain of Being*.

[2] As far as I know, this phrase is Kivy's; see his "Melville's *Billy* and the Secular Problem of Evil: The Worm in the Bud."

[3] See Arendt, *Eichmann in Jerusalem: A Report of the Banality of Evil*.

a significant hint as to the nature of the world and existence."[4] It is, therefore, through tragedy and our responses to it that I shall consider evil and how it affects our aspirations to live good lives.

Tragedy shows our vulnerability to evil. We learn from it the contingency of human existence, the indifference of nature to human merit, and the presence of destructive forces as part of human motivation. But the most painful lesson of all is not that our vulnerability to evil is merely the consequence of adverse external causes but that we ourselves are also agents of the contingency, indifference, and destructiveness that jeopardize the human aspiration to live good lives. The tragic view[5] depicts human motivation as the arena in which our virtues and vices wage their endless battles, and it forces us to recognize that the issue remains undecided. Thus, tragedy prompts us to see human character as fundamentally flawed. The flaw is not a specific vice, like selfishness or intemperance, but a general propensity to live in a state of tension between our virtues and our vices.

This is a deep and profoundly depressing view of human life. It is superficial to respond to it with well-intentioned common sense and resolve to put our will and intellect behind our virtues and endeavor to suppress our vices. For if the tragic view is right, our will and intellect are also infected by the vices that this response supposes they may overcome. According to the tragic view, we are tainted through and through, and this is one main reason (although not the only one) why evil is prevalent and why human aspirations to live good lives are so rarely realized.

In contemporary moral thought there is considerable reluctance to accept the tragic view. The opposition to it is not just a defensive maneuver, aiming to protect us from disillusioning truths; there is a reasoned case behind it, even if many who share the reluctance are unaware of the case. It will be conceded that many people, including ourselves, are often guilty of evil actions, of actions that cause undeserved harm. Yet when we survey those we know—our families, friends, acquaintances, not to mention our own selves—we rarely find individuals whom we might reasonably identify as evil. The more intimately we know others, the more familiar we are with their motivation, circumstances, the information they have, and the constraints under which they operate, the less likely it is that we would be willing to allow their evil actions to reflect on their characters. Intimate un-

---

[4] Schopenhauer, *The World as Will and Representation*, 1:252–53.

[5] My label "the tragic view of life" echoes the English title of Unamumo's book *Tragic Sense of Life*. Unamumo writes in a Christian context. He sees as the source of tragedy the conflict between reason and faith, and he thinks that faith should prevail. As will become obvious, I proceed differently.

derstanding of human conduct tends to reveal complexities disguised from superficial acquaintances. These complexities, then, function as excuses, preventing us from judging the agents of evil actions as harshly as would be entailed by calling *them*, and not only their actions, evil.

Of course, there are some moral monsters, but they are extremely rare, especially among the people we know. This is not because each of us knows only a few people. Moral monsters are also rare in history and literature. We have to look far and wide to find the likes of Stalin or Hitler; Iago is probably the only truly evil character in Shakespeare; and in Greek tragedy, the sole candidate for whom no excuse seems possible is Polymestor in Euripides' *Hecuba*.

This reluctance to allow evil actions to count as evidence for their agents' being evil I shall call *the soft reaction to evil*. That there is something wrong with the soft reaction may begin to become apparent if we ask its defenders to explain the prevalence of evil. It is implausible to attribute evil actions to uncharacteristic episodes in otherwise blameless lives. Although such episodes undoubtedly occur, being uncharacteristic, they are bound to be rare. It is as implausible to suppose that when people cause evil, they usually act out of character, as it is to attribute most evil actions to the conscious malignant designs of moral monsters. Nor does it carry conviction to blame external causes for all evil, such as natural disasters, epidemics, or the scarcity of resources, for the preponderance of evil afflicting us is caused by human agency, and people respond to adverse external influences with differing degrees of moral merit. So the soft reaction has no obvious answer to the question that if we reject the suggestion of the tragic view that evil actions are often caused by evil people, then how is it that evil is as prevalent as it is?

One alternative to the soft reaction may be called *the hard reaction*, the position I aim to defend in this book. According to it, much of the evil that jeopardizes human aspiration to live good lives is caused by characteristic but unchosen actions of human beings. These actions are the results of various vices. And people cause evil when they act naturally and spontaneously, without much thought or effort, in accordance with the vices that have achieved dominance in their characters. They may be cowardly, lazy, intemperate, thoughtless, cruel, vain, or envious, and these vices are reflected in their actions. They do not *choose* to act in these ways. They predominantly *are* in the ways shown by their actions. In appropriate situations, they spontaneously and naturally respond according to habitual patterns ingrained in their characters. Of course, characters are, at least to some extent, formed; and people often have choices about what they become. But from the point of view of understanding evil, the primary fact is that many people have vices of which evil actions are the predictable outcome; how they come to have their vices is secondary.

Consider, therefore, the moral standing of people who, when they act in their habitual and characteristic ways, predictably, regularly, and over a long period of time cause undeserved harm; yet their actions are not chosen. In the distant past, as their characters were being formed, they may or may not have had choices, depending on the strength of the innate and environmental influences acting on them. But now, since their characters are firmly established and their vices have gained motivational force, their actions are the natural consequences of their defects. If evil is undeserved harm and if these people habitually cause undeserved harm, then the hard reaction prompts us to regard as evil, not only their actions, but also the agents themselves, insofar as they are the causes of evil.

The guiding thought behind the hard reaction is that one central task of morality is the minimization of evil, and if we care about morality, we must face evil. But if the evil we are enjoined to face has its main source in the habitual unchosen actions of people, and if these actions are the products of defective characters, then there is no reasonable way of avoiding the conclusion that people dominated by vices that regularly result in evil actions are themselves evil. The implications of this conclusion are far-reaching. They lead us in the direction of a radical reorientation of a central part of contemporary Western sensibility. Part of my concern is to explore these implications and to indicate the nature of the perspectival shift they demand.

In doing so, I must contend with a general unwillingness to accept the legitimacy of the hard reaction and to abandon the soft one. For the conclusion that much evil is caused by the unchosen actions of people ruled by various vices, and that such people are not merely the exceptional moral monsters but our neighbors, acquaintances, and perhaps even ourselves, runs counter to a widely and deeply held conception of morality that I call *choice-morality*. Choice-morality is the background from which the soft reaction follows. I shall briefly sketch some crucial assumptions of choice-morality and give, equally briefly, some preliminary indications of my reasons for doubting them.

The first of these assumptions is that the appropriateness of moral condemnation depends on the possibility of choice. If people could not choose their actions, then it is wrong to condemn them for having performed them. This is often encapsulated in the principle that "ought implies can." The principle translates into the claim that the judgment that agents ought or ought not to have done something presupposes that they could have chosen to act differently from the way they have acted. Against this claim counts the plain fact that people who regularly cause undeserved harm are habitual evildoers, and they do not cease to be that if it turns out that they have not chosen to have the vices of which their evil actions are the natural consequences. If we are concerned with minimizing evil, then the salient fact is the evil that has been done; how it came to be done is a subsidiary matter. The vices of some people are lasting and predictable sources of evil, and calling people dominated by their vices evil merely registers this fact. Of course, those who habitually choose to do evil are even worse than those who habitually do evil without choice. But the existence of worse possibilities does not alter the badness of less bad ones.

The second assumption of choice-morality is that human beings have equal moral worth, and because of it, they are entitled to equal respect and equal protection of their rights to freedom and well-being. But if we were to accede to the hard reaction and condemn moral agents acting on their vices as evil, then we would imply that they have less worth than others. As a result, we would fail to give them the respect and the protection of their rights to which they are entitled. We must recognize, however, that morality is not an egalitarian institution. Moral agents are not equal but better or worse, and they are so not merely in respect to specific talents or skills they may or may not possess but qua moral agents. Moral worth and the respect and rights consequent upon it are not independent of what people deserve. And it is contrary to the aims of morality to suppose that habitual evildoers have the same moral worth and deserve the same protection of their freedom and well-being as habitual benefactors of humanity.

The third questionable assumption is that the primary potentialities implicit in human nature are for the development of virtues that, when properly cultivated, result in good actions. Vices are thought to result from the corruption of the virtues, rather than being independent potentialities competing with them. This is one reason why it is supposed that people cannot lose their moral worth and why choice is so important. For if the potentialities for the virtues are dominant in human nature, then the way to moral improvement lies through choice informed by thought and effort. The rights to freedom and well-being, protecting the conditions in which our will and intelligence can shape our choices, are grounded on this optimistic view of human nature. But it is just this view that tragedy teaches us to doubt. Vices are not aberrations due to adverse external influences; they are equal partners of the potentialities for the good. Their sources are such internal propensities as greed, selfishness, aggression, malevolence, and envy, which also exist as fundamental human motives. In evil people, vices have achieved dominance. That is the fact we must face, and the question of whether vices got the upper hand by choice or otherwise should not distract our moral attention.

I argue that these assumptions of choice-morality, the props of the soft reaction, are dangerously mistaken. They prevent us from facing evil, and they lead us to collude in the prevalence of evil. If it is true that much evil is caused by characteristic and unchosen actions, then the insistence on the necessity of choice in morality, the unwillingness to regard habitual evildoers as having diminished moral worth, and the supposition that human nature is primarily good conspire to render us helpless in the face of evil. Hence, the title of this book is both a description of its chief goal and an injunction to pursue it in opposition to choice-morality.

As an alternative to choice-morality and as a justification of the hard reaction, I develop *character-morality*. My claim for it is that it provides a far more adequate response to the secular problem of evil than does either the tragic view of life or choice-morality. The content of character-morality is given by nine theses. They emerge from the discussion of the nature of evil, the requirements of human welfare, and the inadequacies of the assumptions of choice-morality. The justification of these theses is that they are required by the ideal toward which character-morality aims: that people ought to get what they deserve; and what they deserve depends on their moral merits. The aim of character-morality is to approximate this ideal as closely as circumstances allow.

Character-morality has both an institutional and a personal dimension. The first prescribes a set of rules, principles, values, customs, practices, and ideals whose aim it is to avoid evil. These partly constitute a moral tradition, and part of the purpose of moral education is to inculcate them. The second prescribes an attitude to evil—the reflective temper. The extent to which moral agents increase their control over their lives and conduct depends on their development of the reflective temper. Reasonable people would do what they can to follow these prescriptions because by doing so they are more likely to avoid evil than otherwise. The significance of the secular problem of evil is that it points to the most serious obstacle in the way of realizing the ideal of character-morality.

Character-morality has political and social implications. Its acceptance would bring with it an impetus to reform many of our institutions and practices. But it is not the purpose of this book to propose programs of reform; its purpose is to call attention to the need for such programs. It aims to change our sensibility, so that we shall face evil. We have to do that before we can attempt to work out the nature, direction, and scope of reforms.

The argument of the book falls into three parts. The first contains the first four chapters. They state the secular problem of evil, discuss the tragic view of life as a response to it, explain the key terms, such as "evil," "human welfare," "desert," and "morality," and argue for the central importance of the moral phenomenon of unchosen evil. The second part is the consideration of the soft reaction to the secular problem of evil through the critical examination of choice-morality and of its three key assumptions. The explanation and criticism of these assumptions form the subject-matter of chapters 5–7. The discussion in these two parts, however, is not merely explanatory and critical but also constructive. For the nine theses of character-morality are formulated as arising from these explanations and criticisms. The third part is composed of the remaining five chapters. They formulate and give reasons for character-morality, discuss its institutional and personal dimensions as the best available responses to the secular problem of evil and the best justification of the hard reaction, and, lastly, consider what changes would be required in our sensibility by the acceptance of character-morality.

CHAPTER ONE

True and False Hope

WHAT MAY I HOPE?

Let us begin with the secular problem of evil. It arises because our aspirations to live good lives are vulnerable to evil. We all stand in jeopardy because, as I shall show, the contingency of life, the indifference of nature, and human destructiveness often cause us undeserved harm and frustrate even the most reasonable and decent projects. The problem arises for contemporary Western heirs of the Enlightenment, people whose sensibility is formed, negatively, by the rejection of all forms of supernaturalism and, positively, by the combined beliefs that whatever exists or happens is natural, that the best approach to understanding their causes is scientific, that while human beings are part of the natural world, we still have some control over our lives, and that one chief purpose for exercising the control we have is to make good lives for ourselves. I call this *our sensibility* to indicate that many people in contemporary Western societies and elsewhere share it and that I do so as well. I concede right away that there are also many people who reject it and, moreover, that among those who accept it there are important disagreements that my loose characterization does not capture.

If it is true that evil presents a serious obstacle to good lives, then what hope can we have of overcoming it? The subject of hope does not loom large in our sensibility, but I think, with Kant, that it should. He wrote that "all the interests of my reason, speculative as well as practical, combine in the three following questions: (1) What can I know? (2) What ought I to do? (3) What may I hope?"[1] By and large, we have concentrated on the first two questions and ignored the third.[2] It is, however, no less important than the others because it prompts us to reflect on the point of striving for knowledge and conforming to morality.

The general object of hope is a good life. Its realization, however, is endangered by evil. That this is so—that between hope and its ob-

---

[1] Kant, *Critique of Pure Reason*, A805.

[2] The great exception is Nietzsche. For a superb interpretation of his thought, see Nehamas, *Nietzsche: Life as Literature*. For two more recent exceptions, see Nagel, *The View from Nowhere*, and Nussbaum, *The Fragility of Goodness*.

ject there stands evil, that we are vulnerable no matter how reasonable and decent we may be—is one of the important lessons we can learn from tragedy. True hope can follow only after we have faced evil, while false hope is fueled by a denial of evil. Facing evil is an attempt to come to terms with the fact that many conditions of life are inhospitable to the human aspiration to live good lives. Tragedy compels us to face evil by forcefully reminding us that these conditions exist.

The plan of this chapter is to approach the secular problem of evil by describing what seems to be the most reasonable ideal of good lives that we can hope to achieve—the Socratic one[3]—and then showing, with the aid of tragedy, how even it stands in serious jeopardy.

THE SOCRATIC IDEAL

Good lives may be thought to depend on personal satisfaction or on moral merit. The Socratic ideal is that good lives should combine these components; they should be both personally satisfying and morally meritorious. Thinking of good lives in this way requires understanding the relation between these two good-making components.[4]

One possibility is that personal satisfaction and moral merit are quite unrelated aspects of good lives. But this is implausible because it is not morally indifferent what personal satisfactions people seek, because morally meritorious character traits and conduct are often personally satisfying, and because, as a matter of moral psychology, good lives normally exclude the inconsistency of motives and of actions prompted by them that unrelated aspects of lives are likely to produce.

Another possibility is that personal satisfaction and moral merit are due to partially overlapping and partially conflicting aspects of good lives and that when conflicts occur, one aspect should dominate the other. The difficulty here is in justifying the judgment implied by the imperative that "should" expresses. If it is a moral "should," it means that morality requires one aspect of our lives to prevail over the

---

[3] "Socratic ideal" is a loose label. It is meant to identify what has been called *eudaimonism*. It refers primarily to the views regarding good lives held by Plato's Socrates and by Aristotle. Of course, there are important disagreements between Platonic and Aristotelian eudaimonism, and it is unclear how much is Socrates and how much is Plato in Plato's Socrates. But since the details of the Socratic ideal are irrelevant for my purposes, I shall ignore the complexities of these issues.

[4] Nagel in *The View from Nowhere*, chapter 10, discusses their relation in terms of what he calls the good life and the moral life. His tentative answer is that the moral life should override the good life if the two conflict. As will be apparent, I think otherwise.

other. But if the favored aspect is the one that has moral merit, then the judgment is question begging; while if morality is said to require personal satisfaction to override moral merit, then the judgment is self-contradictory. On the other hand, the "should" may not be moral. In that case, however, it conflicts with the moral "should," and the conflict between aspects reappears as a conflict on a higher theoretical level, where it remains at least as intractable as it was on the lower level.

These difficulties make attractive the Socratic ideal that in good lives there is no conflict between personal satisfaction and moral merit, because they coincide. Indeed, lives are good, according to this ideal, precisely because of the coincidence of these two aspects. The key to seeing that personal satisfaction and moral merit need not conflict is through understanding the nature of the goods whose possession makes lives good.

Every good life is a way of life: an amalgam of personal projects and various relationships ranging from the intimate to the impersonal, guided by a more or less clearly formulated conception of a good life. Goods are external or internal to such ways of life.[5] Internal goods are satisfactions involved in living according to our conceptions of good lives. External goods are satisfactions derived from possessing the means required for living in the ways we do and from receiving appropriate rewards for it. Typically, understanding, good judgment, clarity, and sensitivity are internal goods, while physical, psychological, and financial security, honor, prestige, and influence are external goods.

Now the Socratic ideal is that *if* the conceptions of good lives aimed at are reasonable, then they will maximize our chances of achieving both personal satisfaction and moral merit—the former, because the external and internal goods such lives yield are satisfying; the latter, because the projects and relationships that constitute such lives are generally beneficial. If the assumption about the correlation between rationality and human welfare is granted, it follows that all reasonable people will share at least one fundamental attitude: the desire for good lives. And this means that they will want lives in which personal satisfaction and moral merit coincide. Thus, reason, morality, and human well-being are neatly combined by the Socratic ideal.

One recurrent theme in philosophical discussion of this topic is that

[5] The distinction between external and internal goods is Aristotle's; see especially book 1 of *Nicomachean Ethics*. Aristotle's account is short and obscure. For interpreting it, I am indebted to Cooper's *Reason and the Human Good in Aristotle* and "Aristotle on the Goods of Fortune." See also MacIntyre's *After Virtue*, chapter 14.

good lives should be independent of the vicissitudes of luck.[6] Thus, Nussbaum writes: "I shall use the word 'luck' . . . closely related to the way in which the Greeks themselves spoke of *tuchē*. I do not mean to imply that the events in question are random or uncaused. What happens to a person by luck will be just what does not happen through his or her agency, what just *happens* to him, as opposed to what he does or makes."[7]

I shall not follow this usage, because luck connotes chance events (see any dictionary), and there is no reason to doubt that the obstacles to good lives are law-governed, causally connected events, not random or uncaused ones. What does not happen through our own agency need not happen by luck. Obstacles to good lives appear to be matters of luck only because we lack the capacity to understand and control them. It is, therefore, more perspicuous to refer to the vulnerability of human lives than to their being subject to luck.

The recurrent theme, then, is that the good-making components of our lives must be our own contributions, dependent on our own efforts and not on the state of the world around us. For this reason Socrates could seriously claim that good people cannot be harmed and that virtue is its own reward. Of course, he did not deny that we can be treated unjustly and be injured, but he thought that these sorts of injustice and injury are irrelevant to the goodness of our lives. For their goodness depends on what we are and do, not on what is done to us. The importance of this point for the present discussion is that it is implicit in the Socratic ideal that, since internal goods depend on exercising our dispositions, while external goods depend on circumstances beyond our control, good lives require only internal goods. I think that this is one of the great mistakes in moral philosophy. We can trace to it the dangerous idea that morality requires turning inward, working for our own salvation, while ignoring as much as possible the soiling, corrupting influence of the world.

INTERNAL AND EXTERNAL GOODS

Let us approach external and internal goods through the distinction between moral and natural goods, although I shall come to question this distinction eventually. Moral goods are benefits produced by human beings, while natural goods are benefits enjoyed without appreciable human intervention. Possessing innate talents, escaping injury

---

[6] For a historical account, see Cioffari, "Fortune, Fate, and Chance." For a contemporary discussion, see Williams, "Moral Luck," Nagel, "Moral Luck," and Nussbaum, *The Fragility of Goodness*.

[7] Nussbaum, *The Fragility of Goodness*, 3.

in accidents or natural disasters when others around us are killed or maimed, being constitutionally immune to prevalent illnesses are natural goods; living in a stable society, cultivating one's talents, and being loved are moral goods. External and internal goods are moral because they are due to human agency. One difference between them is that in the case of internal goods, the human agency is primarily oneself, while external goods are benefits conferred on us by others, and frequently by others acting on behalf of institutions.

Internal goods are achieved only as a result of personal effort. They are due to the cultivation of our talents, to working hard at some project, to becoming proficient at the skills required by our way of life. Internal goods are not accidental but require considerable effort; they do not come from the outside but are the by-products of our own activities; and they cannot but be deserved, because the agents are always responsible for achieving them. When technique becomes effortless for violinists, when historians are so familiar with their period that it seems much like lived-through experience, when mothers, through deep love, are intuitively attuned to the needs of their children, when teachers communicate to students the importance, excitement, and complexity of their subjects, then some of the internal goods necessary for making good these ways of life are present.

By contrast, individual effort is neither necessary nor sufficient for obtaining external goods. It is not sufficient, for we can be worthy and deserving of prestige, honor, respect, security, or influence, and yet they may elude us because their distribution is unjust or because our merits are unrecognized. Nor is personal effort necessary, for external goods may be given unfairly to the undeserving, and passing fashions, stupidity, or moral failings may corrupt the distributing institutions. External goods should depend on the appreciation of merit, but the hard fact is that merit may be unappreciated; the distribution of external goods is a fickle affair, and their possession need not signify desert.

Nevertheless, it does not follow that in possessing external goods we are entirely vulnerable or that good lives depend only on our own efforts to gain internal goods. We are also vulnerable in possessing internal goods because they partly depend on natural goods and the possession of natural goods is independent of our efforts. Internal goods involve the successful cultivation of our talents and capacities, and this, of course, requires effort. But the effort presupposes that we have the talents or the capacities to cultivate, and whether we do depends on the outcome of the genetic lottery. So, internal goods are not the pure products of human endeavor.

Furthermore, although external goods are often capriciously distributed, they need not be. The institutions and people in whose power it is to give or to withhold them may be just or unjust. In the long run, it is in everybody's interest that they should be just, because what they reward, then, are achievements that contribute to making lives better. Just distribution is due to the recognition of merit and to the general support of the institutional framework in which people produce and enjoy the relevant benefits. It is natural and expected to use some of the external goods one possesses for strengthening the institutions that justly distribute them. One of the uses of honor, influence, and so forth is to defend and improve the future distribution of these rewards. The reason for doing so is not simply to perpetuate the status quo but to do our share in strengthening the endeavor in which we participate and from which we and others benefit.

Thus, we are not invulnerable in possessing internal goods, and the possession of external goods need not be entirely capricious. Both external and internal goods are required for good lives, for reasons I shall now go on to give, and thus the goodness of lives is, to some extent, vulnerable to conditions beyond our control—the Socratic denial notwithstanding.

THE GOODS OF GOOD LIVES

Some things are good in themselves, others are good as means to something else, and yet others are good in both ways. I shall refer to these goods as intrinsic, instrumental, and mixed. In agreement with Plato,[8] I think that mixed goods are the best. External and internal goods are mixed. Insofar as they are good in themselves, they are constituents of good lives; and insofar as they are means, they help to bring good lives about.

Internal goods are produced by the exercise of our talents and capacities. They are indications that our lives are going well, although they are not infallible, because the satisfactions they give us may be outweighed by frustrations encountered in other aspects of our lives. Nevertheless, internal goods are enjoyed as a result of successful engagement in our projects. Thus, they are satisfying both as confirmations that our conceptions of good lives are indeed good and as genuinely enjoyable experiences. They come to us when we are living and acting as we think we should, and they give us reasons to believe that we are correct in so thinking.

External goods are also mixed. The instrumental part of their mix-

[8] Plato, *The Republic*, 357–58.

ture consists in being direct means to internal goods and, thus, indirect means to good lives. External goods are means to internal goods because they play a necessary role in establishing the conditions in which talents and capacities can be exercised. The optimal conditions for the appropriate activities differ from project to project and from person to person engaged in the same project. Athletes require one thing, scholars another; some athletes and scholars function best when left alone, others need competition to do well. If we are engaged in a project, we must be able to cope with adversity, for the conditions are rarely optimal. But adversity can grow so strong as to undermine the conditions in which even the most steadfast of us can carry on. When scholarship is politicized and scholars' lives depend on the conclusions they reach, when war or revolution wrecks the society in which creative artists work, when lifelong brutalization leads one's children to become vicious, when soldiers are forced to fight against their convictions in an unjust war, when circumstances compel statesmen continually to choose between recognized evils, when students contemptuously jeer at the traditional values teachers aim to impart, then the internal goods these ways of life normally yield recede beyond reach. And even if they are achieved against such heavy odds, their enjoyment must appear to be morally suspect, given the context. They will seem like fiddling while Rome burns, and the corruption of the enjoyment thus achieved is not mitigated by the fiddler's not having started the flames. When the conditions for living any kind of good life are undermined, the appropriate response is to strengthen the conditions rather than to feast on the remaining dregs.

But the dissolution of society is only one way in which the lack of external goods can jeopardize the achievement of internal ones. Another is personal hardship, which can handicap us even in societies hospitable to our projects. Extreme poverty, poor education, recurrent physical or psychological abuse, not being taken seriously by fellow participants in our projects, systematic discrimination, having to earn a living by doing a soul-destroying job, or happening to be out of step with the dominant fashion and thus receiving no recognition may make it impossible to do whatever our ways of life call for with sufficient concentration and energy to derive the internal goods more fortunately situated people can enjoy.

It may also happen that people are deprived of external goods through pride, bitterness, stupidity, timidity, pettiness, self-doubt, or envy. But a lack of external goods often has nothing to do with character defects. Poverty, crime, discrimination, and injustice frequently handicap people through no fault of their own. In any case, the general point, put negatively, is that external goods are instrumental to internal ones, and if people lack the first, whether culpably or not, they cannot have the second. More positively, we can say that at least some degree of physical and financial security, justice, and respect are external goods necessary for continued engagement in our projects, and hence for the enjoyment of internal goods derivable from them.

But external goods are also intrinsically good if they are rewards for our achievements. Security, prestige, respect, and status make our lives better. They are good in themselves because they are indications that our achievements are valued. Those who contribute to the well-being of others ought to receive recognition, and external goods are these recognitions. Justly earned rewards are intrinsically good, partly because they are public confirmations that we are doing well at our ways of life. They provide an objective corollary to the enjoyment of internal goods our activities yield by showing that others appreciate what we are doing. But external goods are intrinsically good also because the specific forms of appreciation are enjoyable in themselves. They confer privilege upon the recipients by giving them a greater share of scarce goods than to others. If the system of distribution is just and if the goods received enhance the recipients' enjoyment of their lives without injuring others, then there is nothing objectionable about such privilege.[9] It is fitting and proper that a great violinist should have a Stradivarius to use, that parents who raise their children well should be especially respected by them, that administrators responsible for the smooth functioning of organizations should have greater influence than others have, that first-rate scientists, artists, or scholars should have the prestigious task of evaluating the performance of others, or that great actors should have the first pick of roles.

Of course, this rosy picture assumes that the distribution of external goods is just, so that reward is commensurate with achievement, and that justly received external goods will not be misused. Both assumptions can and often do fail. And because they do, deserving people may be deprived of good lives. But this is not an acceptable reason for denying that external goods are both intrinsically and instrumentally good. On the contrary, it should act as a spur for assuring that people receive the external goods that are their due.

Thus, external goods make our lives better, if we have them, and worse, if we do not. But since the distribution of external goods is an unreliable affair, the question of whether and to what extent we can

[9] On this point, see Vlastos, "Justice and Equality," section 4.

do without them often arises. The Socratic ideal is that we should learn to do without them altogether and that if we fail to do so and are made miserable by their lack, we are to be blamed. For it is the beginning of wisdom to understand that in trying to live good lives, we can count only on our own efforts; in every other respect we are vulnerable. Thus, we now have a further reason for questioning the Socratic ideal. Just as natural goods are both necessary for internal goods and beyond our control, so, often, are external goods. Hence internal goods and, consequently, good lives cannot be made invulnerable.

However, the Socratic ideal has proved extremely tenacious, and it would not have, unless it had some important truth to it. My account of external goods as being both intrinsically good (as rewards) and instrumentally good (as means to internal goods) makes it possible to identify what is true and what is false in the Socratic ideal. The truth is that good lives are possible without external goods as rewards; but this does not mean, as it has been falsely supposed, that good lives are possible without external goods as means. We can live enjoyable and morally meritorious lives without basking in the wealth, respect, status, prestige, and influence that a juster distribution would bestow on us. It is true that many otherwise good lives have been ruined by the resentment, anger, envy, jealousy, and bitterness produced by the frustrated expectation of just rewards; Socrates is surely right to warn us against this danger. Nevertheless, social instability, physical insecurity, extreme poverty, personal hardship, and living in the midst of war or revolution do jeopardize and often make impossible the enjoyment of internal goods. The external goods from which these adversities deprive us are often beyond our control. Yet by being means to internal goods, they are, contra Socrates, required for good lives.

SOME MISUNDERSTANDINGS

There are several ways of misinterpreting the distinction between external and internal goods. One is to confuse it with the distinction between public and private goods. In one sense, both external and internal goods are private. Part of what makes them good is that they are satisfactions, and satisfactions are private experiences. In another sense, internal goods are often private and external goods are public because the objects of the satisfactions involved in them are usually private and public in their origin. The usual objects of satisfaction, in the case of internal goods, are our own activities, while for external goods, they are the high regard others have for us. But the activities that may occasion our satisfactions need not be always private. It may be that the activities we find satisfying are our growth in understanding, aesthetic appreciation, or depth, and these are indeed private. However, the activities may also be performing in a first-rate chamber music group, playing an excellent game of chess, or putting a case so persuasively as to change the opinions of many people. Hence, the private-public distinction cuts across the distinction between external and internal goods.

Another, closely related misunderstanding fuels the suspicion that the pursuit of external and internal goods is a form of selfishness. It may be objected to the search for good lives I have been describing that it is a search for selfish lives, that the satisfactions are self-satisfactions, and that the goods sought benefit ourselves, not others. The truth in this charge is that the lives made good are indeed ours and that they are made good by the satisfactions we seek and enjoy. Yet the accusation of selfishness is unfounded because the projects that make our lives good and occasion our satisfactions may be altruistic. Part of what may make the lives of physicians, teachers, mothers, statesmen, novelists, and firemen good is that they benefit others. These people and others want good lives for themselves, but achieving them depends on promoting other people's welfare. Thus, wanting good lives for ourselves not only is compatible with wanting them for others but often presupposes it.

A third confusion about the distinction between external and internal goods is due to ignoring the fact that both are intrinsically and instrumentally good. The confusion is to think of internal goods as the true satisfactions and of external goods as merely conditions—perhaps grudgingly admitted to be necessary conditions—of the satisfactions internal goods may give us. This is doubly mistaken.

First, external goods are not only means to internal goods; they can be good in themselves. It is hypocritical to deny that the security, comfort, prestige, or honor we justly receive are intrinsically enjoyable. Of course, we do not merely bask in them but put them to various uses. However, I see no good reason for supposing that having uses is incompatible with being intrinsically enjoyable. Why could not a recipient of the Nobel Prize both find it satisfying in itself and also make use of the money?

Second, internal goods are also instrumental, and if the distributing institutions are just, they are instrumental to external goods. For in that case, external goods are rewards given for the very activities whose enjoyment constitutes internal goods for the agents. The goodness of the lives of violinists, poets, scholars, and inventors consists precisely in finding satisfaction in the activities for which just institutions may reward them.

All three of these misinterpretations of the distinction between external and internal goods are traceable to the supposition that moral merit and personal satisfaction are at odds with one another. If moral merit is thought to consist in controlling our base urges, of not doing what we want to do, then it is indeed hard to reconcile it with personal satisfaction; for how could it be satisfying to frustrate ourselves? And of course it would be wrong to deny that we have base urges that ought to be controlled. But if moral merit is understood only in this negative way, then it becomes incomprehensible why reasonable people wish to have it. It is readily understandable why people or society would demand moral merit from others, but not why those who are not duped by this insidious coercion would fall in with it.

The alternative is to recognize that moral merit has to do not only with the avoidance of harm to others but also with the achievement of benefits both for ourselves and for others and with the avoidance of harm for ourselves. Given this recognition, it becomes obvious that reasonable people wish to live morally meritorious lives because they wish to have the benefits and avoid the harms; that since benefits for ourselves normally involve engagement in activities that benefit others, reasonable people are not selfish; and that moral merit and personal satisfaction coincide because it is personally satisfying to have the benefits morality makes possible. For this reason the Socratic ideal requires good lives to be both morally meritorious and personally satisfying.

THE ESSENTIAL CONDITIONS OF LIFE

I have been arguing that the achievement of good lives, thus understood, requires natural and external goods, and whether we have these goods is often beyond our control. If the general object of hope is the achievement of a good life, then how realistic this hope is depends on the seriousness of the danger that we shall be deprived of the goods we deserve and require for good lives. I shall now proceed to argue that the danger is very serious. Our vulnerability is not a small flaw in the Socratic ideal but a structural defect that poses a fundamental problem for it. To show that this is so, let us consider three tragic situations.

The first is depicted by Sophocles in *Oedipus the King*. Before Oedipus was born, it was prophesied that he would kill his father and marry his mother. To circumvent it, his parents arranged to have the newly born Oedipus killed, but he survived and grew into adulthood, believing himself to be the son of the king and queen of Corinth. The prophecy was then repeated to Oedipus. To prevent it from becoming true, he left Corinth to remove himself from the proximity of his supposed parents. Yet his prudent efforts to avoid the calamity actually hastened its occurrence, for it was to Thebes, the city ruled by his real father, that his self-imposed exile brought him. On the way to Thebes, Oedipus was provoked into a fight and killed several men, not unjustifiably given the prevalent mores, one of whom was his unknown father, the king of Thebes. Upon arriving at Thebes, Oedipus solved the riddle of the Sphinx, thus liberating the city from its oppression, and as a reward, he was made king and was given as a wife the widowed queen, his unknown mother. As the play opens, all these events are in the past. The story concerns Oedipus's discovery that he is guilty of parricide and incest, crimes that he, in agreement with his society, finds deeply immoral. In the course of his discovery, Oedipus realizes that he was unknowingly and unintentionally the agent of evil and that he has caused great and undeserved harm to Thebes, to his wife and mother, to his father, to his children and half-siblings in one, and to himself. Yet throughout his life, Oedipus acted as well as it is reasonable to expect from a highly intelligent and decent human being. He took due account of such facts as he had, and his intentions were morally praiseworthy. Yet he saw himself, and others saw him, as stained by the evil he caused.

For my purposes, the relevant feature of Oedipus's situation is that he is shown to be a plaything of the gods. He had choices, and he made them; but the alternatives between which he had to choose, the conditions in which he could do so, and his inevitable doom were all set by the gods. Oedipus was not responsible for the evil he caused, nor did he deserve the evil he suffered. The fact is that through no fault of his own, Oedipus was manipulated by the gods for their own inscrutable purposes, and he was made to suffer a terrible fate by them. Sophocles' suggestion is that Oedipus's situation is a characteristic human situation, that we are all liable to becoming the playthings of the gods.

The first reaction our sensibility prompts to Sophocles' suggestion is that this cannot be a characteristic human situation because there are no gods. This is true, but it does not dispose of the matter, because the description can be easily reformulated. Instead of gods, we can talk about circumstances we have done nothing to produce and that can and often do make us and others suffer, no matter what we do. Even if we are reasonable and decent, we may find ourselves in wars, revolutions, tyrannies, natural disasters, epidemics, and concentration camps; in the middle of crimes and emergencies; in predicaments created by our jobs as politicians, physicians, firemen, administrators, judges, and officials of public health, criminal justice, or social welfare; in having to make hard decisions as parents, spouses, friends, and lovers, when we have to choose on the basis of very imperfect knowledge between alternatives forced on us. We may, then, become unwitting agents of evil, and we may bring serious and undeserved harm upon others and ourselves whatever we do.

We can take, then, as the suggestion of the play that human life is vulnerable to *contingency*.[10] Our sensibility allows for contingency because it allows that there are vast areas of our lives in which we lack understanding and control. At present, and for the foreseeable future, contingency is our lot. We may not be the playthings of gods, but we are often at the mercy of natural forces. As a result, we may be reasonable and decent, and we may still find ourselves forced to do evil that we abhor in circumstances we are not responsible for.

The significance of contingency is that much evil is beyond human control. Often it is not our ignorance or destructiveness that causes undeserved harm but natural forces. Since evil threatens good lives and our efforts are often unavailing against evil, we are not in control of our destiny.

A second tragic situation is illustrated by *King Lear*. Lear acted foolishly in dividing his kingdom, trusting his two wicked daughters, and disowning Cordelia, who truly loved him. Lear's judgment was impaired by his vices of pride, vanity, and impetuosity. The play shows Lear paying for them in the currency of his own suffering, brought about precisely by the vices that were responsible for his foolish decisions. But he did pay. And not only did he pay, but as he was doing so, his character improved. He came to understand what he had done and how his actions followed from his defective character. Having lost all he valued, enduring gross humiliations, and being deprived of all civilized protection, he then discovered and began to cultivate in himself gentleness, pity, and remorse for what he had been and done. Then he is reunited with faithful Cordelia, who has, of course, forgiven him, and we expect Shakespeare to give us the happy ending they, and we, deserve. What we get, however, is the shocking execution of blameless Cordelia and the broken heart and death of Lear. We learn that goodness may be punished, that suffering and moral growth need not be compensated for, and that people come to undeserved harm.

This situation is caused by the *indifference* of the scheme of things toward human merit. There is no cosmic justice: the good may suffer,

---

[10] In fairness to Nussbaum, I should note that she often puts her point in terms of contingency rather than luck.

and the wicked may flourish.[11] And it is not just that we may enjoy undeserved benefit and suffer unmerited harm but also that the books may not be balanced even in the long run, because there is no superhuman accounting agency. The order of nature is not a moral order; it is not evil, rather than good, nor is it Manichean. It is indifferent. Indifference is worse than neutrality, for the latter implies the presence of an umpire, or perhaps some spectators, who are there as witnesses but stand above the fray and remain uncommitted. That would give ground for some hope, for we could say that they at least know that injustice occurs, and perhaps, if things were really bad, their neutrality might be temporarily suspended. But if there is nobody overseeing the fortunes of humanity, then there is no reason to suppose that what happens to us is or ever will be proportional to our merit.

Our common experience confirms this indifference. Vicious dictators live out their lives in comfort, continuing to wield their evil power amid the adulation of people they have duped. Good causes supported by good people lose out to unscrupulous defenders of deplorable conditions. Crimes, accidents, and disease befall us, regardless of our merit. Living a reasonable and decent life is neither necessary nor sufficient for overcoming the moral indifference of nature. As Mill clearly saw: "The dictum that truth [and, I add, goodness] always triumphs over persecution is one of the pleasant falsehoods which men repeat after one another till they pass into commonplaces, but which experience refutes. History teems with instances of truth [and goodness] put down by persecution. . . . It is a piece of idle sentimentality that truth [and goodness have] . . . any inherent power denied to error."[12]

A third tragic situation is Kurtz's in Conrad's *Heart of Darkness*. Kurtz was an exemplary product of European civilization. He had a strong sense of moral and cultural values; he was a decent and upright man—an eloquent speaker, a talented painter, musician, and writer. He went to Africa, into the deepest, darkest, unexplored region of nineteenth-century Africa, to spread civilization and overcome barbarism, not by the force of arms, but by his exemplary character and intelligence. He established a distant outpost in the jungle, many weeks of travel away from the nearest white settlement, and there he lived among what he regarded as primitive, barbaric, unpredictable tribes. The natives came to regard him with awe; he seemed

[11] See the very interesting article by Wolgast, "Intolerable Wrong and Punishment," and the fuller development of it in *The Grammar of Justice*.

[12] Mill, *On Liberty*, 27–28.

to them to be a supernatural being; his word became law; his power over life and death, and lesser matters, was absolute. There was nothing to restrain him, no obstacles in his way, except those he found in himself. He could do exactly as he wanted. And so the question of what he wanted was naturally forced on Kurtz. In the absence of public opinion, tradition, law, and moral conventions—the institutional structures that hitherto restrained him—he looked inside himself and found there what his last words report: "The horror! The horror!" Underneath his civilized persona, below the layers of education, moral conventions, and decency, he found the barbarism he had gone to Africa to civilize. The heart of darkness was inside himself. He was led by it to enlist his powerful charisma in service of abominations, horrible midnight rituals, impaled heads on the fenceposts surrounding his house, ceremonies involving the dark mixture of sex, violence, and cruelty—all testifying to the destructiveness he found in himself.

What we can glimpse in Conrad's story is that the barbaric and life-diminishing force of evil, appearing this time in the form of *destructiveness*, is an active force in us. It may show itself in the motiveless malignity of Iago, in the uncontrolled excess of the rage of Medea, in the fanaticism of terrorists, ideologues, and fundamentalists of various persuasion, in the cruelty of the Marquis de Sade, and in the selfishness of people in whose scale nothing can outweigh even some small benefit they seek for themselves. Destructiveness is not adequately explained as an external force acting on us, for corrupting influences can take hold only if we are ready to receive them. Nor is destructiveness merely the absence or diminution of the good, because malevolence, rage, fanaticism, cruelty, and selfishness are active and regular performers in the repertoire of human motivation.

The third tragic situation is that morality requires us to cultivate self-knowledge, which then reveals in us the destructiveness we deplore. Thus, the cost of moral merit is to deny part of what we are. If we are reflective, we cannot help being split at the core of our selves, and the question of why one rather than the other part of our split selves should be cultivated is bound to be asked whenever we face serious internal conflicts.

The three tragic situations are alike in some ways and different in others. They are alike in being concerned with evil, understood as undeserved harm, and in showing our vulnerability to it. But they also differ in depicting different forms of evil. The differences among the three forms of evil can be traced to the combination of two factors: the different sources they have and the different ways in which agents collaborate in their production.

In all three cases, the immediate causes of evil were the tragic figures. Oedipus, however, caused the evil he did as if he were an agent of the gods. He abhorred incest and parricide, there is no reason to attribute a secret desire to him (Freud's appropriation of the case notwithstanding), and in fact he did all he could to avoid causing the evil the gods manipulated him into causing. He was at the mercy of contingency, as shown by the futility of his pitting himself against it, and he became the instrument through which contingency assailed Thebes, Laius, Jocasta, Creon, and Oedipus's children. Lear had a hand in setting into motion the evil-producing events. If he had not initially been morally stupid, no tragedy would have occurred. But the world conspired to worsen the ghastly consequences of his failings. And after he paid for them and wanted actively to alter the course of events, he could not. So he paid more, and the innocent Cordelia, Gloucester, and the Fool did so as well. Thus, Lear became the unwitting agent through which cosmic indifference to injustice created havoc. Although his vices made him a suitable candidate for the role he was made to play, they were not serious enough to cause the calamity that occurred. Kurtz had the source of evil in himself. He was not only the immediate cause of it, but his vices were the origin of the force behind it. In his actions, his destructiveness came out. He was not manipulated into unwitting agency; he acted according to the part of his nature that was ruled by vices. But not even Kurtz cultivated his vices. He did not choose to have them, he was unaware of having them until he found himself overpowered by them, and then they horrified him. Indeed, he became a victim of his own vices.

These tragic situations arise, then, because of the contingency of human existence, the moral indifference of nature, and the presence of destructiveness in human motivation. I shall refer to them as *the essential conditions of life*.[13] I do not mean that these are the only essential conditions, but only that they are among them. They are essential because they define some human limitations within which we must pursue whatever good lives we choose. And since they are beyond human control, they are conditions we cannot alter. The best we can do is to plan our lives so as to minimize their influence. For, we must be clear about it, these essential conditions of life are often inhospitable to the human aspiration to live good lives. Any attempt to answer Kant's question of what we may hope must begin with the real-

[13] I borrow this phrase twice over. Leavis, in *Lectures in America*, used it first. It was then borrowed by Mason, in *The Tragic Plane*, 83. Leavis used it as part of his interpretation of Blake; Mason to interpret Sophocles; and I to do duty for all of us.

ization that this is so. Part of the trouble with the Socratic ideal is that it grossly underestimates just how vulnerable we are to these conditions.

FALSE HOPE AND THE VULNERABILITY OF GOOD LIVES

But if even our best efforts are incapable of altering the essential conditions of life, if no matter what we do, we remain at the mercy of contingency, if the connection between what happens to us and our merits is fortuitous, and if we exist in a state of civil war between two parts of our selves, then the answer to Kant's question may well be that, insofar as hope is reasonable, we may hope for nothing. If we allow the significance of this answer to sink in, it becomes very hard to explain why we should seek knowledge and conform to the requirements of morality.

Now Kant did not accept this answer. He instead postulated ideas of faith: God, immortality, and the supreme good, in which "happiness stands in exact relation with morality, that is, with worthiness to be happy."[14] It seems that since reason led Kant to a subversive answer to his question about hope, he looked for a less bleak answer beyond reason. Kant was not the first, nor was he alone, in succumbing to what I shall call *the transcendental temptation*.[15] The Socratic ideal has also succumbed to it, although it took another form. The reason why, according to the Socratic ideal, we can be so confident that if we live rationally and morally, then our lives will be good is that the scheme of things is itself rational and moral. The key to living good lives is to live in harmony with the rational and moral order of the world. The transcendental temptation is to give in to false hope and suppose that behind what appear to be the essential conditions of life there is a deeper order that is favorable to humanity.

This search for false hope has taken different forms, depending on what the nature of this deeper order is supposed to be. In our history, the most influential form has been Christianity. It is instructive to reflect on how it handles the tragic situations I have used to illustrate the essential conditions of life. Instead of having Oedipus manipulated by the gods, we have Job first being tested by God to see whether his faith is strong enough and then receiving ample compensation as a reward for proving himself true. Instead of the unredeemed suffering of Lear, we have the prodigal son forgiven and

---

[14] Kant, *Critique of Pure Reason*, A810.

[15] I borrow this phrase from Kurtz's *Transcendental Temptation*, although my use of it differs from Kurtz's. See also the interesting discussion by Kalin in "The Intent of Romanticism."

reunited with his loving father. Instead of the horror Kurtz discovered in himself, we have the repentant thief dying at Jesus' side, being assured of salvation. In each case, we are promised rescue by God. The contingency and moral indifference of nature, as well as human destructiveness, are allowed to exist; indeed, their existence is insisted upon. But the consequent sense of hopelessness is allayed because there is said to be an infinitely powerful benevolent force assuring that in the long run all will be well. The Christian answer is to add to the essential conditions of life a supposedly even deeper condition: the power and goodness of God.

Christianity is one way of succumbing to false hope; the ways of the Socratic ideal, Hegel, and of most non-Christian religions are others. The fundamental idea behind them all is that reality is governed by a rational and moral principle and that it is tending toward a final purpose. The human significance of whatever the plot of reality is supposed to be is that hopelessness, produced by our perception of evil, in the form of contingency, indifference, and destructiveness, comes from insufficient understanding. The source and ground of hope is our achievement of great enough understanding to discern the plot and live according to it. If we do so, we shall have good lives; otherwise not. On this view, the various tragic situations I have described are due not to the inhospitality of reality to humanity but to our irrational impulses to pit ourselves against the rational order. Thus, understanding, hope, and the plot in reality form a complex, mutually reinforcing whole.

I shall not belabor the well-known criticisms of this approach. The basic objection is that there is no reason for postulating a plot behind nature because any reason we could give must come from within nature. The most we can reasonably say about nature is that there is much in it we do not know and there is much in what we do know that we do not understand or cannot control. There is no rational warrant for going beyond this and mythologizing the unknown. One distinguishing mark of our sensibility is that it does stop here, that it resists the transcendental temptation, that it refuses to alleviate hopelessness by false hope based on a fictional plot that would render tolerable the contingency, indifference, and destructiveness we encounter.

And this brings us finally to the explanation of why hope is such a serious problem for our sensibility. If hope comes from the discernment of a plot in reality and if there is no plot, then there will be no hope either. Since we are at the mercy of the essential conditions of life, what good does it do to worry about them? People of sturdy common sense will carry on with their lives, do as well as they can, and keep out of deep waters. To do otherwise, by dwelling on the hope-lessness the essential conditions of life produce, is to undermine the motivation for effecting such improvements in our circumstances as we can.[16] I used Oedipus, Lear, and Kurtz as illustrations of how people come up against the essential conditions of life, endure unde-served or disproportionate suffering, and end by being destroyed. Why should we not, then, avert our gaze so that the contemplation of their misfortune will not sap our will?

The answer is that the adversities created by the essential condi-tions of life are not rare and freakish concatenations of unfavorable circumstances but daily occurrences in the lives of all of us. To culti-vate blindness in view of this threat is to collude in weakening our capacity to rise to the challenge; it is to cultivate the attitudes of sheep on the way to the slaughterhouse.

Contingency permeates all lives; it comes to us in the form of traffic accidents, cancer, muggings, terrorism, mistakes by manufacturers in producing what we buy or by pilots or controllers of the planes we fly, the crazed acts of drug addicts, the impurity of the blood trans-fused into us, the explosion of gas lines and nuclear reactors, the col-lapse of bridges, not to mention such old standbys as lightning, fire, earthquake, and flood. And of course whether these threats claim us as their victims often has nothing whatever to do with our merits. They are indifferent to our moral or intellectual accomplishments, our past suffering, our future promise, the number of dependents we have, the importance of our pending projects, or the grief, relief, or unconcern our destruction would produce. But the malevolent, selfish, cruel, fanatical motives we find in ourselves and the excessive rage, jealousy, or ambition we discover ourselves exhibiting are the most unpleasant surprises of all. We can blame the world, gods, con-spirators, or civilization for causing the disasters and injustices con-tingency and indifference make us suffer, but for the undeserved harm we cause, our own destructiveness is to be blamed. And when we find ourselves deficient on account of what we recognize as serious flaws in our characters, we are assailed where we really live. Since none of us is likely to be free of some character defects, we are all prone to the experience of turning against ourselves. So, vulnerabil-ity to the essential conditions of life is likely to be experienced, in some form or another, by all of us.

In conclusion, we can see that the Socratic ideal prompts a funda-mental attitude shared by reasonable people—the aspiration to have

---

[16] For two examples of this approach, see Flew, "Tolstoi and the Meaning of Life," and Hare, "Nothing Matters."

good lives. But we must also realize that there is a second fundamental attitude reasonable people will share: the recognition that the essential conditions of life render this aspiration vulnerable. It would be an exaggeration to say that these two attitudes are logically inconsistent. But it is plainly realistic to regard them as creating a tension in the sensibility of reasonable people. One pulls us in the direction of hope, optimism, effort, and achievement; the other, in the direction of hopelessness, pessimism, futility, and failure.

It seems to me that both of these attitudes are reasonable. So, I do not think that we should try to defuse the tension by squelching one of them. We must somehow live with both *and* with the tension. That this is so, that life demands of us both attitudes, is what I take to be one great significance of the lesson tragedy aims to teach us. And this lesson is a reminder that our lives and circumstances are the battlefield on which good and evil wage war and that the issue is undecided. The tension between the two attitudes is the reflection cast by this war on our sensibility. This is the problem—the tension, how to live with it, and what to do about it—that I am going to struggle with in this book. I propose to get a better view of it by discussing the view of life many tragedies imply.

CHAPTER TWO

The Tragic View of Life

THE MORAL IMPORTANCE OF TRAGEDY

We concluded at the end of the previous chapter that the attitude represented by the Socratic ideal exists in a state of tension with the attitude prompted by the recognition that the essential conditions of life render our aspirations to live good lives vulnerable. Both these attitudes are reasonable, and neither should be abandoned. But one fuels optimism and hope, while the other suggests pessimism and hopelessness. The tragic view is that life is like that. The human situation, according to the tragic view, is that we have aspirations and that they are vulnerable to adverse conditions over which we have no control. We call the realization of our aspirations good and the jeopardy they are subject to evil, but this is merely to try, futilely, to impose our wishes on the inhospitable scheme of things. I shall eventually reject the tragic view, but my present purpose is to understand it. One reason for doing so is that it helps us to look at evil unflinchingly.

The view of life great tragedies express is as profound as great works of moral philosophy. The view is not always the same, and we can mine tragedies for many riches in addition to their commentary on life. But I shall be concerned here with a view expressed by only some tragedies, one that presents a stark contrast to the Socratic ideal. As we have seen, the view is one of tension, and the tension is between the human desire to live good lives and the essential conditions of life.[1]

The contrast between the Socratic ideal and the tragic view has occasioned philosophical work of the highest order. The reaction of Plato was to reject the tragic view as morally pernicious. The scheme

---

[1] This conflict is the topic of Nussbaum's *The Fragility of Goodness.* My thinking has been influenced by this book, but I have serious disagreements with it. Put briefly, these concern four points. First, what Nussbaum takes to be luck, I regard as a form of evil; second, in the conflict between the Socratic ideal and tragedy, Nussbaum sides with the latter, while I think that the tragic view is as flawed as the Socratic one; third, Nussbaum embraces a view according to which life is to be lived in clear recognition of luck, while I think that, since what she regards as luck is in fact evil, this view leads to an impoverishment of human possibilities; fourth, she celebrates the tension I have been describing, while I think that human welfare requires finding a way to resolve it.

of things is rational and good, so the evil of which this tragic vision reminds us must be based on a misrepresentation of reality. Since the misrepresentation is couched in an aesthetically pleasing, emotionally appealing, and imaginatively tempting form, it is much the more dangerous.[2]

Aristotle was more moderate. He acknowledged that there was truth in this tragic view. The flaws (*hamartia*) in human character and the role of luck (*tuchē*) in human life are responsible for the failure of many human projects. Tragedies show that this is so, and by leading us to the clarification (*katharsis*) of our emotional responses to this state of affairs,[3] we shall be better able to conduct our lives. If human beings were divine, tragedy would not apply to us. But since we are flawed, we have much to learn from it.[4]

Hegel thought that the contrast between the Socratic ideal and the tragic view is an inevitable by-product of the historicity of human lives. The ideal is perfection, the end toward which human lives gradually evolve. But the process of getting there is as tragedy depicts because the morality by which we live at different stages of our evolution contains conflicting elements. Tragedy occurs when two moral imperatives, regarded as absolute at a given stage of development, conflict. Thus heroes, motivated by the highest moral standards, confront each other, or different parts of themselves, in destructive encounters. Philosophical reflection enables us to understand that the conflicts are produced by the inconsistency of the prevailing morality and that this inconsistency is actually a creative force, propelling us onward to an improved morality that incorporates the salvageable parts of the old and brings us a step closer to the state of perfection in which all conflicts will disappear.[5]

Nietzsche agreed with Hegel in thinking that the conflict tragedy reveals is inevitable, but he disagreed about the nature of the conflict. According to Nietzsche, the conflict is between the dark, chaotic, primitive, irrational forces that are the ruling elements in reality and the attempt to bring them under rational control by giving them form, by civilizing their barbaric tendencies. He referred to these conflicting forces as the Dionysiac and the Apollonian. Nietzsche thought that neither side can be denied but that the Dionysiac forces

---

[2] For Plato on tragedy, see Nussbaum, *The Fragility of Goodness*, part 2.

[3] I follow Nussbaum in interpreting *katharsis* as clarification; see Nussbaum, *The Fragility of Goodness*, 378–94.

[4] The literature on Aristotle on tragedy is immense. For a review of an amazing portion of it and for an interpretation, see Nussbaum, *The Fragility of Goodness*, part 3.

[5] See Paolucci and Paolucci, *Hegel on Tragedy*. This is an anthology of Hegel's relevant writings. It also contains Bradley's classic essay "Hegel's Theory of Tragedy."

are basic and vastly more powerful than the Apollonian attempt to control them. Tragedy, according to him, showed that this is so, that the Socratic ideal is a feeble cultural artifact, and that tragedy breaks down the systematic deception by which most people dupe themselves and others. Yet Nietzsche did not think that the proper response to this was the pessimism of Schopenhauer, by whose views on tragedy he had been strongly influenced. Nietzsche thought that, since we are part of nature, the Dionysiac forces dominate in us too; health lies in recognizing that this is so, instead of denying it, and then living freely, joyously, and dangerously on the crest of these forces. But Nietzsche also thought that the Dionysiac influences have been denied and the Apollonian ones were given pride of place. This is why our culture is sick, why our rationality and morality are hypocritical shams, and why only a few great and creative men can break through the veil of deception.[6]

The four views I have so superficially surveyed are, in their original forms, systematic attempts to work out possible reactions to the realization that evil—in the forms of contingency, indifference, and destructiveness—threatens human welfare. To express the same point differently, they are responses to the lamentable fact that living reasonably and morally is not sufficient to give us good lives. Plato's reaction is on one extreme; his remedy is to strive to be more reasonable and moral. Nietzsche occupies the other extreme; his prescription is the transvaluation of values, the subordination of our false rationality and morality to the primitive and creative forces that alone, if anything, can make our lives good. In between these extremes are Aristotle and Hegel. Aristotle, by and large, tends to attribute the gap between the essential conditions of life and our success in living good lives to human weakness. Hegel, when it is all said and done, is inclined to think that the gap is created by the inevitable hardships of the long march toward perfection in which all must participate. But all four agree that tragedy reveals the tension between good lives and the essential conditions of life, or between good and evil, as I have been describing them.

However, we should not make too imperialistic claims on behalf of such phrases as "the tragic view" or "what tragedy reveals" or "the tragic conflict." Tragedy is a literary genre, and there are very many and varied examples of it. The attempt to define "tragedy" yields di-

---

[6] Nietzsche's views changed throughout his working life. My account is of the early stage, when he wrote *The Birth of Tragedy*. For an excellent account of his views and of the cultural context, see Silk and Stern, *Nietzsche on Tragedy*.

minishing returns.[7] The more embracing the definition is, the less likely it is that all the plays that fall under it will have philosophically interesting features. On the other hand, if we restrict the term to plays possessing the deep significance that concerns us here, then we are bound to exclude plays legitimately regarded as tragedies by knowledgeable and thoughtful literary critics. I am afraid that each of the accounts I discuss above has been used to disparage plays that do not quite conform to it. Nietzsche did this to Euripides' plays; according to Aristotle's definition, *Hamlet* would not qualify as a tragedy; Hegel's account does not fit *Medea* and *Othello*; and Plato is so eager to get rid of the whole lot of them that he failed to provide a way of distinguishing between the vastly different aims of the various dramatic genres.

TRAGIC SITUATIONS

I propose to avoid the danger of arbitrariness by sidestepping the thankless task of trying to define "tragedy"; nor will I try to construct anything like a theory of tragedy. Instead, I offer a distinction between tragedy, the literary genre, and tragic situations, which many tragedies depict. Tragedies are philosophically interesting mainly because they bring us face to face with tragic situations and prompt us to confront their significance for our lives. Instead of concentrating on tragedies, I shall concentrate primarily on tragic situations. Tragedies are relevant to my present purpose because they characteristically depict tragic situations in a manner that combines intellectual, imaginative, and emotional appeal. Thus, they force us to see something about life that is otherwise difficult to hold steadily in the focus of our attention. "In the full tragic experience there is no suppression. The mind does not shy away from anything, it does not protect itself with any illusion, it stands uncomforted, unintimidated, alone, and self-reliant. The test of its success is whether it can face what is before it and respond to it without any of the subterfuges by which it ordinarily dodges the full development of experience. . . . Tragedy . . . forces us to live for a moment without them."[8]

It is compatible with this account to acknowledge that some tragedies may not deal with tragic situations and that literary or artistic works other than tragedies may have tragic situations as their subject matter. Furthermore, approaching tragedies in this manner emphatically does not mean that the overall excellence of tragedies is deter-

---

[7] Quinton's "Tragedy" goes as far as one reasonably can toward offering a definition that balances the claims of the genre and the claims of philosophical significance.

[8] Richards, *The Principles of Literary Criticism*, 246.

mined by how well they lend themselves to my sort of philosophical treatment.

So, I turn to the characterization of tragic situations. We must begin by noting that the adjective "tragic" is used to describe very many different situations. Since only some of these have philosophical significance, I shall concentrate on them. The account I am about to give will therefore be incomplete because it is intended to apply only to one type of tragic situation. For the sake of brevity, I shall omit this qualification, but it should be understood to hold.

In tragic situations, then, we first find agents who pursue some quite acceptable project in a reasonable and moral manner, although not faultlessly. The fault may be some manifestations of the general condition of human fallibility, so that every agent is liable to it; or the fault may be peculiar to the individual agent. But in neither case has the fault become an inexcusable vice. It is a vice, but not an excessive one; it has remained merely a flaw, a shortcoming, a weakness; it has not grown into a grievous form of irrationality or immorality. In any case, the agents intend to act in accordance with what they rightly recognize as the requirements of rationality and morality, but the execution of their intention is flawed because of their understandable vices.

Second, the agents in tragic situations, and often also others who depend on them, suffer evil, understood as undeserved harm. The harm may be totally undeserved, or it may be grossly disproportional to what is merited by the agents' life and conduct. Moreover, the evil is serious. It is often irremediable, like dishonor or mutilation, and it leaves a lasting mark on the agents or on others whose welfare the agents are committed to protecting. One consequence of the serious evil is that the agents can no longer pursue their projects. And since the projects were essential to their conceptions of a good life, the harm they suffer causes the failure or the radical disorientation of their aspirations because it goes so deep that it basically alters them. Having experienced what they had, they cannot just pick up the pieces and carry on. Their experience is not like a long illness from which they might recover; it is more like a deeply committed nun being forced into prostitution, or like surviving in a death camp by being one of those who clear out corpses from gas chambers. The agents' response may be suicide, madness, a radical reevaluation of life and their own lives, or a desultory, deadened half-life without hope, engagement, or attachment.

The third characteristic of tragic situations explains why the agents are so deeply altered by the evil that befalls them. The explanation is that they realize that the evil they, and others who depend on them,

suffer would not have occurred if they had not had their characteristic vices. The evil occurred because they were the sort of people
they were. To be sure, they did not choose to cause it, yet they were
instrumental in bringing it about. Their characters were not sufficient for it, but if they had been different, the calamity would not
have occurred. It was not an accident that it happened to them and
to those they cared about. If only they had been less ambitious or
tired, been less proud, had more energy, or been more attentive, sensitive, or thoughtful, it could have been avoided. We cannot fault
them, and they cannot fault themselves, for choosing to cause evil. In
fact, being reasonable and moral, they would have avoided it if they
could. But they could not, and part of the reason why they could not
is their character. After the fact, they realize this, and so they find the
evil they brought upon themselves and others a devastating experience.

Fourth, the agents are powerless to alter the tragic situations in
which they find themselves, either because they often do not understand their own role in it or because, while they do understand it,
they have not chosen it. So they are incapable of changing even their
own participation in tragic situations, since the part they play dawns
on them gradually or perhaps only in retrospect. When people go
about their business in day-to-day life, when they act routinely, spontaneously, in characteristic ways, then they may well not be aware of
the influence their genetic inheritance, upbringing, interests, level of
energy, tastes, sympathies, habits, past experiences, and similar factors have on their conduct. There is an acceptable degree of unre-
flectiveness, a point beyond which questioning ourselves is unreasonable, a stage at which we must simply get on with living and stop
analyzing. But when we do act in this way, the faults in our characters, faults peculiar to us or inherently human, inevitably find expression. Sometimes their expression is harmless or merely irksome,
but in tragic situations they become significant because as an otherwise innocuous spark can cause a conflagration in a dry forest, so an
understandable fault may produce great evil that would not have
happened without it.

Last, I come to the feature of tragic situations that connects them
to the preceding discussion. Tragic situations essentially involve a
conflict between the essential conditions of life and the human aspiration to live good lives. In tragic situations, the attempt to live good
lives founders on the contingency, indifference, and destructiveness
we find in the world; these forms of evil prevent us from achieving
the good we aim at. The characteristic feature of tragic situations is
that evil presents an obstacle to living a good life, partly because the

agents' characters are faulty. Thus, it is not merely the accidental intrusion of the world that creates a difficulty for our projects but the conjunction of the difficulty and a flaw in ourselves, in the only agency that can pursue our projects. Tragic situations force us to realize that the contingency, indifference, and destructiveness that exist in the world also exist in ourselves, since we are part of the world and thus we are bound to embody its general features. So, it is not just that in the world there are conditions adverse to human welfare and that these conditions tragically prevent us from living good lives regardless of how reasonable and moral we are, but rather that the adverse conditions are often located in us. What is tragic is that part of ourselves colludes in sabotaging the efforts of the other part, and it does so without our choice, just when we act naturally, spontaneously, routinely.

What makes situations tragic, then, is the tension between the essential conditions of life and our desire to live good lives. But the tension is internal to us, produced in part by our equally natural yet opposing tendencies, and it results in great evil, which we, ourselves, are instrumental in producing, although we do not choose to do so. We must live with this tension, since we cannot get rid of an essential part of ourselves, and to live with it reasonably is to know that our divided selves may handicap our reasonable and moral aspirations. The significance of tragic situations is that by reflecting on them, we learn this about ourselves in particular and about the human situation in general.

TRAGIC SITUATIONS AND THE ESSENTIAL CONDITIONS OF LIFE

I think that this account of tragic situations fits many tragedies.[9] It also has a natural extension to tragedies in which the tension exists, not *within* individuals, but *among* individuals.[10] But I shall discuss in a little more detail how it fits what I regard as two of the greatest tragedies: *Oedipus the King* and *King Lear*, as well as Conrad's *Heart of Darkness*; these three, it will be remembered, illustrate how contingency, indifference, and destructiveness affect human lives.

[9] E.g. Aeschylus's Agamemnon sacrificing Iphigenia and Orestes killing Clytemnestra; Sophocles' Creon causing devastation by opposing divine law, Ajax dishonoring himself in a fit of madness, and Deianera causing Hercules' death; Euripides' Hyppolitus and Theseus suffering the consequences of Phaedra's passion and Helen living with her reputation in ruin; and Shakespeare's Othello, Macbeth, and Coriolanus.

[10] E.g. between Aeschylus's Orestes and the Furies; between Sophocles' Creon and Antigone, and his Odysseus, Philoctetes, and Neoptalamus; and between Euripides' Medea and Theseus.

Oedipus and Lear both ruled a kingdom by and large rationally and morally, given the expectations of their different contexts. Rationality and morality are matters of degree, and it is obvious, I think, that we must rate Oedipus quite a bit higher than Lear. Both had vices, but Lear's were much more serious and blameworthy than Oedipus's. It was imprudence that led Lear to abdicate and to divide his kingdom, and his pride and impetuosity were responsible for disowning Cordelia and trusting her wicked sisters. Oedipus's vice was excessive self-confidence and the inclination to respond to situations by asserting himself and attempting to take control. If Lear had not disowned Cordelia and Oedipus had not insisted on taking responsibility for discovering the murderer of Laius, neither tragic situation would have occurred. Of course, given the characters of Lear and Oedipus, they could not have acted differently. Their conduct followed naturally from what they were. And they both caused great evil to themselves and others. Lear brought his humiliation upon himself, and without his instrumentality, Cordelia, the Fool, and Gloucester would not have met their undeserved fate. If Oedipus had been less confident and assertive, his parricide and incest would have remained buried in the past, and his self-mutilation, his wife's and mother's suicide, and the disgrace of his children would not have occurred. There is a case for saying that the evil Oedipus caused and suffered was undeserved, and while Lear did deserve some hard knocks to awaken him to what he had done, he got disproportionately more than he deserved, and of course Cordelia, Gloucester, and the Fool were innocent. Furthermore, both Oedipus and Lear were powerless to change the course of events. The coincidence of their characters and circumstances made them incapable of acting otherwise. They became active and yet helpless agents of their own and other people's misfortune. Anything they might have done would have had to come from their characters, but since their characters were flawed, the only agency capable of affecting a change was hopelessly compromised. If it had not been, their predicament would not have occurred in the first place.

Kurtz's project was to civilize barbarians, and his fault, much greater than Oedipus's or Lear's, was that his own cruel and perverse urges were considerably closer to the surface than it is usual. Nevertheless, Kurtz had them under his control with the help of the paraphernalia of his civilized life in Europe. But when the constraints were unwittingly removed, Kurtz caused great evil to innocent people. He came to understand this fact about himself, and when he saw that his natural, spontaneous, unchosen actions were precisely what he abhorred, he disintegrated. He saw that he caused evil because his vices made him evil, even though he did not know this about himself when he was engaged in his project and he did not choose to cause the evil he did cause. A more balanced view of Kurtz—one he understandably could not take, but one that Marlow, Conrad's spokesman, took—was to see him as divided between his virtues and vices. When the changed conditions of his life favored his vices, he acted accordingly.

What makes the situations of Oedipus, Lear, and Kurtz tragic is thus not merely the great reversal of their fortunes, their own suffering, or the evil they caused to innocent people they were committed to protecting. Their situation is tragic because they realized both that they themselves unintentionally conspired in causing undeserved harm to themselves and others and that they did so when they were conducting themselves in their characteristic ways. Contingency, indifference, and destructiveness took their toll because they found a receptivity in their characters. None of them chose to cause evil. Rather, they lived lives in which the virtuous part of themselves aspiring to the good existed in a state of tension with the part of themselves ruled by vices, the part that was a fertile soil for the growth of evil. When circumstances added their decisive force, they could not help becoming agents of the vice-ridden part of their characters, and they caused evil. Their tragedy is that they came to understand this about themselves.

ONE RESPONSE TO TRAGIC SITUATIONS

If it is accepted that tragic situations are as I have described them and that many tragedies portray people in tragic situations, what, then, can we learn from facing them? Here I think we can turn to Aristotle for the beginning of an answer. I have indicated my doubts about his definition of tragedy, but at least one part of it seems right. He says that tragic incidents arouse in us "pity and fear," and thereby they achieve the "catharsis of such emotions."[11] And he explains, "Fear may be defined as a pain or disturbance due to imagining some destructive or painful evil in the future . . . [which] we feel has great power of destroying us, or harming us in ways that tend to cause us great pain."[12] And "pity may be defined as a feeling of pain at an apparent evil, destructive or painful, which befalls one who does not deserve it, and which we might expect to befall ourselves or some friend of ours."[13] So, from Aristotle we get the suggestion that the

[11] Aristotle, *Poetics*, 1449b28.
[12] Aristotle, *Rhetoric*, 1382a22–30.
[13] Ibid., 1385b13–16. See note 3 above.

reasonable reaction to tragic situations is to attempt the clarification (*katharsis*) of our feelings of pity and fear aroused by the spectacle of evil. The clarification of our emotional responses to tragic situations should touch, I think, on two points: the personal significance of tragic situations and the expectations we have about our own projects in the light of tragic situations. I begin with the first of these.

Many people fail to appreciate tragedies because they suppose that the reaction required of them is identification with the protagonist. But they find it understandably difficult to put themselves, say, in the position of an incestuous parricide or of a king who foolishly loses both a kingdom and love. Tragic heroes are larger than life, their sufferings are extraordinary, their situations are peculiar and extreme, and thus they are unlikely to be encountered by ordinary mortals. Identification in these circumstances often calls for greater imaginative resources than most people possess.

The appreciation of tragic situations, however, requires the opposite of identification. It calls for a detached understanding of the protagonists' predicament. We are not expected to re-create vicariously the struggles of Oedipus, Lear, or Kurtz, with ourselves in the title roles, but to appreciate the nature of the forces that produce their struggles. If we succeed in this endeavor, we do experience fear and pity. However, the connection between tragic situations and our emotional reaction to them is less direct and more complicated than the misguided attempt we are urged to make to imagine ourselves as the protagonists.

Although the attempt to reach a detached understanding, rather than identification, is on the right track, it is not without its pitfalls. Leavis's reflection on tragedy illustrates both the merits and faults of this approach. He begins, rightly, by noting that "it is an essential part of the definition of the tragic that it . . . establishes . . . a kind of profound impersonality in which experience matters, not because it is mine . . . but because it is what it is, the 'mine' mattering only in so far as the individual sentience is the indispensable focus of experience."[14] And he goes on to give an account of the source of impersonality. "The sense of heightened life that goes with the tragic experience is conditioned by a transcending of the ego. . . . It is as if we were challenged at the profoundest level with the question, 'In what does the significance of life reside?' "[15] Leavis, then, locates the answer in "a view of life, and of things giving it value, that makes the valued appear unquestionably more important than the valuer, so

[14] Leavis, "Tragedy and the 'Medium,' " 130.
[15] Ibid., 132

that significance lies, clearly and inescapably, in the willing adhesion of the individual self to something other than itself."[16] Leavis does not explain what he means by this, and the natural explanation produces an untenable view.

The natural explanation is that the source of impersonality in tragic situations is that the protagonists commit themselves to something they recognize as more valuable than they are themselves and then live according to this commitment. What is tragic is that fate, the gods, or their own faults make it impossible for them to realize their aspirations, and yet they nevertheless heroically struggle against hopeless odds. The spectacle of this noble and doomed struggle is what makes, on this account, tragedies uplifting and inspiring.

But this explanation cannot be right. First, it does not fit many tragic situations. In particular, Oedipus, Lear, or Kurtz did not commit themselves to the achievement of something greater than they were. Oedipus just wanted to continue to be the king he was, to carry on with the life he was proud of; Lear wanted to grow old in peace, surrounded by loving daughters and respectful subjects; and Kurtz wanted to impose his own view of life on another culture. The adversity they encountered was not a fateful intervention with their pursuit of something more valuable than themselves but a disruption of their ways of life and of their projects, which were essential parts of their ways of life.

Second, even if we take tragedies to which Leavis's account applies,[17] we do not find the "transcending of the ego" of which Leavis speaks as the source of impersonality. On the contrary, we find characters who know very clearly that they want love, honor, purity, revenge, or removal of the stain of shame. They want it partly for themselves, and they go about getting it with conspicuous strength of character, with a clear sense of themselves, and continually drawing, as the going gets tougher, on the great resources of their will and intelligence. Of course, these resources prove to be insufficient, and that is in part why their situations are tragic. But we do not witness the willing subordination of their selves to something greater. We witness heroic selves whose commitments and struggles would not be possible unless they were the strong, intelligent—indeed, willful—people who could and would pit themselves against odds that would daunt weaker ones. Leavis is right about the importance of imperson-

---

[16] Ibid.

[17] E.g. Aeschylus's *Agamemnon*, *The Libation Bearers*, or *Prometheus Bound*; Sophocles' *Antigone* or *Electra*; Euripides' *Medea* or *Hyppolitus*.

ality, but he is wrong to suppose that its source is "the willing adhesion of the individual self to something other than itself."

What, then, is the source of impersonality that characterizes our appreciation of tragic situations? It is the recognition that tragic situations reveal something about life, not merely about our own lives. Their significance is not that they threaten the projects of individual observers but that they threaten human projects. What they show is not that I am at risk but that we are all at risk. They do elicit my pity and fear, but the source of these emotions is that I see human life as pitiful and fearsome. My jeopardy has, in one sense, nothing to do with me. I am threatened not qua the individual I am but qua a member of the human race. And if I succeed in changing myself and my circumstances, the jeopardy would not be removed but would merely take on another form. Contingency, indifference, and destructiveness, being essential conditions of life, endanger us as we live, and they do so regardless of how, in what manner, or in pursuit of what projects we live. The impersonality of tragic situations comes from our appreciation of them as showing human fate, not my fate; from our understanding that in responding with fear and pity, our feelings are engaged by the human situations.

Of course, human fate is an abstraction. Human fate is the fate of individual human beings insofar as they resemble each other. Tragic situations drive home to us that, in some respects, we are all in the same boat. Nevertheless, we are so constituted that we have an immediate concern for the inhabitant of the boat who is ourselves. Thus, beyond the impersonal understanding looms the question of what *I* should do about *my* lot to cope with *my* fear and to avoid *my* becoming an object of pity. And there is much that I can do, much that we can all do, to lessen the threat of evil, to ameliorate the essential conditions of life, to make ourselves less open to injury by contingency, indifference, and destructiveness. However, after we have done all we reasonably and decently can, we still remain at risk.

The protagonists in tragic situations are brought to the realization of this risk, and they react in different ways. They see themselves at the mercy of fate, as the playthings of the gods, and then they may rage, despair, go mad, and die of a broken heart, as Lear and Kurtz did. Or they may summon up their remaining resources and in a glorious act assert themselves once more to prove that they are in control of their lives, like Oedipus blinding himself.[18] These are understand-

---

[18] His memorable words were:

Apollo, friends, Apollo—
he ordained my agonies—these, my pains on pains!

able and characteristic reactions, but they make matters even worse than they were because they add the evil the protagonists inflict on others and themselves to the evil they caused antecedently. Can we do better?

THE TENSION TRAGEDY REVEALS

This question brings us to the second point I mentioned above as being involved in the clarification of our emotional responses to tragic situations. We have just seen that the first point about the personal significance of tragic situations is that we are brought to understand the vulnerability of our own projects as part of the human condition, which inevitably affects us all, and not, as it were, a personal matter between the peculiar individuals we are and the cosmos. The natural next question is about the influence this understanding should have on our expectations regarding our various projects and, through them, on our chances of living good lives.

In characterizing tragic situations, I argued that they essentially involve a tension in *us*, between our desire to live good lives and the part of our nature that is receptive to evil in the forms of contingency, indifference, and destructiveness. What makes situations tragic is that the agents who cause great evil to themselves and others through their characteristic but unchosen actions and the agents who endeavor to live good lives are one and the same. Seeing tragic situations in this way presupposes the Socratic expectation that if we conduct ourselves reasonably and morally, then we shall have a good life. Without this expectation, all the facts involved in tragic situations would remain the same, but the element of tragedy would be removed. If we did not have this expectation, we would not feel as strongly as we do about the spectacle of great evil besetting representatives of humanity. We would not respond to tragic situations with fear and pity if they did not represent a profound challenge to our expectation that the world is so constituted that at least in the long run virtue will bring benefit and vice will bring harm to their agents. The significance of tragic situations is that they show the hollowness of this Socratic expectation. In Euripides' words:

So I have a secret hope
of someone, a God, who is wise and plans;
but my hopes grow dim when I see

But the hand that struck my eyes was mine,
mine alone—no one else—I did it all myself!

Sophocles, *Oedipus the King*, 1466–71

the deeds of men and their destinies.
For fortune is ever veering,
and currents of life are shifting
shifting wandering forever.[19]

Given our sensibility, this secret hope, this expectation of cosmic justice, must be abandoned. The philosophical significance of tragic situations is to force us to realize that this is so, that evil, understood as undeserved harm, is an ineliminable element in reality and in ourselves and that it endangers human projects, regardless of their merits.

At the end of the previous chapter, we reached the conclusion that the secular problem of evil is the existence of a tension between our aspiration to live good lives and the essential conditions of life, which render our aspirations vulnerable. In this chapter, we have seen that the philosophical significance of tragic situations is that they help us to understand that the tension exists in its most acute form in ourselves, that we are among the causes of our own vulnerability to evil.

[19] Euripides, *Hyppolitus*, 1105–10.

CHAPTER THREE

Evil, Desert, and Character-Morality

THE WIDE AND NARROW SENSES OF "EVIL"

Up to now, I have interpreted evil as undeserved harm. The time has come, however, to make the interpretation more precise, for the simple formula disguises various complexities. To keep the discussion manageable, I shall confine it to evil as it affects human beings. A full account would have to consider animals and perhaps also plants, other organisms, and possible sentient beings not presently known, but I shall ignore all of them here.

According to the *Oxford English Dictionary*, the primary sense of "evil" is "the antithesis of GOOD in all its principal senses." This may be interpreted widely or narrowly: "In the widest sense: That which is the reverse of good; whatever is censurable, mischievous, or undesirable . . . [E.g.] *moral, physical* evil." In the narrower sense, evil is "what is morally evil; sin, wickedness." Thus, the narrow sense is specifically moral, while the wide sense includes it, as well as all other forms of evil.

In the wide sense, contingency, indifference, and destructiveness all qualify as forms of evil because they are various antitheses of the good, understood as that which fosters the human aspiration to live personally satisfying and morally meritorious lives. In the narrow sense, contingency is often not a form of evil; destructiveness frequently is; and whether indifference is evil depends on whether people's not getting their due is morally censurable.

As an initial indication of the ground of the distinction between the wide and narrow senses, we may say that in the narrow, moral sense the question of whether the agent is liable to censure for causing evil is always appropriate while in the wide sense it may or may not be appropriate because, for instance, there may not be a censurable agent. Mass starvation caused by drought is an instance of contingency and of nonmoral evil, provided the drought is due to adverse climatic conditions and not to human stupidity or viciousness. The systematic extermination of a group of innocent people is an instance of destructiveness and of moral evil if, say, the murderers are moved by some noxious ideology. But this initial account still needs to be refined.

The distinction between moral and nonmoral evil does not coincide with the traditional distinction between moral and natural evil. The latter distinction suggests that moral evil is not natural. The source of this suggestion may be belief in a supernatural world to which evil is supposed to belong or the belief that evil is in some sense artificial, perhaps because it is a product of human conventions and not part of the basic furniture of the world. The reason for rejecting the first belief is that human knowledge is restricted to the natural world, since it is only about that world that we can obtain any information, so there can be no evidence for the existence of a supernatural world. The reason against the second belief is that there is a perfectly good sense in which evil is as natural as a multitude of other facts. I shall not argue further that belief in a supernatural world is unfounded; but I shall consider shortly and in greater detail the reason why belief in the artificiality of evil is false. In any case, in agreement with what I have called our sensibility, I shall proceed on the assumption that human beings are part of nature. Consequently, what we do, including the evil we cause, is as natural as the behavior of any other entity in nature. It follows from this that the distinction between moral and nonmoral evil is not the distinction between moral and natural evil.

We might try the suggestion, then, that the distinction between moral and nonmoral evil should be assimilated to the distinction between two kinds of natural events: those brought about by human agency and those that are not. But this suggestion is still unclear because "human agency" is ambiguous. It may refer either to what human beings choose to do or to what they do, regardless of whether they have a choice about it.

If choice is taken to be necessary for human agency, then it would follow that no unchosen action could be morally evil, since moral evil presupposes human agency. Hence, if mass murderers have been motivated by a pernicious ideology that they have accepted without choice because of early indoctrination, then it would be not merely questionable but self-contradictory to call their murderous actions morally evil. This is dubious, to say the least. It is central to the argument of this book that unchosen actions may be morally relevant. This, indeed, is part of the significance of tragic situations. For in such situations human agents act, as it were, not on their own behalf but as instruments of the essential conditions of life. They become the last links in causal chains through which contingency, indifference, and destructiveness jeopardize the human aspiration to live good lives. As we have seen, Oedipus, Lear, and Kurtz did not choose to be the way they were, nor, in the sense that matters, did they choose to act in the evil-producing ways they have acted. If unchosen actions were not morally relevant, then the consensus of intelligent readers of Sophocles, Shakespeare, and Conrad that, through their fictional characters, they are addressing moral questions of the first importance would be grotesquely mistaken. I shall keep returning to this point and argue for it at length. For the moment, I hope that enough has been said to prevent us from taking for granted that moral evil is identical with evil that people choose to cause.

If we do not restrict moral relevance to chosen actions, then we may say that evil that is not caused by human agency is nonmoral, while evil caused by human agency may or may not be moral, depending on the answer to the difficult question about the moral status of unchosen but evil-producing human actions. Thus, the distinction between moral and nonmoral evil can be said to rest on human agency being an indispensable condition of moral evil, while nonmoral evil involves nonhuman agency and may also involve some unchosen human acts. A human being causing undeserved harm by choice is necessary and sufficient for moral evil, while nothing qualifies as nonmoral evil if it is caused by human choice. This leaves the status of unchosen evil caused by human beings, for the time being, indeterminate; such evil may or may not be moral, and which it is will be discussed in the next chapter.

Throughout this book, "evil" will be used in the wide sense to include chosen evil caused by human beings, which is certainly moral, evil caused by nonhuman agency, which is necessarily nonmoral, and unchosen evil caused by human agency, whose classification needs yet to be considered.

The Primary and Derivative Senses of "Evil"

In its primary sense, "evil" may be said to refer to people being undeservedly harmed. I shall postpone discussion of what is deserved and undeserved and shall concentrate on harm. Of course, there are countless ways in which people may be harmed, and the harm may be the effect of a multitude of causes. But we can get a theoretical grip on evil if we bear in mind two considerations. First, evil is of moral concern because it is an obstacle to the human aspiration to live good lives; thus, what makes being harmed a form of evil is that it constitutes such an obstacle. Second, from the moral point of view, the important organizing principle behind the numerous causes of evil is the distinction between human and nonhuman causes. The moral importance of the distinction emerges from one central concern that morality must be acknowledged to have, namely, with minimizing evil in human lives. This concern makes morality into a practical enterprise: it aims to make things better, at least for human beings; or to put it less ambitiously, it aims to prevent things from becoming worse. So, morality is essentially connected with the possibility of control. Now control is exercised, if at all, by human beings. The first step toward the approximation of this aim must, therefore, be to try to control the human causes of evil. For the possibility of controlling nonhuman causes of evil depends on the commitment of those engaged in the task to the minimization of evil. Thus, we may say that in its primary sense "evil" refers to the undeserved harm human beings cause one another and themselves. And since such harm is caused by the actions of human agents, the subjects of which "evil" in its first derivative sense is predicated are human actions.

But "evil" also has various further derivative senses. We can identify one of these if we notice that the evil actions of individual agents often fall into patterns. The various forms of undeserved harm agents cause may not be isolated episodes but predictable expressions of settled dispositions to act in certain ways in certain situations. Selfishness, cruelty, envy, malice, jealousy, cowardice, and self-deception are some examples of such evil-producing dispositions. Thus, in one derivative sense of "evil," it may be used to refer not to human actions but to character traits of which the appropriate actions are expressions. These character traits are vices.

Character traits, of course, are possessed by people, and each of us has many of them. Whether a character trait is morally relevant depends on whether it prompts beneficial or harmful actions. Some character traits routinely do so, others only exceptionally. It is very hard for cruelty not to result in harmful actions, for kindness in beneficial actions, while it is exceptional for spatial memory or writing style to have moral relevance. People are complicated largely because their characters are constituted of many conflicting, competing, and coexisting traits. But there are people in whose characters some traits acquire dominance, and the preponderance of their actions is attributable to these dominant traits. Such people become notable examples of certain ways of being and acting. If the dominant character traits are vices, then their agents are regular sources of evil. In another derivative sense, we can then identify them, and not merely their actions and character traits, as evil.

"Evil" has additional derivative senses, but I shall not dwell on them, since they will not form an important part of the discussion. Customs, laws, rules, ceremonies, and rituals may be evil in a derivative way if conformity to or participation in them causes much undeserved harm. Often such practices are embodied in groups or institutions, which come to be dominated by them, as people may become dominated by vices; and then the groups or institutions themselves deserve to be called, derivatively, evil.

One important point to bear in mind is that the justification for the ascription of "evil" in its derivative senses is that there has been a pattern of primary evil that can be reasonably attributed to a character trait, person, practice, group, or institution. Thus, only if undeserved harm has been regularly inflicted is it proper to characterize its source as evil. Suspicion, fear, or caution, if reasonably based, are proper responses to the possibility of evil, but the condemnation implied by the ascription of "evil" is warranted only if a pattern has been established.

THE MORAL RELEVANCE OF EVIL

One consequence of interpreting "evil" in the wide sense is that, while evil must be recognized as a moral phenomenon of primary importance, its occurrence does not always imply immorality. In the first place, evil is sometimes nonmoral, because it is caused by nonhuman agency, and then there is no agent who could be reasonably censured for causing it. Second, evil may be caused by human beings but without the possibility of choice, and then they might not be liable for it. Unavoidable accidents that are due, say, to mechanical defects in the machines we operate might cause this kind of evil. Third, evil may be caused by choice, but only because it would require extraordinary resources to opt for the alternative to it, and so the agent choosing evil might be acquitted. Cases in point are soldiers doing their sworn duty in an unjust war. Fourth, people may choose to cause evil because they rightly judge that doing so is necessary for avoiding greater evil. Thus, one may kill an innocent person in order to save the lives of many other equally innocent people. In such cases, the evil-producing agents may actually deserve approbation rather than censure.

Just as these examples show that causing evil is not necessarily immoral, so too we must recognize that immorality need not involve causing evil. It is true that morality is centrally concerned with the minimization of evil and that immorality often takes the form of causing evil. But morality also has the other central concern of maximizing good. Thus, immorality may consist, not in causing evil, but in merely doing one's best to cause it but failing to do so, like attempted murder, or in refusing to contribute to someone's welfare when it is one's responsibility to do so, as in withholding affection in marriage or parenthood.[1]

[1] The complexities of the notion of immorality are well discussed by Milo in *Immorality*.

One deep problem about evil is how to decide whether its occurrence is an appropriate subject, first, of moral concern and, second, of moral censure. This leads us back to the idea that morality is practical because it aims at control. The commitments to minimizing evil and to maximizing good are necessary to participation in morality. But for these commitments to be other than quixotic gestures, it must be at least possible for morality to be effective. It is supposed by many that the area within which morality can be effective is defined by choice. Their assumption is that morality can be effective only if it can influence agents, and influence takes the form of guiding their choices.

Although this assumption may seem to be obvious, it is actually false. Certainly, morality includes the sphere of chosen actions, but it goes beyond it. As a preliminary indication of this being so, consider people who habitually cause undeserved harm without choosing to do so. I have in mind people ruled by vices that cause them to act in certain ways, yet they have not chosen either their vices or their evil-producing actions. Cruelty due to lifelong brutalization, prevalent prejudices accepted as moral principles, an inability to love, or cowardice masquerading as prudence are often such unchosen failures. Nevertheless, they do not cease to be moral failures on that score. If choice were necessary for the appropriateness of moral concern, we would have to regard it as self-contradictory to say that people, insofar as they are ruled by the vices just described, are moral agents and possible subjects of moral censure. I take it as obvious that such judgments are not self-contradictory, no matter how controversial they may be. What form our moral concern should take and how severe our moral censure should be are often agonizing questions. My point here is merely that the absence of choice does not disqualify us from asking the questions about the agents.

But if choice is not necessary for moral concern and moral censure, then how can morality be effective in minimizing evil? How can unchosen actions be controlled? How is moral censure related to being an agent of unchosen evil? Are we accountable for our characters? Should we be liable for vices we cannot help having? The first requirement of grappling with these questions is to consider more concretely the content of the evil actions that reflect the vices and characters of evil people.

SIMPLE EVIL AND CHARACTER-MORALITY

Evil is undeserved harm, and some occurrences of it are as hard, factual, observable, and empirical as other items in the furniture of the world. Harm can be simple and complex. Torture is simple harm; emotional blackmail is much more complex. The hardness of the fact of undeserved harm derives from simple harm. Simple harm is to deprive people of the minimum requirements of their welfare. To give content to the notion of simple harm, I need to specify some of the minimum requirements of human welfare. In doing so, I shall only repeat what everyone knows, but the repetition has a point, because the significance of these commonplaces tends to be overlooked.

The minimum requirements are universally human, culturally invariant, and historically constant features of human life.[2] Our physiology imposes requirements on all of us: we need to eat, drink, and breathe to survive; we need protection from the elements. Rest and motion, maturing and aging, pleasure and pain, consumption and elimination, and sleep and wakefulness form the rhythm of all normal human lives. If uninjured, we perceive the world in the same sense modalities; and within a narrow range, we are capable of the same motor responses. So, part of human nature is that all healthy members of our species have many of the same physiological needs and capacities for satisfying them.

We can go beyond these truisms by noticing that we do not merely want to satisfy our physiological needs by employing our capacities but that we want to do so in particular ways. These ways differ, of course, from person to person, culture to culture, age to age. But there is no difference in the psychological aspiration to go beyond necessity and enjoy the luxury of satisfying our needs in whatever ways happen to count as desirable to us. We all know the difference between a primitive state of nature, where our resources are exhausted by the requirements of survival, and a civilized state, where we have leisure, choices, and the security to go beyond necessity. And we all prefer the civilized state to the primitive one. Furthermore, we are alike in having the capacities to learn from the past and plan for the future; we have a view, perhaps never articulated, about what we want to make of our lives; we have likes and dislikes, and we try to have much of the former and little of the latter; we have capacities to think, remember, imagine, use language, have feelings, emotions, moods, and motives, make efforts, go after what we want, or restrain ourselves.

[2] "There is a massive central core of thinking which has no history—or none in recorded histories of thought; there are categories and concepts which, in their most fundamental character, change not at all. Obviously these are not the specialities of the most refined thinking. They are the commonplaces of the least refined thinking, and are yet the indispensable core of the conceptual equipment of the most sophisticated human beings" (Strawson, *Individuals*, Introduction).

These psychological needs and capacities also form part of human nature. But the facts so far described, constituted by these needs and capacities, concern primarily the agents themselves. We can go still further in describing human nature because personal and impersonal contacts with others are also inevitable features of human life.

We are born into families and depend on them or on surrogates during the first years of our lives. We live in a network of relationships with those responsible for our upbringing and with those who depend on us, with family members and with sexual partners; and we extend it when we enter the larger community of which these smaller units are parts. We acquire friends and enemies, we cooperate and compete with, look up to, help, teach, learn from, imitate, fear, love, admire, envy, and get angry at people we come to know. We share the griefs and joys of those close to us, we have positions in life that others recognize, we like and dislike others, and we are made happy or sad by them. These are also parts of human nature, and they concern the elements of our intimate relationships with other people.

Beyond them are more impersonal matters. Human vulnerability, scarce resources, the requirements and benefits of the distribution of labor, the need to adjudicate conflicts, and limited strength, intelligence, energy, and skill force cooperation on us. Social life exists because only within it can we satisfy our physiological and psychological needs in the ways we want, create and protect conditions in which we can exercise our capacities, and establish and maintain close relationships. The form social life takes is the establishment of some authority, the emergence of institutions and conventional practices, and the slow development and the deliberate formulation of rules; all these demand conformity from members of a society. Different societies have different authorities, institutions, conventions, and rules. But no society can do without them, and we cannot do without some participation in social life, provided we seek the satisfaction of our physiological and psychological needs.

These commonplace facts and others like them form a universal and unchanging aspect of human nature. There are, of course, innumerable other facts, and they form the individual and variable aspect of human nature. But I have concentrated on the universal aspect because of its connection with morality. Given that one primary concern of morality is with minimizing evil, it is not surprising that understanding human nature should be morally important. For it helps us to identify at least some of the things that are harmful for all human beings, and it helps us to see the reason why they are so. Consequently, if we have reached the right conclusions about the universal aspect of human nature, conclusions sketched in my list of truisms, then we can identify a large number of things that will be harmful for everyone, always, everywhere. These constitute what I mean by *simple harm*.

Simple harm is caused by frustrating the needs and curtailing the exercise of the capacities I have included in the description of human nature. The importance of this list of physiological, psychological, and social facts of human nature is that they constitute some of the minimum requirements of human welfare. In the absence of countervailing moral arguments, to jeopardize the conditions in which physiological needs are satisfied, so that people's lives and health are endangered, is obviously evil. Death, dismemberment, lasting physical pain, and prolonged hunger and thirst are normally evil. The same air of obviousness surrounds the satisfaction of psychological needs. If there are no moral reasons for it, it is evil to deprive people of the opportunity to direct their lives, assess what they regard as important, develop their capacities, and do what they can to make good lives for themselves. The facts of social life provide the conditions in which physiological and psychological needs can be satisfied. In an anarchic society, the failure to guarantee security and some freedom, and the breakdown of established authority and rules for settling disputes and adjudicating conflicts are evil, provided there are no overriding moral considerations prompting us to think differently.[3]

Thus, we can distinguish between simple and complex evil. *Simple evil* is to cause simple harm to people who do not deserve it. *Complex evil* derives from particular conceptions of good lives. These conceptions are historically, culturally, and individually variable, and they presuppose, but also go beyond, the minimum requirements of human welfare. I shall concentrate on simple evil from now on. And the first claim I take to be established about it is that since one of the primary concerns of morality is with minimizing evil, it has a presumption in favor of avoiding simple evil.

My argument has proceeded from truisms about human nature to the moral presumption against causing simple evil. It implies three intimately connected theses. The first thesis is that simple evil provides morality with some objective content. Since morality is concerned, among other things, with minimizing simple evil, there are

[3] My list of truisms has obvious affinities with several recent attempts to provide similar arguments. My position is closest to Gert's in *The Moral Rules*, especially chapters 5 and 6. But it is also similar to Rawls's account of primary goods in *A Theory of Justice* (see the index for relevant entries) and to Gewirth's discussion of necessary goods in *Reason and Morality*, especially 52–65.

some objectively true or false moral judgments. They are objective in the sense that they concern factual matters, and whether the facts are as judged is independent of the moral attitudes of the person judging. Let us call this the thesis of *the objectivity of simple evil*.

Of course, this thesis does not license the claim that moral judgments are objective when they are about complex evil or other matters. From this thesis, there follows no conclusion regarding the objectivity of higher-order moral judgments. But it does have the consequence of excluding radical versions of relativism, historicism, and subjectivism. I mean by these the denial of the universality and constancy of simple evil on the ground that what counts as simple evil varies with cultures, historical periods, or individuals. If simple evil is as I have described it, then it does not vary in the ways asserted by these theories.

The second thesis is implied by the first. Whether moral judgments about simple evil are true or false depends on whether or not people have been harmed in certain ways. Thus, their truth or falsehood is independent of the mental states of the agent whose action is being judged. This being so, it is a mistake to claim, as Kant does, that the moral evaluation of actions "consists, not in the effects which result from them, not in the advantage or profit they produce, but in the attitudes of mind . . . which are ready in this way to manifest themselves in action even if they are not favored by success."[4] The moral evaluation of simple evil depends not on its agents' being in the appropriate mental state but on the undeserved simple harm they cause. The connection between mental states and simple evil is contingent. As a matter of fact, some mental states do tend to result in morally censurable actions. But if they do, it is this fact that they usually produce simple evil that makes them morally suspect, and not, as Kant asserts, any quality intrinsic to mental states and independent of the consequences that may follow from them. I labor this point because, as we have seen, Kant and his followers identify the sought-for intrinsic quality with choice, and they regard its presence as a necessary condition for the appropriateness of moral censure. It follows from the second thesis, however, that what counts as simple evil depends on its connection with undeserved simple harm, and not on the mental state of its agents. I shall refer to this as the thesis of *the irrelevance of choice to simple evil*; I discuss it further in the next chapter.

The third thesis is about the consequences causing simple evil has for the moral standing of the agents. An action causing simple evil

[4] Kant, *Groundwork*, 102–3.

may be chosen or unchosen, characteristic or uncharacteristic, part of a pattern or an isolated episode. Simple evil may be caused by the unchosen vices of some agents. What makes some character traits into vices is that people who have them regularly, predictably, and habitually cause simple evil. The character traits of moral agents form various patterns in which one may outweigh, balance, or be overwhelmed by the others. If vices achieve dominance in the character of moral agents, then it is proper to characterize such agents as, derivatively, evil. They are evil because, being ruled by their vices, they frequently and predictably cause evil. So, there is a progression from being an agent causing simple evil by one's actions, to being moved by vices, and from there to being an evil person. This is the thesis of *the reflexivity of simple evil*.

So, the truisms about simple evil imply three far from truistic theses: simple evil is objective, choice is irrelevant to its moral status, and the condemnation of evil actions often reflects on the moral standing of the agents of these actions. Of course, more needs to be, and will be, said about them, but these three theses may be regarded as the minimum content of *character-morality*,[5] a conception of morality that permits us to face evil with some hope of success.

CHARACTER-MORALITY AND DESERT

Character-morality is concerned with promoting human welfare. We may say that this concern is necessary for character-morality because commitment to character-morality is inseparable from commitment to promoting human welfare. Of course, human welfare includes our own welfare, so commitment to character-morality does not oblige us to be indifferent to our own welfare. And of course what human welfare comes to in many different situations is often controversial, as are answers to the question of how best to promote it in a wide variety of settings. But these are controversies *within* character-morality, not *about* it, because they presuppose commitment to promoting human welfare. Nor am I suggesting that this necessary concern of charac-

---

[5] Character-morality belongs to a family of approaches to morality that have been characterized as eudaimonistic, or virtue theories. The literature on this topic is rapidly becoming unmanageable, but for some of the main works, see Foot, *Virtues and Vices*; MacIntyre, *After Virtue*; Norton, *Personal Destinies*; Nussbaum, *The Fragility of Goodness*; Pincoffs, *Quandaries and Virtues*; Wallace, *Virtues and Vices*; and two collections of representative essays: Kruschwitz and Roberts, eds., *The Virtues* (this has a useful bibliography), and French et al., eds., *Ethical Theory: Character and Virtue*, as well as my own books *The Examined Life* and *Moral Tradition and Individuality*. All of the above concentrate on the good-approximating aspect of morality and on the virtues, while I am interested here in the evil-avoiding aspect and in some of the vices.

ter-morality is the only one it has. Character-morality is also concerned with the rights and obligations of specific positions, like those of a physician, a judge, or a parent, with particular virtues and vices, with various conceptions of good lives, and so on. But these other concerns of character-morality must also satisfy the basic requirement that whatever is found to satisfy them must, at the very least, contribute to human welfare.

The interpretation of what commitment to human welfare involves is left deliberately vague to allow for moral disagreements. Minimally, it involves acting in the interest of the welfare of at least some people apart from oneself; maximally, it is to act in the interest of humanity. In between these extremes, there are numerous more or less inclusive interpretations. My own view is that few people, if indeed any, ever have the opportunity of acting in the interest of humanity. Questions about human welfare normally present themselves as questions about the welfare of some individuals or groups. So, people committed to character-morality typically need to decide what to do in particular contexts in respect to particular individuals. The commitment to human welfare thus translates into the disposition to promote the welfare of those in our context, and moral disagreements about the inclusiveness of the commitment turn on how extensively we should define that context. Be that as it may, the main point is that, given the necessary concern of character-morality, nothing can qualify as a moral concern unless it aims at promoting human welfare; whatever other concerns character-morality has must be subordinated to the necessary one.

Yet this necessary concern is general, not specific. Situations often arise in which the general concern is best served by violating some specific requirement of human welfare. Avoidance of the simple harms included in my list of truisms are specific requirements of human welfare. Thus, character-morality establishes a general presumption in favor of satisfying them. But this presumption may be justifiably overruled on the grounds that the general concern of character-morality is better served by frustrating a specific need or restraining the exercise of a specific capacity. For instance, it is true that in general death is a simple harm, so there is a moral presumption against it. However, the presumption may be overruled in case of incurable illness involving prolonged and extreme pain.

The nature of desert, as the link between simple harm and simple evil, can now be put more precisely. What makes simple harm into simple evil is that it is undeserved, and it is undeserved unless there is an acceptable moral reason for thinking otherwise. Moreover, the only acceptable moral reason for overruling the presumption against simple harm being undeserved is that by doing so the general concern of morality is better served.

What exactly minimizes evil in specific situations is often an immensely complicated question. I doubt that there is any general answer to it. It seems to me that the best answer depends on attending to the details of whatever specific situation happens to be at hand. In any case, my aim here is not to consider the extent to which moral judgments can be generalized but to explain what I take to be the only acceptable justification for overruling the presumption against causing undeserved simple harm—against causing simple evil.

The essential feature of desert is that it is fitting, proper, or appropriate that individuals should receive their due. But it is also essential that the entitlement created by desert should be based on some characteristics or actions of the individuals to whom it is due. What makes individuals deserving is that they have certain characters or they have acted in certain ways. So, desert has its roots in the past, and it is a response to it. Now what individuals deserve varies with circumstances, but in general, it is either benefit or harm. Merit creates an entitlement to some benefits, and demerit does likewise to some harm. The nature of this entitlement, as the content of desert, is general. It translates into the claim that it would be a good thing if the individuals in question received some benefits or harms. And what would make that good is that they have some merits or demerits that create a presumption in favor of their having or not having something.

Moral merit is a special kind of merit. The entitlement created by it derives from the characteristics or actions of individuals that have caused evil or good. Thus, in the context of character-morality, the claim that some agents deserve something is based on their virtues or vices and on their good- or evil-producing actions. This entitlement is to be understood in an unspecific sense. To say that it would be a good thing if particular individuals received some particular benefits or harms is not to say that some institution or person has the obligation to make that good thing happen. There may be such an obligation in some cases, such as entitlements created by debts, promises, or contracts, but not in many other cases, where the entitlement is a claim toward the scheme of things rather than toward specific individuals, as when we say that a good person deserves to be happy or that an evil one does not deserve robust health or riches.

Thus, claims about moral desert express the ideal that life should be such that moral merit receives the appropriate benefit and moral demerit results in the appropriate harm. Part of the reason why we find the tragic situations of Oedipus, Lear, and Kurtz so disturbing is that they violate this ideal. They suggest that our ideal may be grossly unrealistic.

It may be asked, however, why the presumption against causing simple harm is put in terms of desert? Why is simple evil understood as *undeserved* simple harm? We may be quite prepared to share the commitment to human welfare and, at the same time, be reluctant to do so on the grounds of desert. A case in point is Rawls's influential view that "desert presupposes the existence of . . . [a] cooperative scheme."[6] According to this view, desert is a function of institutional arrangements, and so appeals to it cannot be as basic to morality as I suppose. I shall defer detailed criticism of Rawls's view until chapter 6, but the following reasons for the privileged moral status of desert should be considered here.

First, if desert were not a fundamental moral notion, then we would be deprived of one of the strongest reasons for criticizing institutions. A very good moral reason for being opposed to an institution is that it causes undeserved harm to people. If desert were a product of institutions, then, provided an institution functioned in accordance with its own rules, it could not cause undeserved harm, because its rules, according to this suggestion, define what counts as desert. Our constant practice of criticizing institutions on just that ground shows that desert is a more fundamental notion than Rawls supposes.

Second, if desert were not basic, what would occupy the place I am supposing it to have? The currently favored candidates are rights, needs, and wants. The idea is that the basic requirement of human welfare is that people's rights should be protected, or needs be met, or wants be satisfied. But in each case we can and should ask why we should favor whatever people's rights, needs, or wants turn out to be. And the answer must ultimately be that we value people, we are committed to their welfare, and so we think that they *deserve* respect for their rights, needs, or wants, unless there is an acceptable moral reason for thinking otherwise.

The privileged status of desert, however, may be attacked, not on the grounds that something else has the status I mistakenly attribute to it, but on the grounds that nothing has it. Simple evil is not *undeserved* harm, nor is it harm caused by the violation of rights, or by the frustration of needs or wants, but harm itself, pure and simple. According to this suggestion, one fundamental moral notion is that it is evil to inflict harm on people.[7] Although this is an attractive idea, it

---

[6] Rawls, *A Theory of Justice*, 103.

[7] This suggestion is implicit in Gert's *Moral Rules*. My rejection of it constitutes one of my chief, and few, disagreements with Gert.

does not do the job intended for it. Harming people may actually be beneficial because, like surgery, it prevents greater harm in the future; furthermore, morality may require us to harm people if doing so constitutes just punishment, such as depriving murderers of their freedom. Thus, harm, pure and simple, need not be evil. It is evil only if there is no morally acceptable reason for causing it. But to say that evil is *undeserved* harm is just a succinct way of saying that harm becomes evil in the absence of moral justification.

Last, to put the point in favor of the fundamentality of desert positively, rather than negatively, as in the considerations presented above, the idea that people should not be undeservedly harmed expresses one basic presupposition about what people are entitled to simply by being what they are. To have moral concern is, minimally, to believe that the world should be such a place that people are not subject to simple evil, that they should not have undeserved harm inflicted on them.

We must, however, be clear that this justification of desert being a fundamental moral notion is a moral justification. It presupposes commitment to the necessary concern of character-morality, to promoting human welfare. There are people who do not have that commitment, and so the justification will not convince them. The response to such cases depends on why the people in question do not have the commitment. One possibility is that they do not understand that the commitment to human welfare is inseparably connected to the aspiration to have good lives for themselves. Such a life requires personal relationships and a stable society hospitable to one's aspiration, and this, in turn, requires reasonable agents to care about the welfare of at least those people to whom they are connected either intimately or by being members of the same society. If people do not understand that this is so, it can be explained to them. If they are incapable of understanding the explanation, they are mentally deficient and are disqualified from moral agency. If they understand it but reject it for personal, political, or some other reason and habitually cause simple evil by disregarding human welfare, then they become primary candidates for being evil, and they are to be treated in whatever way it is proper to treat evil people.

However, the fact of the matter is that most people are not indifferent to human welfare. Hume, I think, was right about this. "I am of the opinion," writes Hume, "that tho' it be rare to meet one, who loves any single person better than himself; yet 'tis rare to meet one, in whom all the kind affections, taken together, do not overbalance all the selfish."[8] I am less sanguine than Hume was about the actual

[8] Hume, *Treatise*, 487.

numbers in the party of humanity, but I think his general point still holds. And if we are tempted to ask why it holds, Hume replies: "It is needless to push our researches so far as to ask, why we have humanity or a fellow-feeling with others. It is sufficient, that this is experienced to be a principle of human nature. . . . No man is absolutely indifferent to the happiness and misery of others. The first has a natural tendency to give pleasure; the second pain. This every man finds in himself."[9] Those who like to know what experimental evidence there is for such common-sense claims may find it surveyed by Brandt.[10]

Of course, from the fact that people have at least some minimal moral concern, it does not follow that it prevents them from causing evil, for they may not act on the moral concern they have. The reasons for this are various. They may have other concerns that dominate over the moral ones; or they may mistakenly believe that they are acting to promote human welfare because they are guided by a pernicious morality; or they may be in the grip of forces that they cannot withstand, and so they have no choice about causing evil; or they intend to act on their moral concerns, but character-defects prevent them from doing so. Thus, Hume's being right about the general predisposition toward character-morality is not incompatible with believing that there is much evil caused by human agency.

This account of the place of desert in character-morality raises many questions. What exactly are moral merits and demerits? What benefits and harms are appropriate in their cases? What happens or should happen if people do not get what they deserve? What is the force of the claim that it would be a good thing if people got what they deserve? These are difficult questions. Until about 1960, only the most cursory philosophical discussion of moral desert was available. But this situation has changed during the recent past.[11] My thinking about moral desert differs, however, in several respects from what is beginning to emerge as the contemporary consensus. I shall now discuss some of these differences in order to develop further my account of desert.

Many writers think of desert in terms of economic distribution.

[9] Hume, *Enquiry*, 219–20.

[10] Brandt, "The Psychology of Benevolence."

[11] In chronological order, the following contributions seem particularly important: Feinberg, "Justice and Personal Desert"; Barry, *Political Argument*, 106–15; Rawls, *A Theory of Justice*, 310–15; Nozick, *Anarchy, State, and Utopia* (see index for relevant entries); Miller, *Social Justice*, 83–121; Zaitchik, "On Deserving to Deserve"; Galston, *Justice and the Human Good*, 170–91; Sandel, *Liberalism and the Limits of Justice* (see index for relevant entries); and Sher, *Desert*.

The question of what people deserve is interpreted by them as concerning the material goods people ought to have.[12] I think of desert as a fundamental moral notion that includes, in addition to material goods, many other kinds of goods, such as moral, political, psychological, and personal. The goods I regard as relevant to moral desert are the external and internal goods required by good lives.

One consequence of the prevalent narrow focus on desert is that claims about it are generally regarded as merely one among many different legitimate moral claims.[13] By contrast, my view is that claims about desert are fundamental moral claims because they concern all the requirements of good lives. Particular moral claims ultimately presuppose the legitimacy of claims about desert, since particular claims assume that people are entitled to some good or another, and I interpret entitlement in terms of desert. The ground of my interpretation is that human welfare is the necessary concern of character-morality, so that commitment to character-morality involves commitment to the idea that individuals deserve good lives unless there are acceptable moral reasons for thinking otherwise.

Another way in which my interpretation of desert differs from the one accepted by many writers concerns the relation between desert and choice. It is widely assumed that there is a necessary connection between them, so that claims about desert are supposed to be grounded on the free, autonomous, or voluntary actions of agents.[14] However, if desert is the moral response to people having caused evil or good, then choice cannot be a necessary condition of it, because people can and do cause evil or good without choosing to do so. I have introduced this issue earlier and will discuss it in detail in the next chapter.

A much-needed clarification of the idea of desert has been the recognition that claims about desert are various because there are different types of desert. The following list contains some main types of desert, but I make no claim to its being exhaustive. People can be said to deserve (1) high or low ranking in some comparative hierarchy, (2) reward or punishment for something they have or have not done, (3) praise or blame for being or acting in certain ways, (4) gratitude or resentment for their conduct, (5) compensation or penalty for some

---

[12] E.g. Rawls often speaks of desert in terms of "distributive shares"; see e.g. *A Theory of Justice*, 312–13. Nozick, in criticizing Rawls, nevertheless writes about how "holdings ought to be distributed" (*Anarchy, State, and Utopia*, 215).

[13] See Miller, *Social Justice*, part 1; Galston, *Justice and the Human Good*, 171–91; Sher, *Desert*, chapters 4–8.

[14] See e.g. Barry, *Political Argument*, 108 ("a person's having been able to have done otherwise is a *necessary condition* of ascribing desert"); Sher, *Desert*, 158–59.

harm they have suffered or caused, (6) fortune or misfortune affecting their aspirations, (7) flourishing or languishing in their lives, and (8) admiration or obloquy for their accomplishments or failures.[15]

There is a general agreement emerging that, because there are these and perhaps other types of desert, desert is a pluralistic notion. Consequently, it is not to be supposed that all claims about desert have the same basis or the same justification.[16] On my view, however, moral desert, at least, does have a unitary basis and justification, whatever may be true of other types of desert. The basis is the moral merit of the agents who are said to deserve something. And moral merit depends on the good or evil the agents have caused in the past. Of course, there are many forms of good and evil, many ways of having merit, and many kinds of moral desert. There is no doubt that desert is a pluralistic notion. But underlying the plurality, there is a unity established by the necessary concern of character-morality with promoting human welfare. Good actions contribute to it, and evil actions detract from it, but both reflect on the moral merits of their agents, and so they constitute both the basis and the justification of claims about desert.

This way of thinking about desert has the advantage of recognizing the plurality of different types of moral desert without sacrificing the simplicity and force of having a unitary account. It also provides a relatively simple way of distinguishing between moral and nonmoral desert. Many writers make use of this distinction, but without offering a justification for it.[17] On my account, however, moral desert has to do with moral merit, and moral merit derives from having caused good or evil. Thus, moral desert is justified by reference to the necessary concern of character-morality. Nonmoral desert, then, is constituted of forms of entitlement that derive from agents' being or acting in ways that have no obvious connection with good or evil, such as athletic or aesthetic achievement, or outstanding accomplishment as a collector, stylist, or inventor of ingenious gadgets. Yet difficulties remain even on my account—it is impossible to tell a priori whether some way of being or acting could not be morally relevant. I doubt

[15] In compiling this list, I have drawn on Feinberg, "Justice and Personal Desert," 62; Galston, *Justice and the Human Good*, 170–76; and Sher, *Desert*, 6–7.

[16] This is argued most explicitly by Sher in *Desert*, which is the only book-length treatment of the topic. Sher concedes that much simplicity and force is lost by giving up the idea that there is a unitary source or justification for claims about desert, but he finds no acceptable candidate. Yet, in his search for unity, he examines only one candidate, what he calls "the expected-consequence account," and after rightly rejecting it, assumes without further argument that none can be found.

[17] See e.g. Sher, *Desert*, 129–31.

that this difficulty can be overcome in any other way than by examining the claim that a particular candidate is entitled to moral desert. But a ready test is available: the claim is justified if the candidate can be shown to have caused good or evil; otherwise, the claim about moral desert fails.

One of the main contentions I hope to substantiate is that there is a prevalent reluctance to face evil and that it has morally damaging consequences. Current discussions of desert are cases in point, because many authors share the reluctance to face evil. This shows itself in their concentration on the positive side of desert, on claims that people deserve benefits, and in their generally ignoring the negative side, when what people deserve is harm. Even those who find it fitting, proper, or appropriate that benefits should be commensurate with moral merit show a marked disinclination to make harms proportional to moral demerit.[18] The assumptions behind this line of thought run deep, and they ultimately bear on views about human nature and the nature of morality. I shall discuss and criticize these assumptions in chapters 5–7. However, as a preliminary indication, I mention two often-cited considerations against inflicting deserved harm.

First, if people deserve to be harmed, by way of either punishment or deterrence, it is because they have caused undeserved harm. But since "the past wrong, just because it is past, cannot be annulled,"[19] as a result of harming the evildoer "we would have two wrongs now, not one that has been righted."[20] So, if character-morality aims at the minimization of evil, causing deserved harm should not be part of it. The difficulty with this argument is its failure to distinguish between harm and evil. Harming evildoers is deserved harm, and so it is not evil. Thus, the claim that "we would have two wrongs now" is false. Harming evildoers would be wrong only if character-morality were concerned with minimizing harm, but harming people who deserve it may be required by morality, if doing so minimizes evil.

The second consideration against inflicting deserved harm denies that it could minimize evil. The thought behind it derives from a misinterpretation of the type of argument Hume offers about the general predisposition toward benevolence. It is supposed that if moral agents cause evil, they do so because some external interference has corrupted their native benevolence. The remedy is to remove the corrupting influence, rather than to harm the agents. Harming them will

[18] See e.g. Becker, *Reciprocity*, 94–103; Miller, *Social Justice*, 98–100; and Sher, *Desert*, 149.

[19] Mackie, "Morality and the Retributive Emotions," 4–5.

[20] Wolgast, *The Grammar of Justice*, 159.

merely continue the process of reacting to harm by causing more harm. What is needed is to interrupt the process, not to exacerbate it. I say that this argument rests on a misinterpretation of the Humean notion about benevolence because benevolence being a predisposition is perfectly compatible with there being other predispositions that conflict and compete with benevolence. As we have seen, contingency, indifference, and destructiveness may come to dominate the lives and actions of moral agents precisely because their nonbenevolent predispositions make them receptive to these evil-producing tendencies. Thus, the removal of obstacles to the expression of benevolence is insufficient, since the evil moral agents cause may be due to their nonbenevolent predispositions, rather than to the benevolent ones becoming corrupted. As I have said, however, these questions concern fundamental matters that have to be, and will be, considered further. What I hope to have shown here is that character-morality is a conception of morality that pays due attention to evil and that it recognizes the intimate connection between evil and moral desert.

THE MINIMUM CONTENT OF CHARACTER-MORALITY

The tragic view of life locates the source of the secular problem of evil in ourselves. We are so constituted, according to this view, that our aspiration to live good lives exists in us in a state of tension with the inhospitable essential conditions of life that our actions often reflect. These conditions often jeopardize our aspirations to live good lives, and this is at the root of the secular problem of evil. My aim is to come to grips with this problem. The first step toward it is to understand evil. I have made a start and in subsequent chapters will continue to develop character-morality, a conception in terms of which, I believe, evil can be understood.

We have begun with the formula of evil as undeserved harm, and I have been offering an analysis of the phenomenon behind the formula. The evil I am considering includes both moral and nonmoral evil. Paradigmatically, evil caused by human choice is moral, while evil caused by nonhuman agency is nonmoral. I have deferred until the next chapter consideration of evil caused by human beings but without choice. In its primary sense, "evil" refers to undeserved harm; in its derivative senses, "evil" describes human actions that cause undeserved harm and character traits, people, practices, groups, and institutions from which stem actions that are evil in the primary sense. Evil may be simple or complex. Simple evil involves undeservedly harming people by depriving them of the minimum requirements of their welfare. Simple harm is undeserved if there is no morally acceptable justification for causing it. And such justification can only be that causing it is required by human welfare. Throughout the discussion, "evil" will mean simple evil, unless otherwise noted.

The other component of the formula is desert. People deserve to have what is due to them, and what that is depends on their moral merits, that is, on the good and evil they have caused in the past. Character-morality is a conception of morality that unites these concerns with evil and desert. Its minimum content is defined by the objectivity of simple evil, the irrelevance of choice to simple evil, and the reflexivity of simple evil. As the argument advances, this minimum content of character-morality will be expanded.

CHAPTER FOUR

Unchosen Evil

In the previous chapter, I deferred discussion of unchosen evil, and I now propose to take up this topic. Unchosen evil is clearly not non-moral, because it is caused by human beings. But it does not seem to be clearly moral either, because human beings do not choose to cause it. I shall argue that unchosen evil may still be moral and thus an appropriate subject for moral concern and, possibly, for moral censure. This kind of evil occurs when human agents cause undeserved harm without being able to do otherwise. Yet we cannot say that they are causing it accidentally, because their evil actions follow from their unchosen vices, they are symptomatic of enduring dispositions, and they occur when they act naturally and spontaneously, in accordance with vices they have developed but without choosing to develop them. Part of the significance of tragic situations is that they force our attention to such cases.

Concentration on unchosen vices and on the unchosen evil actions that follow from them is not the exploration of an obscure corner of moral psychology. Most of us have some unchosen vices because our characters embody the essential conditions of life. Our unchosen vices are the ways in which contingency, indifference, and destructiveness come to be expressed through our agency, as they have been through Oedipus, Lear, and Kurtz. I shall argue that such vices are ubiquitous and are responsible for much evil.

This is not to deny that our actions are often chosen or that our chosen actions are capable of transforming our characters. It is rather to recognize that alongside the part of our characters capable of choices there is a very large part formed by genetic inheritance, physical circumstances, and psychological and social influences over which we have no, or only negligible, control. This part is the substratum upon which choices may produce alterations. But the extent to which we can choose, the kind of choices we can make, and the effect these choices may have on our characters are themselves dependent on the unchosen part of our characters.

In the light of these considerations, we can now sharpen the questions posed in the previous chapter regarding the connection between character-morality and unchosen evil. First, are unchosen vices and the corresponding evil-producing actions appropriate subjects for moral concern? I shall argue in this chapter that they are. This raises a second question, to be considered in subsequent chapters; namely, what is the appropriate moral reaction to such vices and actions?

THE NATURE OF CHOICE

Let us begin by considering the nature of choice. The literature on this controversial topic is immense,[1] and I shall not attempt to do justice to the complexities of the various issues. Nor is it necessary for my purposes to have a set of criteria enabling us to decide in case of any action whether or not it is based on choice. All we need is a rule of thumb for identifying a large number of typical chosen and unchosen actions. This is compatible with recognizing, as we must, that there are many cases whose classification is bound to be difficult. My procedure will be to list some general conditions, conformity to which entitles us, in normal circumstances, to describe an action as chosen. If an action clearly and noncontroversially fails to conform to one or more of these conditions, then it is unchosen.

The essential feature of choice is that we are in a position where we can perform a number of actions and that we decide to perform one in order to bring about a certain result. The conditions of having a choice are thus the availability of alternatives and the possession and exercise of capacities to make decisions regarding them. Alternatives are available if we are not forced by physical conditions or by serious threats. And having the capacities consists in understanding the situation, not being overwhelmed by emotions, and being able to exercise our will.

In typical chosen actions, then, (1) the agents decide to bring about certain results; (2) they believe that by performing specific actions in appropriate circumstances, their chances of achieving the result will be at least enhanced; (3) they are not forced physically or by threats to aim at the result or to perform the relevant actions; (4) they have the cognitive, emotional, and volitional capacities to aim at other results and to perform both the actions in question and alternative actions; and (5) they understand the situation in which they are to act.

To make this concrete, consider Mrs. Jones's divorce from her husband as an example of a chosen action. She wants to have a better

---

[1] For seminal essays, surveys of the literature, and useful bibliographies, see Davis, *Theory of Action*; Fischer, *Moral Responsibility*; and Watson, *Free Will*.

life. She believes that by divorcing her husband she is more likely to achieve it than by remaining married to him. Mrs. Jones is not forced, say, because gangsters threatened to kill her children unless she divorces Mr. Jones. She is not in the throes of a passionate, overpowering love affair; she is not obsessed by hatred of her husband; and her judgment is not obstructed by low intelligence, drugs, or insanity. Moreover, she understands tolerably well what she has to do to seek and obtain divorce and understands that it will bring about certain obvious and predictable changes in the lives of her family and herself.

So far, I think, this rule of thumb for identifying actions based on choice is fairly clear. But now complications enter because often there is no clear-cut answer to the question of whether the conditions are met. Take the first two conditions to begin with: the results the agents decide to bring about may be impossible, and their beliefs that specific actions will help to achieve them may be absurd. Mrs. Jones may understand by the better life she desires the regaining of her youth and starting all over again as a young woman. She decides to do this, she believes that shedding her husband is an important first step toward it, yet her decision and her belief are so unrealistic as to make us suspect that she may be skirting mental disorder. And if this is so, then we must doubt that her action is chosen, even though it meets the first two conditions.

Similar questions arise about the condition of not being forced, because it is often difficult to tell what constitutes force. Criminals threatening to kill her children unless she divorces probably qualifies, although not in the very strong sense of leaving her no choices whatsoever, for she could go to the police or send her children out of the country. However, this is perhaps stretching things. But suppose that the threat is veiled and unspecific and that it comes from a meanlooking character whom she suspects of being an underworld figure. Is she forced then?

Take the next condition, the cognitive, emotional, and volitional capacity to act otherwise. Imagine that her marriage has been absolute hell; her husband is a monster who has regularly beaten her and raped their children. She has gotten to the breaking point, and she cannot think about anything else but freeing herself and her children. Her emotional resources are exhausted, and understandably but monomaniacally, she wants out. She feels that she has no options left; doing anything else is inconceivable to her. Is her divorce, in that case, a matter of choice?

Consider finally the condition of understanding the situation. Suppose Mrs. Jones is not very intelligent, quite impractical, and rather dreamy and that her marriage is neither very good nor very bad. She has not really thought through what the better life after divorce would be like, but she vaguely imagines it to be like her present one with the irritants removed. She has not considered the children's response, her financial circumstances, the positive aspects of her marriage, or what she will do with herself. Just how poor does her judgment have to be before the action based on it ceases to be chosen?

In all these cases, the conditions of choice shade into lack of choice. It is useless to try to fix a line and say that it marks the distinction. But this need not disconcert us. Let us acknowledge the existence of numerous borderline cases that are due to the difficulty of establishing what precisely are the necessary and sufficient conditions of choice and whether particular instances conform to these conditions. Yet alongside unclear cases, there are also clear ones, and it is upon these that my discussion will focus. Actions are clearly unchosen if the agents did not decide to perform them, if they had no strong reason to believe that the actions would produce the results they did produce, if they were forced to perform the actions, if they were psychologically incapable of doing anything else, or if they lacked understanding of their situations.

My interest in the coming discussion will be in unchosen actions of a particular kind: those that bring about undeserved harm and so are evil, yet they are not isolated episodes in the lives of agents but follow from the agents' vices. My view is that a great deal of evil is due to unchosen vices. Actions based on choice are like the tip of an iceberg, and beneath them lie submerged the vast mass of genetic, environmental, psychological, and social forces that form our characters and are thus indirectly responsible for both our chosen and unchosen vices and actions. The plausibility of this view rests on showing that there indeed are many generally shared unchosen vices and that there really may not be a choice involved in acquiring and acting according to them. Thus, my argument must become concrete and focus on specific vices.

I shall consider three types of widespread and unchosen vices: insufficiency, expediency, and malevolence. The reason for considering these is that they are typical ways in which the essential conditions of life inform our characters and exert their influence on our conduct. Often, contingency appears as insufficiency, indifference as expediency, and destructiveness as malevolence. Of course, there are numerous other vices, and of course these are not the only ways in which the essential conditions of life affect our characters.[2] But I shall ignore other vices and ways, for I do not aim at a complete account.

[2] For an account of some such vices, see Shklar, *Ordinary Vices*.

For the sake of clarity, I shall discuss these three vices in their pure forms. Actually, life is messy, vices are rarely pure, and choice is a matter of degree. But it is useful to have clear cases if we want to understand the complications inherent in unclear ones. I call insufficiency, expediency, and malevolence vices because in some people they form enduring character traits and predictably manifest themselves in evil actions. Yet—and this is crucial to my case—neither the evil actions nor the vices that prompt them are chosen. The agents do not decide to cause evil, yet they do so as a regular by-product of their characters and actions.

Two qualifications should be borne in mind about the coming discussion. The first is that my aim here is merely to establish the moral relevance of unchosen vices and of the evil actions that follow from them. There is an important further question about the appropriate moral reaction to unchosen evil. It will be discussed, but only after the question of relevance is settled.

The second qualification is that the discussion of unchosen evil is naturally related to the perennial problems of determinism and responsibility. Insofar as determinism is a metaphysical problem, I shall ignore it here. My view is that all human actions are in principle capable of causal explanation, yet this is compatible with the possibility that human agents control at least some of the things they do. But I shall not argue for this view here.[3]

Another reason for bypassing the various questions raised by determinism is that I doubt that whatever may prove to be acceptable answers would have substantive bearing on the distinction between chosen and unchosen actions. If some radical version of determinism were correct, it would still remain true that the causes of the actions we now identify as unchosen are different from those that produce what we currently regard as chosen actions. Among the causes of chosen actions, the beliefs and intentions of the agents occupy an important place; while in the case of unchosen actions, beliefs and intentions play at best only a negligible causal role. So, even if all actions were fully determined by some set of causes, we would still need to distinguish between different sets of causes. And this distinction would duplicate the one I am interested in, namely, between chosen and unchosen actions. Thus, the moral consequences of the distinction are, I believe, independent of the outcome of the metaphysical problem.[4]

[3] I argue for it in *The Examined Life*, chapter 6.
[4] For a similar view, see Rawls, "The Independence of Moral Theory," and Miller, *Social Justice*, 99–102.

My view about responsibility is essentially Strawson's.[5] People do various things, and they and other people react to what they do. Sometimes they hold themselves and other agents accountable for their actions, sometimes not. Responsibility is not a question independent of our reactive attitudes. Whether agents are responsible for their actions and whether particular reactive attitudes toward their actions are appropriate are not two different questions but two different ways of asking the same question. My discussion will focus on the question of what reactive attitude is appropriate toward agents with the unchosen vices I shall consider—namely, insufficiency, expediency, and malevolence.

INSUFFICIENCY

This vice is due to the inadequate development of some capacity required for acceptable moral conduct. The lack may be cognitive, emotive, or volitional. Let us begin with cognitive insufficiency. One form it can take is dogmatism. Dogmatic people may have a strong commitment to moral principles, and they may act according to them, but their principles are mistaken. If they were more independent minded, inquiring, or questioning, they might discover that their commitments are faulty, but as a matter of fact, they have not developed the required critical faculty. Such dogmatists may cause great evil if they come to believe that some groups or individuals live in gross violation of their (mistaken) moral principles. For they may suppose, then, that the violators are guilty of grave offenses and deserve the serious harm these dogmatists knowingly cause them. Dogmatists may acknowledge that they are causing harm, but they believe, sincerely and yet falsely, that it is deserved punishment, necessary corrective, justified self-defense, or the only way of instilling discipline. And so they may righteously flog slaves, burn witches, treat infidels as vermin, torture criminals before execution, or gas Jews and Gypsies.

There are many explanations of why dogmatists come to hold their mistaken principles uncritically. One explanation that makes one kind of dogmatism relevant for my purposes is that its agents have been brought up to hold mistaken principles, the same is true of everybody around them, and such doubts as they may have are allayed by the authorities whom they have been taught to respect. It often happens that people live in surroundings inhospitable to critical reflection on the prevailing morality. It is not that the habit of question-

[5] See Strawson, "Freedom and Resentment," and Bennett, "Accountability."

ing is defensively discouraged. Rather, there is no scope for questioning because the morality, which to outsiders may appear as pernicious, is simply taken for granted by them and by everybody who counts. Holding these mistaken principles and acting according to them is an essential part of their form of life. Their identity and sense of belongingness to society, the respect they give and receive, their moral status and moral judgments, and their own appraisals of themselves are all inseparably tied up with their pernicious principles. Such were the circumstances of many slaveowners in the antebellum South, of just about everybody during the sixteenth-century European witch craze, of Crusaders slaughtering Moslems, of Moslems waging holy war against infidels, of the institution of judicial torture in medieval Christendom, and of countless obedient functionaries in Nazi Germany and Stalinist Russia.

It can hardly be denied that the actions of these dogmatic people caused simple evil. But the actions were merely expressions of their dogmatism, and the dogmatism, in turn, was due to the insufficient development of the cognitive capacity to question their vicious morality. Since choice requires both the capacity to act otherwise and to understand the situation in which one is to act, we must conclude that these evil actions and the vices from which they sprang were unchosen. Their agents did not develop their critical capacity, because there was no reason why they should and there were good reasons why they should not. Nor did they understand their situation, because their mistaken principles made them misperceive what they were doing.

Another kind of insufficiency is emotive, and one form it can take is insensitivity. Consider people who are temperamentally cold and unimaginative about the suffering of others. Perhaps they are insensitive because they are themselves stoic or ascetic, have a high pain threshold, and, not being attuned to others, expect everyone to be like them. When they witness signs of pain, elicited by what they regard as meager provocation, they treat them as signs of weakness to which people should not give in. Thus, their reaction to evil is often contempt for the victims.

Now imagine such insensitive people in intimate relationships in which others expect, and are entitled to expect, their sympathy, help, and understanding. They may be parents, teachers, spouses, friends, or lovers, but when they are confronted with the effects of evil done to their intimates, they deny that it is evil. But matters can be much worse than a mere failure to understand what others suffer. Insensitive people may actively cause simple evil because they do not see it as evil. If they understood it, they would not cause it, but they cannot understand it because they lack the imagination, sympathy, or emotive agility to recognize that others are vulnerable where they are not. They fail to appreciate that this vulnerability may be not a weakness but a result of openness and receptivity, the very capacity they lack. And so they become archetypal figures of the stern and unforgiving father, the teacher with unsatisfiable demands, or, the most dangerous traitor of all, the intimate enemy who knows our vulnerabilities.

Thus, insensitivity is yet another form of insufficiency, and it is a vice because it regularly causes evil. But it is unchosen because it comes from an impoverishment of one's emotional life. Its source may be genetic or hormonal, or it may be a function of one's environment being conducive to the development of some character traits and to the suppression of others. Yet the evil that insensitive people may cause is not diminished by their not being able to control it.

A third form of insufficiency is weakness as it affects the capacity to do what the agents recognize they ought to do. Dogmatic and insensitive people believe that they are acting in a morally unobjectionable way. Of course, they are wrong, although they do not realize it, and so they do not feel guilt, shame, regret, or remorse about their actions. By contrast, weakness is often recognized by the agents, and they then blame themselves for their incapacity, although, in the cases I have in mind, there is nothing they can do about it.

Consider, for instance, people who are cowardly, lazy, or intemperate. The cowardly cannot control their fear of physical, psychological, or social injury; the lazy cannot make themselves exert sufficient energy to do what they ought to do; and the intemperate extravagantly squander their inner resources in some intense activities and, resources being limited, become incapable of discharging their obligations in other areas. In all these cases, the agents may be led by correct moral principles and may know what they ought to do; nevertheless they cannot do it, because they have not developed the necessary capacity. Others around them count on these weak people to stand up for what is right, to do their jobs, to work diligently for some worthwhile goal, but these legitimate expectations are disappointed. People whose welfare depends on the principles the cowardly ones desert or on the job the lazy ones fail to perform or on the obligation the intemperate ones are incapable of honoring are undeservedly harmed. Thus, weakness causes evil.

What makes the evil caused by weakness unchosen is the agents' incapacity to make the required effort. It is not that they are reluctant, hesitant, or unwilling; rather, it is truly beyond them because they have no control over the relevant aspect of themselves. Nor is the required effort extraordinary, since other people in similar situations often make it. Yet the weak ones cannot, because they have failed to develop in the right way. Their vices have left deep marks on their characters, and whatever may have been true at an earlier stage, they are now established, stable traits against which they cannot go.

But what about that earlier stage, before the vices became fixed? Cowardice, laziness, intemperance, and many other kinds of weakness usually begin as uncertain predispositions that may or may not be reinforced. There may be exceptional cases in which the reinforcements are the systematic, deliberate decisions of the agents to cultivate their defective predispositions. But the pursuit of a conscious policy to make oneself morally weak is surely quite rare. What usually happens is that circumstances conspire to provide the reinforcements. Sickly children whose anxious parents protect them from all danger until they reach adulthood are likely to fan their natural fear into full-fledged cowardice. The normal disinclination to push oneself beyond what is comfortable may be encouraged by an environment in which exertion is viewed as a sign of vulgarity, and so there are sociological pressures toward the development of laziness. A social context in which verve, imagination, adventurousness, and dilettantism are highly prized will tend to strengthen preexisting tendencies in people to make short, intense spurts in many directions and thus will foster intemperance.

It would be a misunderstanding to regard the forms of weakness developed in the ways I have just described as being necessarily based on choice. Cowardice, laziness, and intemperance incapacitate people and make them into agents who predictably cause evil in certain situations. Yet it often happens that neither their evil-causing actions nor the vices that these actions express have been chosen by them. All the same, when the agents see what they have become, how the evil they caused followed from their defective characters, they blame themselves. And others, witnessing the consequences of their actions and understanding how the agents came to be possessed by vices, may agree with the agents' appraisal of themselves.

Thus, we can see that through the various forms of insufficiency, moral agents may become instruments of the contingency of life. They do not choose to be dogmatic, insensitive, or weak, and they cannot help it if their actions reflect their characters. The fact remains, however, that people dominated by the vice of insufficiency are extremely likely to cause, and keep on causing, serious evil. Insufficiency renders them unfit for the sort of life and conduct we expect from moral agents. But this unfitness is not of their own making. They did not choose, intend, plan, or cultivate their insufficiency; it was something that happened to them. Nor could they have done much to alter the course of their own development, since doing so would have required of them a sustained effort to act contrary to their own predispositions and to the social context that favored their development in a particular direction. If they had been more critical, sensitive, or strong, they might have been able to draw on these virtues in their struggle against the current. But since they lacked the virtues, they had nothing with which to resist the pressures on them to become unfit moral agents. So, when people fall afoul of them and suffer undeserved harm as a result of their insufficiency, we cannot attribute the undeniable evil either to conscious design or to unfortunate accidents. The evil is characteristic, hence predictable; yet it is unchosen.

EXPEDIENCY

In the normal course of events, people live their lives aiming at what they believe are various internal and external goods. Expediency is the vice of pursuing these supposed goods without regard for the evil that may result from the pursuit. Expedient people are committed to their goals, and they have made themselves into efficient instruments for achieving them. Their energy, attention, and intellectual and emotional preoccupations are largely directed toward success. In the course of their goal-directed activities, they encounter difficulties, opposition, and problems, and they do what is necessary to prevail over the adversity they face. Thus, they naturally end up causing frequent and undeserved harm to those who have the misfortune of being obstacles in their paths.

Expediency may or may not involve choice. I shall discuss two forms of unchosen expediency: selfishness and fanaticism. Expediency may take other forms, and selfishness and fanaticism need not be unchosen. However, my discussion will focus on agents dominated by these forms of expediency; agents who cause evil, but not by choice, because they fail to see the moral significance of their own conduct. They see their situation under the description of working to achieve their goals. They do not choose to exploit, humiliate, maim, or ruin people in their way, yet when their actions produce these results as by-products, they take as little cognizance of them as a bulldozer does of the wildlife in its way. If their attention is called to the evil they cause, their response is a shrug. If forced to explain, they talk about the importance of their goals.

They do not set out to harm others, they do not enjoy doing so, but they do not care either. They just do what is necessary. And their strong commitment to their goals provides them with a rationale for conducting themselves as they do. One cannot make an omelette without breaking eggs, they say. It is perverse and feeble to worry about the eggs; one just gets on with it. If people did not act in this manner, they claim, nothing would ever be accomplished. Add to this that the goals they pursue may be approved by their society and that there may be a tradition of pursuing them. Expedient agents need not be ruthless pioneers; they may come out of and perpetuate an accepted practice. Success is honored and rewarded; failure is shameful. Politicians, businessmen, soldiers, artists, and athletes can easily fall into this pattern; as we all know, many have.

Take selfishness, to start with. Imagine people born into very poor families living in brutal circumstances. There is fierce competition for the available meager goods and opportunities. Everyone's lot is terrible, and those few who have the energy, intelligence, will, and imagination not to be defeated by their wretched environment are, of necessity, pitted against each other. In such contexts, there may be little scope for friendship, generosity, or altruism. Acting from soft sentiments is normally a sign of unaffordable weakness. When the chips are down, reasonable agents have to favor themselves against all comers, for there are no second chances. Indeed, even first chances are rare. Hence, people learn to harden their hearts, become tough, and think of the degradation they are trying to escape and of the promise success holds out.

This learning process is long and arduous, and of course it shapes the characters of those who undergo it. They learn to think of themselves first. The pattern is thus established, and it serves these people well because it removes scruples from pursuing their goals. Thus, they acquire an advantage over many of their competitors, opponents, and rivals because their priorities are crystal clear. What they want takes precedence, and everything else has its importance merely as a means to it. If such people fail, they may well attribute it to not having been sufficiently tough and determined. But what if they succeed? What if they achieve their goals, become secure, and gain for themselves the luxury of being able to reflect on their career? They may come to see, then, what they have done and why, and they may even realize the selfishness at the core of their characters. Those few who achieve this remarkable feat have, perhaps for the first time, a choice about their selfishness. But just as the combination of their initial talents and circumstances naturally gave rise to their selfishness, so now the combination of the goals remaining yet to be achieved and their characters, incorporating their developed talents and the justified confidence nourished by success, reinforces their vice of selfishness. So, even the possibility of choice provided by exceptional success may be preempted by the influence of the past and the attraction of the future.

Of course, success is rare, and its conjunction with self-critical reflection is rarer still. The usual situation of the kind of people I am describing is to be somewhere along the road toward their goals. As they see it, their resolve needs to be strengthened, rather than weakened by too much reflection. Of course, the initial spur of selfishness need not be poverty and a brutal environment. It may be keenly competitive siblings, exclusion by one's peers, powerful, loving, and ambitious parents, or resentment about being regarded as inferior. But the vice is the same regardless of its wellspring. What the agents want has the highest priority, opposition is to be overcome, and everything else has merely an instrumental value. There are many people whom this characterization fits, and many of them have not chosen or deliberately cultivated their selfishness; indeed, its development was a natural response in their situation. Yet the evil they regularly and predictably cause is none the less for that.

Consider fanaticism next. The pattern is again the ruthless pursuit of some goal, but this time it is not the agents' interests that dominate but something external to them, something that may even seriously endanger their interests. The goals may be ideological, religious, racial, or nationalistic, or they may be connected with honor, justice, pride, or shame. In any case, the agents' commitments to the goals are absolute and overpowering. Everything else is subordinated to them, including the agents' own well-being. Assume for the sake of argument that the moral credentials of the goals are impeccable. What is at fault is the manner in which the agents pursue them. They recognize no limits. They do not feel the need to balance their goals against the competing claims of other worthy goals, for they do not see them as standing in competition. The claims of one are held by them to be so clearly superior to those of others as to nullify the possibility of conflict.

People can fall into this pattern by a combination of some event that they see—sometimes accurately, sometimes not—as a great provocation and of a disposition to be swayed by passion. The provocation and the disposition coincide, and their joint forces fan their passions, which may then be reinforced by further provocations, seen as even more horrendous. Thus, their passions are intensified in an ascending spiral to a state of perpetual readiness for frenzy. It lends considerable force to fanaticism that reasonable people may often recognize the justified moral force of the fanatics' commitments, as well as what is frequently the reality of the provocation. Nations, races, justice, and honor often are inexcusably trampled upon, and it is right to respond, at the very least, with indignation. This is the reasonable kernel of fanaticism, which is then embedded in a swamp of exaggeration, misperception, lack of balance, self-deception, emotional volatility, and blindness to proportion.

The conditions producing these handicaps to seeing things as they are may often be so influential as to remove the possibility of choice. Given the provocation of a mass murder, a lynching mob, the show trial of innocent people, or the use of brute force to suppress just complaints, and given also a passionate predisposition, people may just be galvanized. Once that happens, the next provocation will not need to be as strong; the claims of competing considerations will have already begun to weaken, and a start toward fanaticism will have been made. So, although fanaticism may be the result of indulging one's passions and encouraging them to get out of hand, it need not come about in this way. The passions may be uncontrolled because in some people they are naturally more intense than in others and because these intense passions may come to be provoked by real outrages.

The effect of fanaticism is ruthlessness toward friend and foe alike. Foes are guilty of the outrages, and so they deserve the worst; friends share the fanatics' commitments, hence they must be prepared to make the sacrifices for the cause the fanatics themselves are prepared to make. The world is divided into "us" and "them." There is a small and dedicated group of true believers pitted against the powerful and threatening group of the enemy. And in the middle there is the large group of naive and uncommitted people whose well-being, allegiance, or recruitment is one chief object of the struggle. But since this group comprises the naive, its numerous members do not understand what is at stake; they are stupid, meek, weak, or unaroused, and they must be forced to awaken by carefully manipulated shocks. Thus, fanatics harm their enemies and themselves and aim to force the rest into the position where they will become their accomplices.

Selfishness and fanaticism are forms of the vice of expediency. People who possess them as dominant character traits regularly and predictably cause evil. Both expediency and the actions that flow from it may be unchosen. For if the vice is an established character trait, then the actions are the natural consequences of the agents' being that kind of person. Selfish and fanatic people rarely need to choose to act in characteristic ways; they just spontaneously respond to the many routine situations they encounter in their daily lives. Nor is it necessary that the agents should have to take an active part in encouraging the growth of their vices. They may begin with a predisposition whose development is then fostered by circumstances, and so it is strengthened until it becomes dominant. And the predisposition itself is not monstrous. Who does not have the tendency to go after the satisfaction of a want without paying much attention to anything else?

Yet the character that was formed in this understandable way is a rich source of evil. Through selfish and fanatical people, indifference—one essential condition of life—regularly finds expression. For expediency is the vice of being indifferent to the evil one causes. And the source of this evil is not that the agents choose to inflict it but that their characters have been so formed as to make them concentrate on achieving their goals and ignoring whatever side effects their actions may have. Expedient people lack the virtue of conscientiousness: the disposition to reflect on their actions in the light of the requirements of morality and to be led by that reflection to attempt to control what they do. But neither the presence of expediency nor the absence of conscientiousness is bound to be a matter of choice. It often happens that the development of this vice is an unsought consequence of conditions beyond the agents' control. Nevertheless, evil follows from it, and if we care about morality, we must be concerned with that.

MALEVOLENCE

There is no mystery about how people come to be motivated by the vices of insufficiency and expediency. They may lack some capacity required for acceptable moral agency, or they may be blinded to the evil they cause by their strong commitment to some goal. Malevolence, however, is more puzzling. It is a disposition to act contrary to what is good. Its emotional source is ill will, a desire for things not to go well. Malevolence may be general, directed toward humanity as a whole, or particular, focusing on selected individuals. Hate, resentment, envy, jealousy, rage, vindictiveness, cruelty, and cynicism are some of its forms. But the puzzling thing about malevolence is that it is so very uneconomical. To begin with, it is unpleasant to have the underlying feelings. Other things being equal, people would not wish to have them. Yet other things often are unequal, and these unpleasant feelings may be elicited in perfectly reasonable people by the adversity they face. Nevertheless, having the feelings does not change the adverse situations that elicit them. They fuel reactive attitudes, thus they come after the fact. Nor do they help the agents to cope with future adversity, because these feelings tend to cloud judgment, interfere with cool deliberation, and make people lose their sense of proportion. So, if malevolent feelings are unpleasant, likely to be causally inefficacious, and detrimental to reasonable responses, then why would reasonable people allow themselves to be motivated by them? The question becomes even more puzzling when we note that the various forms of malevolence are frequently responses to situations in which the agents do not face adversity. Cruelty, hatred, rage, and so on are often unprovoked by the people toward whom they are unloosed. Malevolence, unlike insufficiency, is thus active; unlike expediency, it carries with it no prospect of gain. If malevolence succeeds, it makes matters worse. The question is why would people want to make matters worse, often at considerable cost to themselves.

The question is puzzling because it rests on a mistaken assumption. Asking it presupposes that malevolent agents want to be that way, that they *choose* their malevolence. It is possible that there may be some few people of whom this is true. Iago, the Marquis de Sade, and Goethe's Mephistopheles may be like that. But most malevolent people are not, because they do not see themselves and their actions as malevolent. To remove the puzzle, we need to understand how people can be malevolent and act malevolently without choice.

One possibility is that malevolence is the natural reaction elicited by understandable grievances against a society that treats them with contempt. The agents I have in mind are the lifelong losers in a competitive setting, the members of some racial, religious, regional, or ethnic group whose beliefs and practices are found offensive by those in power. Or the agents may be people who lack the physique, education, opportunity, or ability required for improving their lot. Such people may see their lives as hopeless. They may realistically view the past as an unrelieved stretch of humiliation and the future as the continuation of the same. Their lives are informed by futility, indignity, and meaninglessness.

People in this position cannot reasonably deny that they have done badly by the prevailing standards, that they have the characteristics others find objectionable, and that they are handicapped in various ways—they are forced to face it in their constant and inevitable contacts with the defenders of the standards of which they fall short. There are only a limited number of reactions open to them. One is to acknowledge defeat and literally or metaphorically lie down and die. Another is to escape into a fantasy life in which the misery of their existence is ignored, ameliorated, or transformed into a means to some mythical end. Malevolence is a third possibility. It involves saying no to life—to their own, to the lives of people like them, and certainly to the lives of those who adversely judge them. It is not a resigned no but a hate-filled, resentful, enraged no. It involves actively wishing ill to their society, not in order to transform it into something else, but just because by its values they are themselves judged to be inferior. And of course the passionate no is translated into action when the opportunity arises. Casual vandalism, senseless crime, random violence, desecration of symbols, indifference to consequences due to contempt for self-interest, and delight in cruelty are some of the ways in which this form of malevolence manifests itself.

Outsiders who witness the conduct of people thus motivated may come to understand its source, may see why it is that the normal restraints of reason and decency are repudiated by these agents, and yet they can have no other reasonable option than to recognize the evil malevolent conduct regularly causes. But the agents themselves will not share the outsiders' view. Reflection and articulation rarely accompany this form of malevolence, so it is unlikely that its agents would be willing or able to explain their position. It is not difficult, however, to imagine what they could say. Uppermost in their minds would be not the evil they cause but the humiliation to which their conduct is a reaction. To say no to their wretched condition, they could say, is part of human dignity.

Yet it would be wrong to suppose that the resulting cruelty, violence, and brutality is a consciously chosen policy. Given their circumstances, their unwillingness to admit defeat, a personality not open to seeking refuge in fantasy, they have no choice left. Their strong, terrible, destructive feelings must find some outlet, and the simplest one is to vent them indiscriminately on objects that happen to be handy, objects among which, often, the agents themselves are one. Such people do not choose malevolence. They are overpowered by it; it is something that happens to them. Nevertheless, understanding the source of their malevolence must not blind us to the regular and predictable evil such people cause and would continue to cause unless stopped.

Another explanation of why people may be bent on making matters worse, even if it involves going against their own interest, and why following their bent may be based not on choice but on something that takes hold of them is that they are deceiving themselves. Consider people with strong feelings of cruelty, hatred, envy, jealousy, resentment, and so on. They know, of course, at first hand, the unpleasantness of these feelings, and they know also the social sanctions against them. Suppose that they are well-trained moral agents who share the prevailing adverse view of these negative feelings. Yet they are saddled with the feelings, and if they were reflective about their inner lives and honest with themselves about what their reflection might reveal, they would have to judge themselves adversely. Naturally, this is an undesirable prospect, so there is a strong impetus against looking too closely at their own motives. But averting their gaze does not make the feelings go away. If they are indeed strong, they will not be ignored.

The solution is to redescribe them. This accomplishes a lot in one fell swoop. If the redescription is sufficiently nimble, it transforms an unacceptable feeling into an acceptable one. Cruelty becomes the reluctant administration of deserved punishment, hatred turns into righteous indignation provoked by suspected immorality, envy is reinterpreted as opposition to elitism, jealousy is changed into principled objections to one's rival, and resentment is tricked out to look like reasonable skepticism about the dubious ventures of some objectionable people. Thus, rendered acceptable, it becomes permissible to be motivated by the neatly laundered feeling. Moreover, the agents thus put themselves in a position where they can compliment themselves on their moral sensitivity and on their stalwart moral feelings. The key to the success of this maneuver is to disguise it from oneself. But this is not too difficult, since the reason for it is strong, the opportunity is easily seized, and the means to it is merely to construct a story that could be told to others and oneself if the need arose. The result is that these malevolent people act malevolently, while they genuinely believe that they are being and acting in a morally praiseworthy manner.

The self-deception that makes this possible cannot be chosen. For choosing it requires knowing what they do, but the possession of such knowledge would make self-deception impossible. The key is to slide into it. This involves holding their own feelings at arm's length and, without concentrating on them, making themselves receptive to some construction that renders the feelings acceptable. And then a favorable construction suggests itself by something they read, by the praise they hear bestowed on someone else, or by an admiring and uncritical observer. It clicks, and they say to themselves with a sigh, yes, this is how it is, this is how I am. And not without some satisfaction, they go on causing evil to the victims of their cruelty, hatred, envy, and so on.

If we understand the mechanism involved in the malevolence that indignity elicits and self-deception makes possible, then the puzzle of why people would be moved to make matters worse, although without choosing to be so moved, dissolves. Malevolence is the vice through which another essential condition of life, destructiveness, finds expression. It is just a fact about us that destructiveness is part of our makeup. No doubt there is a causal explanation of why it is so. The explanation may be in terms of evolutionary atavism, the structure of the brain, the reaction to having to confront the world after the security of the womb, unsuitable social arrangements, hormonal imbalance, or some combination of these and other factors. But however it comes about, malevolence causes evil; hence it is of moral concern, even if its agents have not chosen to be the way they are.

UNCHOSEN EVIL AND THE LACK OF CONTROL

I have come to the end of cataloging a depressing variety of unchosen vices and corresponding evil-producing actions. My intention has been to present a sufficient range of examples of moral conduct that reasonable people would recognize as widespread, as causing simple evil, and as being unchosen. Since they are not isolated episodes but patterns of action, they are symptomatic of vices, and the agents dominated by such vices must themselves be recognized as evil. The cases I discussed are examples of unchosen evil because they fail the conditions of choice adumbrated at the beginning of this chapter. The agents did not decide to cause evil, or they did not believe that their actions would cause it, or they did not have the capacity to act otherwise, or they did not understand their situation.

Part of the significance of unchosen evil is that it forces us to realize that character-morality should not deal only with chosen actions. For insofar as character-morality is concerned with minimizing evil, it must take account of all human manifestations of it, regardless of their etiology. But it has also been my purpose to show that unchosen evil is not a rarity but a ubiquitous feature of life, while chosen evil, caused by the conscious designs of moral monsters, is quite rare. People dominated by the vices of insufficiency, expediency, and malevolence are deplorable moral specimens, but they are not moral monsters. For they have not set out to be evil and to do evil. They became possessed by it. Through them, the essential conditions of life exerted their baneful influence on the human aspiration to live good lives.

There is a common feature shared by these three vices. Each is brought about by lack of control. In the case of insufficiency, control is lacking because the agents do not have the necessary cognitive, emotive, or volitional capacity to exercise it. Expediency becomes a powerful motive because the agents fail to control their pursuit of goals by setting limits on what they might do to achieve them. Malevolence could dominate people because they do not control their strong and destructive feelings. But whether people are able to exercise control is often not a matter within their control. This is why so much evil is unchosen. The prospect of true hope in the face of unchosen evil is thus intimately connected with the possibility of extending within ourselves the area we can control. The exploration of this possibility is the eventual direction of my argument. But much needs to be said before I can directly address that issue.

CHAPTER FIVE

Morality beyond Choice

THE MORAL REACTION TO UNCHOSEN EVIL

In this chapter, I shall begin to consider the appropriate moral reaction to simple evil. Evil may be moral or nonmoral, and moral evil may or may not be caused by choice. As we have seen in the previous chapter, much simple evil is caused by the unchosen vices of insufficiency, expediency, and malevolence, and it is on the moral reaction to these that I shall concentrate for the following reasons.

The alternatives are to concentrate on nonmoral evil, or either on patterns or on isolated cases of moral evil caused by choice. Yet none of these would take us very far. We can and do use our scientific and technological resources in the hope of ameliorating nonmoral evil. But this attempt is itself subject to the vicissitudes of the human tendency to cause evil, and so it is liable to abuse. We are better advised, therefore, to look first at the prior question of what to do about the human causes of evil.

Isolated cases of simple moral evil caused by choice undoubtedly occur, but they cannot account for most of the evil we cause and from which we suffer, since they are bound to be rare. These episodes do not stem from the agents' characters; they are, rather, infrequent and uncharacteristic actions responding to strong provocation, stressful circumstances, or considerable temptation, or they are symptoms of the agents' being disturbed, overpowered by some strong emotion, or unable to think clearly. If the episodes were not rare and uncharacteristic, they would be part of a pattern of chosen evil.

The reason why we should not focus on patterns of chosen simple evil is that its agents—moral monsters—are rare. There just are not many people who habitually choose to cause undeserved harm. Being a moral monster is very difficult. In addition to legal sanctions, there are extremely strong social pressures on people not to behave monstrously. These prohibitions force most potential monsters either in the direction of hypocrisy or in that of self-deception. Hypocritical moral monsters know perfectly well what they are doing, but they hide it from others. A successful hypocrite is "a very cunning liar and actor . . . he is prepared to treat others ruthlessly, but pretends that nothing is further from his mind. Philosophers often speak as if a man could thus hide himself from those around him, but the supposition is doubtful, and in any case the price in vigilance would be colossal. If he lets even a few people see his true attitude he must guard himself against them; if he lets no one into the secret he must always be careful in case the least spontaneity betray him."[1] I suppose there are such people, but the talents, if that is the word, required for living in this way are so exceptional as to make it unlikely that many would possess them.

The other alternative for moral monsters is self-deception. If it is successful, the monsters convince themselves of the truth of some account that makes their habitual evildoing appear in an acceptable moral light. They may tell themselves the sort of stories that we have seen told by one kind of malevolent evildoers, although, of course, self-deception is not restricted to this kind of malevolence. Whatever may have been true at the beginning, success at self-deception requires people to come to believe their own stories. Thereby they succeed in cultivating in themselves some vices of the intellect or of the will that undermine the conditions of choice. Thus, they are gradually transformed into agents of unchosen simple evil, and these are the cases I propose to consider.

An additional reason for this focus is that agents of habitual and unchosen evil present the most difficult questions about the appropriate moral reaction. There is little scope for a moral reaction in the case of nonmoral evil. We may be saddened by it; we may sympathize with its victims and resolve to do something about it, but since it is not caused by human beings, there is no one to censure. Isolated episodes of chosen evil are bound to be uncharacteristic, and this serves to weaken our condemnation of them. And the appropriate moral reaction to agents of habitual chosen simple evil is the strongest censure morality permits us. But what are we to say about the agents of habitual unchosen simple evil?

THE SOFT REACTION

Our sensibility does not prompt a clear answer to this question. It is consistent with both a soft and a hard reaction, and the disagreement between them discloses one of the deep moral divisions of our age. The two reactions agree about censuring evil actions; they cause undeserved harm, and if we care about morality, we must want to oppose evil in all of its forms. The disagreement arises over the question of how habitual patterns of unchosen evil actions reflect on the moral

[1] Foot, "Moral Beliefs," 129.

standing of their agents. The soft reaction is to excuse the agents, while the hard one is to censure them. The reason behind the soft reaction is that since the agents did not choose to do the evil they have done, they should not be held morally accountable. According to the hard reaction, however, the morally significant fact is that the agents of unchosen evil habitually cause undeserved harm, and this should affect our moral evaluation of them. Few writers have considered this disagreement directly; those who have, have defended the soft reaction.[2] I shall proceed by discussing the soft reaction and its inadequacies and then developing the hard reaction as a more adequate alternative.

The soft reaction, in Hofstadter's words, is as follows: "In true moral evil the actor is convinced that the norm he violates is morally right. He is convinced that he is setting himself against what he ought to do, intentionally doing what he ought not to do. Evil cannot exist save in and through this active opposition to what is perceived as good and right."[3] In Benn's version, "Indispensable . . . to the notion of a wicked person is a cognitive capacity [leading one] to act on evil first-order maxims, or . . . so order . . . first-order maxims as to exclude what ought nevertheless to be taken account of."[4] And acting on a maxim is explained as the "capacity to act on principles . . . that are one's own because one has made them so by a process of rational reflection on the complex principles and values one has assimilated from one's social environment."[5]

Thus, according to the soft reaction, we can describe people as evil only if they choose to cause evil. As Benn puts it, discussing what he calls the psychopath: "He is capable . . . of instrumental deliberation, though he may be prone to discount future satisfactions heavily in favor of immediate gratification. So he may be liable to do evil impulsively to satisfy a whim. But the more significant point is that he does not see it as evil, except, perhaps, in a conventional sense: This is something that I know most people do not like being done, so I had better conceal the body. But the kind of considerations that might justify and rationalize conventional disapproval can get no purchase on his understanding. . . . Such a person cannot be

---

[2] I found the most thoughtful expressions of the soft reaction in Benn's "Wickedness" and Hofstadter's *Reflections on Evil*. There is a large body of psychoanalytic literature on evil, but I do not discuss it because I find the theoretical assumptions these writers make untenable. The only work I know of that defends something like the hard reaction is Adams's "Involuntary Sins."

[3] Hofstadter, *Reflections on Evil*, 5–6.

[4] Benn, "Wickedness," 796–97.

[5] Ibid., 803.

wicked."[6] Psychopaths may *do* evil, but they cannot *be* evil, because they did not choose the evil they have done.

One reason for rejecting the soft reaction is that, while it fits some cases of evil, it cannot account for many others. Consider, for instance, people whose evil takes the form of expediency. Throughout their lives they step on others when the achievement of whatever they want requires it. They do not take delight in harming those in their way, but they do not agonize over it either. They simply do what is necessary, and it is often necessary to inflict serious harm on people who present obstacles to them. For some people, this vice may be the result of "a process of rational reflection on . . . complex principles and values," but for many others it is more like the accent with which they speak, the way they move, or their attitude to pets. It is a question of habit or style. No doubt it is learned, but the learning is closer to unconscious habituation than to the rational reflection Hofstadter and Benn suppose to be a requirement of evil.

People whose vice is the kind of insufficiency that manifests itself in dogmatism present further counterexamples. Their evil actions follow from a mistaken moral belief, but they do not realize that it is mistaken. They were brought up to hold it and to act according to it; people around them also either accept the same belief, or they are censured; and the justification of their belief is readily available from their religious or secular leaders. And so they righteously persecute some minority, treat members of another culture as barely domesticated animals, or regard dissenters as wicked. Benn says about Eichmann that while he acted according to a mistaken moral belief, he ought to have taken steps to examine it critically.[7] But it often happens that the need for critical examination is not felt, because the belief is unquestioningly accepted by all. This was not true of Eichmann's beliefs in his context. It was, however, true of the beliefs of the Jews of the Pentateuch in slavery and human sacrifice, of the Puritan's belief in the sinfulness of sex outside of marriage, and of the belief in many traditional societies in the depravity of the deformed. It seems to me that insofar as people habitually inflicted simple and undeserved harm on slaves, sacrificial victims, sexual dissenters, and the deformed, they were evil, even though they had not examined critically their moral beliefs.

Expedient and dogmatic evildoers may thus fail the requirement of the soft reaction that evil should be done with clear understanding to make it justified to regard the agents as evil. People whose insuffi-

[6] Ibid., 799.
[7] Ibid., 802–4.

ciency takes the form of weakness may, by contrast, fail the requirement of being willing to do evil. If people habitually fail to perform
what their jobs require, because they are lazy, or if they regularly
betray those who love or depend on them, because they are cowardly,
or if they have no energy left to do what they should, because they
have intemperately squandered it elsewhere, and if, as a result, they
inflict simple harm on others, then I see excellent reasons for regarding them as evil, although they are not moved by evil will.

But defenders of the soft reaction would not accept these cases as
counterexamples. They would reply that if it is indeed true that the
people in my cases did not choose to cause the evil they caused, then
it would be wrong to regard them as evil. Their *actions* may be evil,
but their actions do not reflect on them, because they have not chosen
to perform them. Thus, we are forced to go deeper to examine the
assumptions behind the refusal to accept my cases as counterexamples.

There are three such assumptions. They are of increasing depth,
and they lie at the core not merely of the soft reaction but also of
much contemporary thinking about morality. The first is that *the domain of morality coincides with the domain of choice.* This is why moral
reactions are appropriate only to chosen actions and their agents. But
what is so special about choice? Why should it be thought that the
moral standing of people is necessarily connected with the capacity to
choose? The second assumption provides an answer. The capacity to
choose frees human beings from necessity. Agents who have this capacity possess a basic worth because they can, at least to some extent,
control their lives. And *since all normal human agents have this capacity,
they possess a certain basic worth equally.* Yet it is obvious that this capacity
may be used for evil purposes. Why should people who habitually
make evil-producing choices have the same worth as those whose
choices are beneficial? And so we arrive at the third and deepest assumption upon which the soft reaction rests. *Human beings are basically
good.* Evil is not a constituent of human nature but a corruption of it.
Human beings cannot lose their worth because their potential for
good is basic, while their potential for evil is merely a by-product of
something going wrong. But if nothing goes wrong, people will use
their capacity for choice to perform good rather than evil actions.

I shall argue that all of these assumptions are mistaken. Yet they
are not totally false, because they capture important features of our
central moral concerns. The trouble is that these features are mistakenly generalized, and the generalizations are used to exclude equally
important moral phenomena to which the generalizations do not apply. The most important of these insufficiently appreciated moral
phenomena is that within human beings the evil-producing essential

conditions of life exist in a state of tension with the aspiration to live good lives. As a result, both chosen and unchosen actions can systematically produce evil; lives dominated by such patterns have less worth than lives that are beneficially directed; and whether the primary potential of individual moral agents is for good or for evil is an open question.

Part of the trouble with these assumptions is that they fail to take account of what tragic situations reveal about life. They fail to consider that the human capacity to resolve the tension between the aspiration to live good lives and the essential conditions of life is itself subject to the tension it is supposed to resolve. Thus, the problem lies not with the failure to exercise the capacity or with exercising it badly but with the capacity itself being tainted by contingency, indifference, and destructiveness. If the antidote is also poisoned, taking it will not help. Thus, the assumptions behind the soft reaction to unchosen evil are superficial, for they move at a level insufficiently deep to address the questions raised by tragic situations.

The first assumption will be discussed and criticized below; the others, in the two subsequent chapters. I shall then describe, justify, and explore some of the implications of the hard reaction.

The First Assumption of Choice-Morality: Ought Implies Can

The first assumption, that the concern of morality is exclusively with chosen actions and their agents, is often expressed by the principle that "ought implies can." I shall refer to it as the *Principle* and interpret it as follows: the moral censure of agents for performing evil actions is appropriate only if the agents had a choice in performing the actions. And, drawing on the discussion in the previous chapter, the agents' having a choice is to be understood as follows: having decided to bring about a certain result; believing that by performing a specific action the result is more likely to be achieved than otherwise; not being forced to perform the action; having cognitive, emotional, and volitional capacities to perform actions other than the one in question; and having a normal understanding of the situation. If any of these conditions is not met, the agents cannot be said to have chosen and thus should not be held morally accountable. Moral accountability, then, presupposes that agents can do or refrain from doing what morality requires of them; that is, it presupposes that they have a choice. This is the idea captured by the Principle that "ought implies can."[8]

---

[8] The Principle has generally been taken for granted in moral discussions at least since Kant. E.g. "The action to which the 'ought' applies must indeed be possible under

If we apply the Principle to the cases of unchosen evil habitually done by insufficient, expedient, and malevolent agents, the soft reaction appears to follow. These agents have caused simple evil, but they are not themselves evil, because they had no choice. Consequently, we should not censure these people or countless others like them, whose lives are dominated by vices leading to habitual but unchosen evil actions.

Against this, we must weigh the judgment that people who are conscientious rather than expedient, reflective rather than dogmatic, strong rather than weak, sensitive rather than insensitive, and benevolent rather than malevolent are morally better rather than worse. And this judgment remains true independently of how the worse ones acquired their vices and the better ones acquired their virtues. Part of the force of this judgment is that we personally want to have the virtues and not the vices, that we also want our children, friends, teachers, and politicians to be virtuous rather than vice ridden, and that we believe that human life would be better if people in general had the virtues rather than the vices. What else does this judgment reflect but our commitment to the appropriateness of moral censure, even if the Principle legislates otherwise?

Of course, moral censure should be mitigated by extenuating circumstances. People who cause evil by choice should be judged much more severely than those who had no choice about it. But this is not to say that we should condone evildoing. We should always censure agents of insufficiency, expediency, and malevolence, although we should also recognize that on occasions there may be extenuations. However, extenuation is needed only when evildoing has occurred.

---

natural conditions" (Kant, *Critique of Pure Reason*, A548); "a rational being can rightly say of any unlawful action which he has done that he could have left it undone. . . . For this action and everything in the past which determined it belong to a single phenomenon of his character, which he himself creates" (*Critique of Practical Reason*, 203); "duty demands nothing of us which we cannot do" and "when the moral law commands that we *ought* now to be better men, it follows inevitably that we must *be able* to be better men" and "we ought to conform to it [to our moral disposition]; consequently we must *be able* to do so" (*Religion within the Limits of Reason Alone*, 43, 46, 55). Recently, the Principle has been questioned on logical grounds. For the controversy surrounding its logical status, see Gowans, *Moral Dilemmas*, and Rescher, *Ethical Idealism*, chapter 2. My own doubts about the Principle are moral, not logical. For a criticism similar to my own of the Principle as a presupposition of Kant's conception of morality, see Larmore, *Patterns of Moral Complexity*, 84–90. In a series of influential articles, reprinted in *The Importance of What We Care About*, Frankfurt also attacks the Principle on the grounds that being able to do otherwise is irrelevant to moral responsibility, provided the agents act for reasons that are their own. My attack goes further, for I hold that people may be morally responsible for what they do, even if they had no reason of their own for acting as they did and could not act otherwise.

Insufficient, expedient, and malevolent agents are thus proper objects of moral censure. The Principle holds that such censure is always inappropriate in the absence of choice, and that restriction shows that the Principle is faulty.

In this dispute, one side makes the appropriateness of moral censure conditional on the agents' powers (such as decisions, beliefs, capacities, and understanding), while the other side includes the agents' powers among the objects of censure. What kind of dispute is this? We may say, initially, that it is a dispute about the limits of morality. One side holds that morality is coextensive with the domain of choice, while the other side extends morality beyond that domain to embrace the evaluation of agents even of unchosen actions. The first position is taken by what I shall call *choice-morality*, in contrast with the second position, my own, which is *character-morality*.

In choice-morality the central question is, What ought we to *do*? Since what we ought to do is one action rather than another, and since what we ought to do frequently conflicts with what we want to do, in choice-morality the primary preoccupation is with choice and action, with the conflict between obligation and inclination, and with training the will to act on the choice guided by obligation. Choice-morality is Kantian in spirit,[9] if not in every detail, and it provides the rationale for the soft reaction.

In character-morality the central question is what sort of people we ought to *be*. The focus is not on action but on character, not on choice but on virtue. The assumption is that what we do normally follows from what we are, that actions follow from character. If our characters embody the virtues, our actions will be morally praiseworthy without our having to agonize over choices, obligations, and the control of our inclinations. The inspiration of character-morality is Aristotelian, although it is unclear how far Aristotle would agree with my present arguments.[10] In any case, the hard reaction is derived from this view of morality.

These two views of morality are not logically inconsistent. Neither excludes any of the elements the other includes. Their dispute is one of emphasis. Choice-morality emphasizes choice and action; character-morality emphasizes character and virtue. In choice-morality,

---

[9] See e.g. Kant, *Critique of Pure Reason*, A800–801 and A805.

[10] Irwin's "Reason and Responsibility in Aristotle" is an excellent discussion of this difficult point. I stress more than Irwin does Aristotle's inclination to approve or disapprove people's characters, regardless of how they came to have them. Without this stress, it would be difficult to understand Aristotle's attitude toward women and natural slaves (see *Politics*, book 1, chapters 4–5). Another illuminating discussion of the complexities of these issues is Kenny's *Aristotle's Theory of the Will*.

what we are is formed by innumerable choices; in character-morality, choice of action depends on character. Action and character are related in both. In the first, action is primary, and character, being formed by action, is secondary; in the second, character is primary, and action, being a consequence of character, is secondary. As Hume put the point, "Actions are by their very nature temporary and perishing; and where they proceed not from some cause in the character and disposition of the person, who perform'd them, they infix not themselves upon him, and can neither redound to his honour, if good, nor infamy, if evil."[11]

A version of the Principle is employed in both kinds of morality, but, as it is to be expected, the versions are different. To distinguish between them, I shall say that the Principle has an *acquitting version* employed in choice-morality and an *extenuating version* employed in character-morality. The acquitting version expresses a necessary condition for the appropriateness of moral censure. We should be censured for what we do only if we can choose not to do it. Thus, in choice-morality the acquitting version of the Principle has the crucial role of demarcating the domain of morality as that within which we can choose. In character-morality, the extenuating version plays a secondary role. Censure attaches to our characters. If they are evil producing, they should be censured, even if it is not in our power to choose to be otherwise. But censure should be mitigated if there are excuses, and the extenuating version of the Principle expresses one possible type of excuse.

I have observed that the dispute between choice- and character-morality is about the limits of morality. But now we can see that it is more than that: it is not just a disagreement *about* morality, it is a *moral* disagreement. For what is at stake is how we should judge people morally. Should we judge them on the basis of what they have become through their choices or on the basis of their characters independently of how they came to possess them? Choice-morality gives the first answer, character-morality gives the second. Regardless of where we stand on this, it is clear that since the dispute is moral, the Principle is a *moral* principle. Its acquitting version prescribes that we should judge people on the basis of the choices they make, while its extenuating version prescribes that we ought not to judge those who lack the power to choose as severely as we judge those who have that power. I think that it is surprising that "ought implies can" turns out to be a moral principle.[12]

---

[11] Hume, *Treatise*, 411.

[12] To the best of my knowledge, only Brown, "Moral Theory and the Ought-Can Principle," makes the same point.

The question I now want to consider is whether it is an *important* moral principle. If its acquitting version is acceptable, it is very important indeed. On the other hand, if the extenuating version is acceptable, it plays only a subsidiary role. But which version is acceptable depends on the outcome of the dispute between choice-morality and character-morality. As we have seen, the dispute is one of emphasis. I shall now consider four contrasting pairs of notions. In each case, choice-morality emphasizes the first member of the pair at the expense of the second, while character-morality reverses the emphasis. I shall argue that in each case character-morality has it far more nearly right. Consequently, I think that the Principle is only of secondary importance; its acquitting version is mistaken; and its extenuating version plays only a subordinate role.[13]

CHOICE-MORALITY VERSUS CHARACTER-MORALITY

The first contrast is between *choice* and *character*. According to choice-morality, at the foundation of morality we find radical choice concerning fundamental values, and morality consists in choosing to make a commitment one way or another. MacIntyre explains why this is so: "Underlying each moral judgment there is a choice that the agent has made—a type of choice in which the individual is at the most fundamental level unconstrained by good reasons, precisely because his or her choice expresses a decision as to what is to count as a good reason for him or her."[14]

This way of looking at morality is obviously inadequate. The mere fact that people find themselves in the position of having to choose demonstrates that they have commitments to the alternatives they confront. Without such commitments, there would be no call for choice. The typical moral problem most agents face is not to choose a commitment but to weigh the hold on themselves of commitments they have already made. Thus, morality enters into such situations long before choices need to be made. Therefore, choice cannot be at the foundation of morality.

A more realistic way of looking at morality is to observe that people are born into a tradition, and soon after birth their moral education begins. By adolescence, they are saturated with the moral views of their tradition. Of course, people may come to reject their tradition and its values, but no one starts with a choice to accept or to reject it.

[13] There is a masterful discussion of how the emphasis has shifted from character-morality to choice-morality in Greek ethics from Homer to Aristotle in Adkins's *Merit and Responsibility*.

[14] MacIntyre, *Revisions*, 8–9.

Those who eventually come to reject it either replace it with another tradition or opt out of humanity. The idea that choice lies at the foundation of morality is mistaken because it ignores the fundamental role tradition and education play.

Tradition and education, however, require an object upon which they can exert their influence. This object is character. Moral education inculcates the rules, values, and ideals of a tradition. It takes young unformed children and influences them to develop in a certain way, to cultivate habits, to strengthen or weaken dispositions, and to judge themselves and others in the light of conventional norms. This is the process by which character is formed. And when people have well-formed characters, then the actions they perform follow from them. Normally, acting in moral situations is a matter not of choosing but of doing what comes naturally. People with well-formed characters spontaneously do what, for better or worse, their tradition prescribes. One reason why people with vices may cause evil is that they act spontaneously on the dictates of a questionable moral tradition that has formed their characters.

This is not to deny that choice has a role in morality. It has to be faced when the tradition in the background is inconsistent, when it is seriously challenged externally or internally, when the agents' characters are formed of conflicting dispositions, or when unexpected or unusual situations occur for which moral education has not prepared agents. But choice is the exception, not the rule. Most people most of the time act in accordance with their characters. And if their characteristic actions are generally good, we praise them for it; if they are evil, we censure them. People are morally accountable for what they do, even though what they do is rarely the result of choice. Usually their actions are merely the surface manifestations of the deeper structure of their characters. For these reasons, choice-morality is mistaken and character-morality is correct in the emphases they place on the contrasting notions of choice and character.

The second contrast is between *action* and *agent.* Choice-morality concentrates on actions at the expense of agents because it places commitments to certain kinds of action at the foundation of morality. Choice-morality allows, of course, that actions require agents, but it claims that becoming a moral agent depends on making the appropriate commitments to acting in certain ways. As Falk puts it: "There is one commitment whose ground is intimately personal and which comes before any other personal or social commitment whatsoever: the commitment to the principled mode of life as such. One is tempted to call this the supreme moral commitment."[15] The claim is

---

[15] Falk, "Morality, Self, and Others," 374–75.

that we are transformed from mere persons to the status of moral agents by the choice of this commitment and by acting according to it. Moral agency is supposed to be the result of the slow accretion of many choices and actions in conformity with the principled mode of life. The idea is that people are, as it were, in place, and then they may gradually become moral agents depending on the nature of their choices and actions.

Character-morality rejects the priority of personhood over moral agency. People are moral agents regardless of their choices and actions. The inseparability of personhood and moral agency is simply a fact of life. Moral agency depends on the capacity to cause good and evil, and we have that capacity because of the nature of our species. If we could fend for ourselves immediately after birth and spend, say, the first twenty years of our lives in solitude, then personhood might indeed be prior to moral agency. But as things are, the two go together, and choice-morality is mistaken in supposing that moral agency begins with choice making.

Of course, it is true that our choices and actions have a formative influence on the kind of moral agents we become. Character-morality recognizes that this is so. What it rejects is the suggestion that choices and actions *create* moral agents. Moral agents are born, and they are shaped by their tradition and education. Choices and actions *alter* moral agents, but they do not produce them. Thus, moral agency is a deeper, more fundamental notion than action.

The third contrast is between moral *improvement* and *achievement*. The emphasis choice-morality places on improvement goes hand in hand with its emphasis on choice and action. The underlying assumption is that people embark on a career of moral agency as they become choosers and actors. Before this happens, they are saddled with genetic and acquired dispositions, talents and weaknesses, capacities and incapacities. According to choice-morality, they are not subject to moral praise or censure for any of these pre-moral characteristics, for they have no choice about possessing them. People should be praised or censured only for what they do with their pre-moral characteristics. Moral progress is moral improvement. But since people start with different pre-moral characteristics, moral improvement comes to different things in different cases. In moral progress, we measure the distance traveled from the starting point. And for some people, the starting point is way back, while others are more fortunately situated.

But this will not do. Consider two men, one of whom starts out as a dyed-in-the-wool racist, yet he brings himself to the point where his racism dictates his choices and actions only in extreme situations. He has gone a long way toward ridding himself of it, but he has not quite succeeded. The other man has never encountered racism. The thought of discriminating against people of other races has never entered his mind. If choice-morality were right, we should have to say that as far as racism was concerned, the first man, having improved so much, is more worthy of moral praise than the second one, who has not improved at all. But this is extremely implausible. Surely, the man who is not a racist at all has better moral credentials on that score than the one who has not quite managed to shake his vicious upbringing. One improved, and the other did not. But the one who did not had no need of it. As far as racism was concerned, he had impeccable moral credentials, so he and the moral tradition that formed him deserve more moral credit than the reforming racist and his moral tradition.

Choice-morality is encumbered with this implausibility because it underemphasizes the actual good and evil moral agents cause and overlooks the crucial importance of the characters and traditions of moral agents in judging their choices and actions. The reason why improvement looms so important in choice-morality is that that is what choices are supposed to bring about. And of course improvement matters, but it is wrong to regard it as one main determinant of moral standing. Considerable improvement in some people may merely bring them to the lower rungs of decency, a position that others have achieved without effort. The truth is that some people are raised in vicious traditions and they are encumbered by many vices. These are moral handicaps. And they are so, even though people do not choose their traditions and characters, at least not during their formative years.

The fourth contrast is between *responsibility* and *desert*. Choice-morality is responsibility centered, while character-morality is desert centered. For a succinct statement of the rationale for focusing on responsibility, we can turn to Kant: "Man *himself* must make or have made himself into whatever, in a moral sense, whether good or evil, he is or is to become. Either condition must be an effect of his free choice; for otherwise he could not be held responsible for it and could therefore be *morally* neither good or evil."[16] Since good and evil depend on choice, their agents must be held responsible. Similarly, given the coincidence of the domains of morality and choice, morality and responsibility mutually entail one another.

In a thoughtful essay, Watson considers contemporary reasons for concentrating on responsibility. He says, "The boundaries of moral

---

[16] Kant, *Religion within the Limits of Reason Alone*, 40.

responsibility are the boundaries of intelligible moral address."[17] And the boundaries of moral responsibility are set by excusing and exempting conditions. People may be excused for evil actions if they perform them, for instance, in emergencies or when being coerced; and they may be exempted if, for instance, they are insane or hypnotized. So, when choice-morality faces agents of habitual evil, its concern is with trying to establish the extent to which the evildoers come under the heading of excusing or exempting conditions.

Watson gives a harrowing case of the cold-blooded, cruel, and gratuitous murder of two boys and goes on to describe, equally harrowingly, the brutalized childhood of the murderer. Watson then agonizes: the murderer "both satisfies and violates the criteria of victimhood. His childhood abuse was a misfortune inflicted upon him against his will. But at the same time . . . he unambivalently endorses suffering, death, and destruction, and that is what (one form of) evil is. . . . [Our] ambivalence results from the fact that an overall view simultaneously demands and precludes regarding him as a victim."[18]

Watson takes the responsibility-centeredness of choice-morality as far as it will go, shows the impasse it produces, and then he stops because he sees no way out. As he eloquently and honestly puts it: "The fact that [the murderer's] . . . cruelty is an intelligible response to his circumstances gives a foothold not only for sympathy, but for the thought that if *I* had been subjected to such circumstances, I might have become as vile. . . . This thought induces not only an ontological shudder, but a sense of equality with the other: I too am a potential sinner. . . . The awareness that, in this respect, the others are or may be like oneself clashes with the distancing effect of enmity. Admittedly, it is hard to know what to do with this conclusion."[19]

It is a remarkable feature of Watson's discussion that almost all of his attention is concentrated on what our reaction should be to the murderer. Great subtlety is employed in probing our sensibility for the right reaction. But nothing is said, after the murder is recounted, about the undeserved harm suffered by the victims. Two boys were brutally murdered; their future was taken away from them; their families were confronted with the loss, with the gory details of the crime, and with their own feelings of grief, rage, and helplessness; and we witnesses see that such things happen in our society, to our fellows, that it may happen to those we love and to ourselves. And Watson, consistently with choice-morality, agonizes over the criminal

---

[17] Watson, "Responsibility and the Limits of Evil," 286.
[18] Ibid., 275.
[19] Ibid., 276.

and glosses over the crime. Surely, there is something seriously askew here.

What is wrong is that choice-morality and Watson do not give sufficient weight to the fundamental moral fact that great evil has been done. *That* should occupy the center of our moral attention; *that* is what it is the task of morality to prevent from happening. And it happened because the murderer caused it. We know enough about him to know that it was not an accident, an uncharacteristic episode in an otherwise decent life; we know that his character is such as to make it likely that he will do it again if he gets the chance. He is an evil person because he is ruled by his vices and he habitually causes undeserved harm. This is the moral fact that we should hold firmly before us. The degree of responsibility is secondary. It is a mistake to suppose, as choice-morality and Watson on its behalf do, that "the boundaries of moral responsibility are the boundaries of intelligible address."[20] There is nothing unintelligible in saying that people like the murderer are evil and that they deserve to be treated as such, even if it was their brutal childhood that caused them to be what they are.

The blindness to this truism has two sources. The first is the Kantian assumption that good and evil are mental attitudes. Discussing the question of what things have intrinsic worth, Kant writes, "Their worth consists, not in the effects which result from them, not in the advantage or profit they produce, but in the attitudes of mind . . . which are ready in this way to manifest themselves in action."[21] Consequently, the evil that people's actions cause is morally irrelevant. What matters, from the moral point of view, is whether agents act with the appropriate attitudes of mind. Responsibility attaches to these attitudes and not to "the effects which result from them." And the agents are responsible for their attitudes only if they have chosen them. However, it is a plain fact of life that evil consequences often follow from even the most saintly attitudes, and people are often moved to cause evil by attitudes they have not chosen. If we accept this Kantian assumption, we shall be left without moral resources to deal with unchosen evil. And since one aim of morality is to minimize evil, we would be ill prepared to pursue it if we agreed with Kant.

The second source of the tendency to concentrate on responsibility at the expense of desert is the confusion of the question of whether moral censure is appropriate with the question of how severe the censure should be. The appropriateness of censuring agents depends on

---

[20] Ibid., 286.
[21] Kant, *Groundwork*, 102–3.

whether they habitually cause evil, not on whether they choose to do so. The severity of the censure, on the other hand, depends on the extent to which these agents had choices. Choice-morality, employing the acquitting version of the Principle, concentrates on the second question, misses the first, and thus leaves people like Watson incapable of formulating an intelligible response to evil. Character-morality, using the extenuating version of the Principle, however, has such a response available, and that is yet another reason for preferring it.

The acquitting version of the Principle is supported by the combined forces choice, action, improvement, and responsibility as the fundamental notions of choice-morality. If morality is coextensive with the domain where actions are chosen, and if the responsibility for chosen actions partly depends on the moral improvement they produce, then we should indeed make the appropriateness of moral censure dependent on whether or not the evil-producing actions were chosen. In choice-morality, "ought implies can" expresses a fundamental condition of morality. As we have seen, however, choice-morality is mistaken in assigning fundamental importance to choice, action, improvement, and responsibility.

Choice, action, improvement, and responsibility matter insofar as they are signs of the deeper, more fundamental considerations of character, moral agency, achievement, and desert. Character-morality gives a more reasonable account of these more basic considerations. But in character-morality, the acquitting version of the Principle has no place, because we are perfectly justified in doing what we frequently do: censuring people for being dominated by vices and for habitually doing evil, even though they have no choice in the matter. This would lead to excessively severe moral judgments if the extenuating version of the Principle were not there to mitigate them. The proper function of the Principle is to remind us that people do not deserve as harsh a treatment for the evil they did not choose to cause as for the evil they inflicted by choice. The extenuating version of the Principle is a civilizing force because it restrains righteous indignation. Let us, however, be clear that "ought implies can" is a rather misleadingly expressed moral call for restraint and not the important standard that legitimizes the soft reaction.

THE PRINCIPLE DEMOTED

Having argued for demoting the Principle, I must now recognize that, notwithstanding its faults, its acquitting version does capture some of our important moral concerns, although in a confused way. If we think clearly, we shall see that we can hold on to what is important about them without having to commit ourselves to an unacceptable view about the appropriateness of moral reactions.

Let us begin with the sentiment that if my arguments about the unchosen evil caused by insufficient, expedient, and malevolent agents are correct, then we should censure the moral tradition whose products these agents are, rather than the agents themselves. Now I think that it is true that moral traditions are liable to moral censure if they systematically produce agents who cause evil. But this being so does not remove the censure from the agents.

Moral traditions are abstractions. They refer to the system of ideals, values, rules, customs, conventions, and expectations that prevail in a society. These can be described, codified, and expressed by novelists, prophets, philosophers, dramatists, statesmen, and other articulate observers or participants. But a moral tradition is living only if there are people who act according to it. To say that moral traditions do this or that is a short way of saying that people adhering to the traditions do this or that. Without people acting on their behalf, moral traditions cannot be causal agents. The claim that moral traditions systematically produce evil agents amounts to claiming that people in those traditions miseducate the young, brutalize their fellows, or set deplorable examples. So, the primary subjects of moral censure are always people, and the censure of moral traditions is always derivative.

Another attempt to shift the censure from evil-producing agents is to concede that the unchosen vices of insufficiency, expediency, and malevolence are evil ways of being but to locate the source of evil in the scheme of things, rather than in the agents. If the agents really did not choose to be in these deplorable ways, then, the feeling is, they are not acting on their own behalf. They are merely carriers of the evil that the world has instilled in them, not originators of it. It is readily agreed that the world would be a better place if people were not made to cause evil by it, but we still should not make scapegoats of those who are affected in these unfortunate ways. What has happened to agents of unchosen evil is that the essential conditions of life—contingency, indifference, and destructiveness—have come to inform their characters. So, the appropriate objects of censure are those formative conditions, not the agents formed by them.

This is an influential sentiment, but it is curiously one-sided. Its prevalence is a testimony to the strong hold choice-morality has on our sensibility. Its effect is that when we try to look evil in the face, we tend to concentrate on the helplessness of evil agents, rather than on the undeserved simple harm they have inflicted on their victims. This one-sidedness diverts our attention from the terrible things evil people do and urges us to try to understand how they came to do them. Understanding means discovering the conditions that formed them, and once discovered, their evil actions become less horrible—the sort of thing anyone might do. To understand is not exactly to excuse; still, understanding tends to lead to excuse. And so we are guided, step by innocuous step, away from one central concern of morality, namely, with minimizing evil, and we are led toward a merely secondary concern, that of assigning the appropriate degree of responsibility for the evil that has been done. But the latter presupposes the former, and unless we face evil, the question of responsibility can have no reasonable answer.

From the moral point of view, the salient fact is that there are many people who habitually cause simple evil because their characters are flawed. If we want to minimize evil, we must be concerned with that. We must want to curtail their activities, to hold them up as examples to avoid, and to use our influence to stop others from becoming like them. Moral censure is the clearest expression of our wanting all this. And while our sensibility may generate some sympathy for the soft reaction to agents of unchosen evil, in much of our actual practice we respond with the hard reaction.

There really is no doubt in anyone's mind that agents who habitually benefit deserving people are morally better than agents who habitually harm those who do not deserve it. We simply do not believe that the difference between virtue and vice becomes a morally neutral fact if it is discovered that their agents did not choose their respective character traits. We do not withhold moral praise from such holy innocents as St. Francis, Melville's Billy Budd, or Dostoyevsky's Prince Myshkin and Alyosha Karamazov, even though they are described as being spontaneously, naturally, instinctively good, rather than having had to work hard to stifle their contrary urges and choose to act the way they did. Nor do we withhold moral censure from their counterparts at the opposite end of the moral scale. Would we think that mass murderers motivated by an ideology they did not choose but into which they were indoctrinated should be exonerated if it turns out that unhappy childhood, strict toilet training, or an incapacity to love caused them to be open to indoctrination?

If morality has to do with minimizing evil, then anything brought about by human agency that contributes to this task has moral relevance. Clearly, actions performed on the basis of choice are paradigmatic moral phenomena. But unchosen actions also aid or hinder the minimization of evil. If evil is to cause undeserved harm, then unchosen actions may cause evil.

Defenders of choice-morality, of course, concede this; what they balk at is allowing the judgment of the evil of actions to be carried over to the judgment of the evil of their agents, unless the actions were chosen. It is here that the three unchosen vices present a very serious difficulty for them. For in each case, the unchosen evil actions are part of a long pattern. They are not fortuitous episodes in which agents accidentally inflicted undeserved harm but habitual, predictable actions that naturally followed from their agents' vices. If agents habitually inflict serious and undeserved harm on others, then there are evil agents who have not chosen their actions. Think of practicing terrorists who have been brainwashed into accepting the ideology they happen to want to force on the world, religious fanatics who simply know that God wants them to punish those who transgress divine commands, people so obsessed with their projects as to have no resources or interest left for moral considerations, and the cowardly, cruel, intemperate, greedy, or malicious ones whose passions are so strong or whose self-discipline is so feeble as to make it impossible for them to control their actions. If we are concerned with morality, we cannot refrain from censuring such people for being evil.

In trying to meet this point, defenders of choice-morality may say that evil is our most severe adjective of censure, and even though the people in my examples are deplorable specimens, it is unjustifiable to call them evil. There are, after all, worse possibilities: if they chose their evil actions, then they would clearly be evil. As it is, we cannot censure them for being evil.

The trouble with this argument is that it confuses two distinct questions. One is whether there is present a dominating vice that results in an enduring pattern of action causing serious and undeserved harm. If there is, it is justified to censure its agents as evil. The other question is about how severe our censure of evil people should be. We cannot consistently identify people as evil and fail to censure them; evil *is* our strongest term of censure. But it does not follow that the censure must issue in some punishment. Punishment is the strongest form of censure, and it should be reserved for the most serious kinds of evil. Chosen evil is a clear candidate for punishment, but so may be unchosen evil, as illustrated by the discussion in the previous chapter. However, the absence of choice does not and should not prevent us from censuring certain ways of being and acting. We can and should say that the brainwashed terrorist, the scourge of God, the obsessed immoralist, and the self-indulgent weakling are, morally speaking, horrible human beings, even though they have not chosen their ways. No doubt, if they became what they are by choice, they would be even more horrible. But lack of choice does not suddenly render these people morally neutral. The salient fact about them is that, because of their vices, they habitually inflict serious and undeserved harm on others, and if we care about morality, we must censure that. How severe the censure should be is a secondary question; in answering it, we should be guided by the extenuating version of the Principle.

It will be asked: what does it mean to censure these people, if it does not necessarily involve punishing them? It means that, although we cannot fault them for choosing the evil they regularly do, we can shun their company, we can hold them up as examples to avoid, we can teach our children not to be like them, we can regard their lives as basically flawed ways of living, we can evaluate the conduct of others by considering, among other things, how much or little they resemble these evil cases, and above all, we can create and maintain institutions to protect us from them and from the evil they do.

So, choice-morality is correct in supposing that evil is often done by choice, but it is incorrect in ignoring the frequent evil that is done without it. It is also correct in insisting that censure and punishment often go together, but it erroneously withholds censure if punishment is inappropriate. The unfortunate consequence is that choice-morality prompts the misguided soft reaction to common types of evil. Hence, it is a poor approach to one main task of morality: the minimization of evil.

The Growing Content of Character-Morality

The minimum content of character-morality is defined by three theses: the objectivity of simple evil; the irrelevance of choice to simple evil; and the reflexivity of simple evil. We have seen that part of the reason why choice is irrelevant to evil is that much evil is unchosen. But there is a reluctance to regard it as moral and to allow unchosen evil to reflect on the moral standing of the agents who cause it. This reluctance finds expression in the soft reaction to evil, and the soft reaction rests on the assumptions of choice-morality. In this chapter, I have attempted to show the illegitimacy of the first of these assumptions, namely, the acquitting version of the Principle that ought implies can. My criticisms have a destructive and a constructive aim. The former is to identify the mistaken emphasis choice-morality places on choice, action, improvement, and responsibility in contrast with character, moral agency, achievement, and desert. The latter, constructive aim is to develop character-morality further by going beyond its minimum content and thereby prepare the ground for justifying what I take to be the more appropriate hard reaction to evil.

The growing content of character-morality may be expressed in the form of theses added to the previous three. The fourth thesis is *the importance of character to moral judgment.* Moral judgments concern good and evil. The moral lives of most people most of the time consist in the routine transactions of everyday life. Family, neighborhood, work, hobbies, friends, colleagues, and acquaintances establish the context of our conduct. The rights and duties, the rewards and punishments, the supererogatory and backsliding actions, and the norms observed or deviated from are familiar to everybody through custom, habit, convention, and moral education. The need for choice usually arises when the familiar pattern of life is interrupted by emergencies, fundamental challenges, the breakdown of the tradition, novel situations, or personal crises. But life is not a permanent revolution, and although it can become so, most of the time it is not a violent process, at least in civilized circumstances. Our characters are formed by the society into which we are born, by the possibilities it provides for the development of our various native capacities, and by the roles, personal relationships, and careers that it recognizes as acceptable. The development of character is the long process of trying to find a fit between our predispositions and the available forms for translating them into action. In some lives, this process is more informed by choices than in others. But even in lives where choices figure prominently, the choices express the capacities and possibilities the individuals have prior to choices. Of course, among the prior capacities choices reflect is the capacity to choose itself. So, from the moral point of view, characters are vastly more important than the choices that stem from them. This is why attention to character is likely to bring us to greater moral depth than attention to choices, which are merely the epiphenomena of character.

The fifth thesis is *the unavoidability of moral agency.* All normal human beings are moral agents. To become such an agent does not require making a basic choice; there is no conscious or tacit contract. No commitment, intention, or decision is required, nor need there be consciousness of one's status as a moral agent. None of these is individually or jointly necessary for moral agency. Moral agency depends on the universal human capacity to cause good and evil to other people and to oneself. We express our agency through actions, and actions are the immediate causes of good and evil. But actions are morally important partly because they are signs and expressions of the kind of moral agents we are. Uncharacteristic actions are usually of negligible moral relevance because they are necessarily rare. Typical actions reflect the characters of their agents. Thus, if we aim to minimize evil, the best policy is to concentrate primarily on moral agents and only secondarily on their actions. It remains true that we can concentrate on agents only through their actions, but since actions are the products of agents, if we want to shape the product, we must attend to the source from which it comes.

The sixth thesis is *the significance of moral achievement*. Moral achievement depends on the balance of good and evil one has caused. From the moral point of view, this is the most important question about moral agency and about the moral judgment of character. Everything else is merely circumstantial evidence. Handicaps, effort, misfortune, the nature of genetic endowments, the influences of the society that proved formative, honest mistakes, and sincerity of belief are considerations that can only reduce the severity of moral judgments. But the objects of moral judgment are good and evil and, especially, habitual patterns of good and evil that reflect the agents' characters. This relentless objectivity of moral judgments follows from the necessary aim of character-morality. If our aim is to promote human welfare, then the good, which does so, and the evil, which does the opposite, are the relevant facts. Agents who regularly cause simple evil, whose actions reflect vices that dominate their characters, are evil agents. They cannot but be appropriate subjects of moral concern and of adverse moral judgment. How severe the moral judgment should be depends on the various extenuating factors that may be present. But these factors can affect only the severity of moral judgments; they cannot expunge its appropriateness.

The seventh thesis is *the centrality of moral desert*. People deserve what is due to them, and what that is depends on their past actions. Desert has a central place in character-morality because evil is understood as undeserved harm, and good as deserved benefit. Since character-morality is concerned with human welfare, it begins with a presumption in favor of people deserving the minimum requirements of their welfare; to put it differently, it begins with a presumption against causing simple evil. But this presumption can be overruled if, and only if, doing so promotes human welfare. In the context of our discussion of evil, the centrality of desert translates into a two-pronged strategy. The first is to minimize the evil people suffer. The second is to give their due to those who cause them to suffer. People who habitually cause evil deserve censure. What form the censure should take, how severe it should be, and what excuses are exculpating are questions that remain to be answered. I go some way toward answering them in the next chapter.

CHAPTER SIX

Human Worth and Moral Merit

CHOICE AND HUMAN WORTH

One purpose of this chapter is to make explicit and to criticize the second of the three assumptions of choice-morality, from which the soft reaction to habitual unchosen simple evil derives. This assumption is that the mere capacity to choose confers worth on agents who possess it. But just as the moral significance of choice is at issue between choice and character-morality, so also is at issue the moral significance of human worth. Behind these issues lie two conflicting moral visions.

Choice-morality regards the capacity to choose as a basic and most important moral fact about us. The chief purpose of morality is supposed to be protection of the conditions in which people may exercise that capacity. This vision is the animating spirit behind the emphasis our sensibility places on a particular interpretation of rights, justice, and freedom. Rights are supposed to protect the conditions in which choice can be exercised; justice is taken to include the social arrangements intended to guarantee that no one is unjustifiably prevented from choosing; and freedom is regarded as the sphere of uncoerced choices. And since all normal and mature human beings have the capacity to choose, rights, justice, and freedom are deserved equally, so that everyone is entitled to the same protections and opportunities for exercising choice.

It is the capacity for choice, according to this view, that bestows basic worth on human beings. This worth is universal and equal, and it can be lost only if the capacity to choose is lost. Thus, the soft reaction to habitual unchosen evil is justified because its agents do not lose their worth. They may cause evil, but they have not chosen it, so their actions cannot reflect adversely on the source of their worth, which is their capacity to choose.

As Kant puts it: "Man (even the most wicked) does not, under any maxim whatsoever, repudiate the moral law in the manner of a rebel (renouncing obedience to it). The law, rather, forces itself upon him irresistibly by virtue of his moral predisposition; and were no other incentive working in opposition . . . he would be morally good."[1] A

---

[1] Kant, *Religion within the Limits of Reason Alone*, 31.

little later he writes: man is "*not basically* corrupt (even as regards his original predisposition to good), but rather . . . still capable of improvement. . . . For man, therefore, who despite a corrupted heart possesses a good will, there remains hope of a return to the good from which he has strayed."[2] This hope is pegged on the universal capacity for choice; it is a capacity that all human beings are supposed to have equally; and it is regarded as the foundation of equal human worth.

Thus, the moral vision animating this assumption of choice-morality is that although contingency, indifference, and destructiveness may jeopardize our aspirations to live good lives, they cannot destroy the deepest source of this aspiration. "Natural inclinations, *considered in themselves*, are *good*, that is, not a matter of reproach, and it is not only futile to want to extirpate them but to do so would also be harmful and blameworthy."[3] Consequently, contingency, indifference, and destructiveness are merely obstacles that we have reason to hope we can overcome; they are perhaps conditions of life, but they are not essential ones. What is essential is the predisposition to the good, which confers equal worth on all human beings. I shall discuss this view by separating its two fundamental claims—one about goodness, and the other about equality. Of course, they are connected, and their connection will not be ignored, but we have to start somewhere, and I shall start with equality in this chapter.

Opposed, then, to this moral egalitarianism is the vision of character-morality. According to it, contingency, indifference, and destructiveness are among the essential conditions of life, and moral thinking should begin with the fact that our aspiration to live good lives is jeopardized by them. People routinely become instruments of the essential conditions of life and cause evil, even though they have not chosen to do so. Those who habitually act in this way are evil, and one purpose of morality is to protect us from them. By holding evil people morally accountable for both chosen and unchosen vices and for actions that follow from them, we call their worth into question. The hard reaction rests on the assumption that evil people do not deserve the same treatment as good ones, because they have less worth. According to the moral vision of character-morality, human worth is not universal and equal, because it is conditional on the various degrees of moral merit different people possess. Thus, there is no universal moral equality, and choice-morality is mistaken in sup-

---

[2] Ibid., 39.
[3] Ibid., 51.

posing that there is. Another purpose of this chapter is to show that this moral vision is reasonable.

THE SECOND ASSUMPTION OF CHOICE-MORALITY: MORAL EGALITARIANISM

It is a depressingly common phenomenon in human history that a false belief pervades the sensibility of an age and exerts a deep influence on the prevailing moral, political, and legal practices. The divine right of kings to rule, the barbarity of people who do not share some favored form of life, the sinfulness of sex outside of marriage, the influence of evil spirits on human affairs, and the wickedness or backwardness of people who fail to worship a particular god are examples of the kind of belief I have in mind. I think that the egalitarian assumption of choice-morality, that all human beings have equal worth independently of their moral merit, is another such belief, and it threatens to exert a deep influence on our sensibility.

Although this belief is presupposed by many social programs proposed and often implemented in liberal democracies, we have to turn to philosophers for explicit statements of it. Thus, Rawls writes: "There is a tendency for common sense to suppose that . . . the good things in life . . . should be distributed according to moral desert. . . . Now justice as fairness rejects this assumption."[4] Dworkin, arguing in support of Rawls, agrees. "Justice as fairness rests on the assumption of a natural right of men and women to equality of concern and respect, a right they possess not by virtue of birth or characteristic or merit or excellence but simply as human beings."[5] Vlastos thinks that "the human worth of all persons is equal, however unequal may be their merit."[6] And Gewirth "prescribes what I shall call an *Equality of Generic Rights.* . . . Directly, this equality sets an obligation for the individual agent to respect in his actions the freedom and well-being of his recipients. Indirectly, the equality must be provided, restored, or reinforced by social rules and institutions."[7]

The practical implication of this egalitarianism is that the vicious and the kind, the cruel and the benevolent, and the just and the unjust deserve equal rights to other people's support of their freedom and welfare. Justice, according to egalitarians, requires that we should ignore the use to which people have and are likely in the future to put their freedom and welfare. Long patterns of good or evil

---

[4] Rawls, *A Theory of Justice*, 310.
[5] Dworkin, *Taking Rights Seriously*, 182.
[6] Vlastos, "Justice and Equality," 43.
[7] Gewirth, *Reason and Morality*, 206.

conduct are supposed to be irrelevant to what we think of the respective worth of people whose conduct form these patterns. The principled and the expedient, the reflective and the dogmatic, the strong and the weak, and the attentive and the negligent have the same human worth and are entitled to the same share of whatever contribution others can make toward their freedom and welfare.

Defenders of egalitarianism attempt to mitigate the implausibility of this belief by the qualification that the attribution of equal human worth is not absolute but prima facie. There is a presumption in favor of all people possessing it and thus having equal rights to freedom and welfare, but the presumption can be justifiably overruled, provided the resulting inequality strengthens the protection of overall freedom and welfare. Thus, criminals, for instance, are properly deprived of their freedom because they have violated the rights of others. But the justification of unequal distribution is, and can only be, that it is required by equal distribution. As Vlastos puts it, "An egalitarian concept of justice may admit inequalities without inconsistency if, and only if, it provides grounds for equal human rights."[8]

This is a step in the right direction, but taking it has two fundamentally damaging consequences for the prima facie case for egalitarianism. The first is that the reasons that can justifiably lead to the defeat of the prima facie case for human worth being independent of moral merit are nothing but appeals to moral merit. We can violate the rights of right violators if they habitually cause simple evil. And since, on any view of morality, morality is centrally concerned with the good and evil people cause, those who habitually cause simple evil are deficient in moral merit, and this is what justifies depriving them of their rights. Hence, if the case for equal human worth is prima facie, not absolute, then human worth is not independent of moral merit.

The response to this may be that the prima facie case rests not only on the presumption of equal human worth but also on that of moral merit. People are assumed not to have caused evil unless there are overriding reasons to believe otherwise. Safeguarding people's rights to freedom and welfare should not be made to depend on the favorable outcome of an investigation into their moral merit. This claim leads to a second damaging consequence.

The presumption in favor of the possession of moral merit may or may not be reasonable; whether it is, depends, among other things, on the general level of morality prevailing in a social context. Consider, therefore, the following description: "Wherever you looked, in

[8] Vlastos, "Justice and Equality," 40.

all our institutions, in all our homes, *skloka* was brewing. *Skloka* is a phenomenon born of our social order, an entirely new term and concept, not to be translated into any language of the civilized world. It is hard to define. It stands for base, trivial hostility, unconscionable spite breeding petty intrigues, the vicious pitting of one clique against another. It thrives on calumny, informing, spying, slander, the igniting of base passions. Taut nerves and weakening morals allow one individual or group rabidly to hate another individual or group. *Skloka* is natural for people who have been incited to attack one another, who have been made bestial by desperation, who have been driven to the wall."[9]

In a social context where *skloka* dominates, the presumption of moral merit is unreasonable because people habitually cause simple evil. Some individuals, of course, may still escape corruption, but *skloka* shows that most do not. The implication is that in such societies the prima facie case is systematically defeated. Consequently, we cannot reasonably attribute human worth to people simply in virtue of their humanity; their moral merit and their social context exerting a strong influence on their moral merit are also relevant.

Thus, the egalitarian belief that people have equal human worth and deserve equal treatment independently of any other consideration ought to fizzle out. The rights to freedom and welfare should be seen as partly dependent on the morality of agents and on the prevailing social conditions. But what should happen does not happen, and this extraordinary belief is continued to be strongly held in spite of its implausibility and the existence of such obvious criticisms of it as I have just adduced. At least part of the reason for this is that, supporting egalitarianism, there are three generally unarticulated beliefs whose truths are assumed, but not argued, although they are actually false. I shall now proceed to make explicit and criticize these beliefs.[10]

Selves and Their Qualities

The first belief concerns the distinction between two aspects of being a person. One is the self, and the other are various qualities. The self is the subject who possesses these qualities. Some of these qualities may exist as potentialities at birth; others are acquired by conditioning, accident, education, or choice. The self is at least relatively en-

---

[9] Mossman, *The Correspondence of Boris Pasternak and Olga Friedenberg*, 303–4.

[10] In formulating these criticisms, I have been influenced by Nozick, *Anarchy, State, and Utopia*, chapters 7–8; Sandel, *Liberalism and the Limits of Justice*; and Sher, *Desert*, chapter 2.

during and continuous; it is the bearer of one's name, the referent of "I," the guarantor of some minimal personal identity. By contrast, qualities are changeable; they can be developed and lost. In some sense, then, people necessarily possess their selves, but the possession of qualities is contingent. It is very difficult to specify the appropriate senses of necessity and contingency, continuity and change, or the nature of personal identity. But I do not think that the use egalitarians make of this distinction depends on having precise logical answers to these complicated questions.

The heart of the egalitarian case is that human worth attaches to selves, while moral merit depends on qualities. One reason why human worth is thought to be independent of moral merit, according to egalitarians, is that selves are distinct from their qualities. Since people possess selves necessarily and universally and qualities only contingently, people also have human worth necessarily and universally and moral merit only contingently.

The proper interpretation of equal human rights to freedom and well-being, according to egalitarians, is not that people are rewarded by these rights for their morally good qualities but that human rights are necessary conditions for people exercising their capacity to choose and thus for developing morally good qualities. Human rights protect selves and make their development possible; and they are equal because all human beings possess selves simply because they are human. Human worth is prior to moral merit because the possession of selves is prior to their development. Justice includes social arrangements guaranteeing equal protection for all people so that they may choose and develop. This is why justice, equality, and human rights attach to people per se, rather than only to those who have morally merited them. To express this in terms of human worth is to indicate that one belongs to the party of humanity, that one thinks that there is a prima facie case in favor of people's development of their selves.

This is behind Vlastos's claim that "if there is a value attaching to the person himself as an integral and unique individual, *this* value will not fall under merit or be reducible to it. For it is the essence of merit . . . to be a grading concept; and there is no way of grading individuals as such."[11] And this is part of the rationale for Rawls's placing prospective agents in the original position where, behind the veil of ignorance, they know, as it were, only their selves, but not their qualities. They are to legislate so as to enable people to develop their selves. "The self," Rawls writes, "is prior to the ends which are af-

[11] Vlastos, "Justice and Equality," 43.

firmed by it."[12] "The parties' aim in the original position is to establish just and favorable conditions for each to fashion his own [plan of life]."[13]

So the first belief supporting the supposed independence of human worth from moral merit is that these two notions should not be seen as competing grounds for the ascription of rights. When they are properly understood, it becomes apparent that human worth is logically and morally prior to moral merit because the self is prior to its qualities, and while human worth is a necessary and universal feature of all human beings, moral merit is merely a contingent one.

The initial problem with the supposed priority of the self to its qualities is that if this were true, then there could not be a reason for attributing human worth to the self. The problem is logical. If the self were regarded merely as the logical subject of which qualities were predicated, then there could be no reason for thinking that the self was a human self. Animals, plants, and material objects also possess logical subjects in this pure sense. But if we go beyond pure logical subjects, so that the kind of logical subjects human beings have could be distinguished from other kinds of logical subjects, then the distinction must be made in terms of some quality or another. In that case, however, the identification of a logical subject as a human self necessarily involves reference to some quality. Consequently, if a logical subject were prior to its qualities, then the attribution of moral worth to it would be illegitimate, since the logical subject may not be a human self. On the other hand, if human worth were justifiably assigned to a self, then there would have to be some quality present justifying the ascription, and then the self would not be prior to *that* quality.

Whatever that quality is, it would have to be one that distinguishes human subjects from nonhuman ones: capacity for choice, rationality, altruism, good will, conscience, and self-consciousness are some of the often-proposed candidates. However, regardless of what the quality is, critics of egalitarianism would reasonably claim that its possession is the minimal ground of moral merit. And then human worth would go hand in hand with moral merit. For if people lost the relevant quality, they would ipso facto be deprived of both human worth and moral merit—the former, because the subject of human worth would not have been shown to be human, and the latter, because moral merit would lose its minimal ground. Contrariwise, if the relevant quality were present, then the ascription of human worth

[12] Rawls, *A Theory of Justice*, 560.
[13] Ibid., 563.

and minimal moral merit would be equally justified and be justified on the same grounds. Therefore, the first belief supporting the supposed independence of human worth from moral merit is vitiated by a logical error.

One of Vlastos's arguments illustrates this error. He writes: "If A is valued for some meritorious quality, m, his individuality does not enter into the valuation. As an individual he is then dispensable; his place could be taken without loss of value by any other individual with as good an m-rating. Nor would matters change by multiplying and diversifying the meritorious qualities with which A is endowed. No matter how enviable a package of well-rounded excellence A may represent, it would still follow that, if he is valued only for his merit, he is not being valued as an individual."[14] The implication is clear: if A is to be valued as an individual, then A must be valued independently of any qualities. Hence A could be a ping-pong ball or a cobweb.

To make clear what he means by the above quotation, Vlastos gives as an example a parent (P) valuing his son (A) in the right way: "P prizes [A's] . . . conjunct of qualities (M), [and] he values A also as an individual. . . . If so, his affection will be for A, not for M-qualities. The latter, P approves, admires, takes pride in, and the like. But his affection and good will are for A, and *not only because* or *insofar as* A has the M-qualities."[15] Thus, P's affection and good will ought not to depend on A's qualities. So, if A turned out not to be P's son, if P had not watched A's growth and development, if A did not have a long intimate relationship with P, then, and only then, would P's affection and good will be directed at A as an individual. Vlastos fails to see that if A's qualities were removed, then A would cease to be an individual whom P could reasonably value, or that if P is reasonable in valuing A, then the valuing must be based on some quality or qualities of A.

Suppose this logical point is conceded by egalitarians. They may attempt to defend the independence of human worth from moral merit by arguing that the identification of logical subjects as human beings does rest on some qualities, and these are sufficient to justify the ascription of human worth, but the qualities are morally neutral and hence insufficient for the ascription of moral merit. Some of Rawls's arguments can be cited in support of this approach. He writes, for instance, that "the natural distribution [of qualities] is neither just not unjust; nor is it unjust that persons are born into society

[14] Vlastos, "Justice and Equality," 44.
[15] Ibid.

at some particular position. These are simply natural facts. What is just and unjust is the way institutions deal with these facts."[16] The suggestion is that some nonmoral qualities are prior to the establishment of institutions, while moral merit is contingent on institutions, since institutions define what a particular society counts as morally meritorious qualities. "A good person . . . is someone who has a higher degree than the average the broadly based features of moral character that it is rational for persons in the original position to want in one another. Since the principles of justice have been chosen . . . each knows that in society he will want the others to have the moral sentiments that support adherence to these standards."[17]

But while the principles of justice may be regarded as establishing what counts as moral merit in some cases, they cannot establish it in all cases. For Rawls himself insists that some moral considerations are appropriate prior to the choice of the principles of justice. "It is characteristic of natural duties that they apply to us without regard to our voluntary acts. Moreover, they have no necessary connection with institutions or social practices; their content is not, in general, defined by the rules of these arrangements. Thus we have a natural duty not to be cruel, and a duty to help another, whether or not we have committed ourselves to these actions."[18]

If we suppose what is obvious, namely, that there are both people who habitually violate their natural duties and people who habitually honor them, then we have clear instances of the presence and absence of moral merit prior to institutions or to people's commitment to them. Consequently, the attempt to separate morally neutral preinstitutional qualities from morally evaluative institutional qualities fails. And so also fails the attempted rescue of the independence of human worth from moral merit. For we cannot reasonably connect human worth with preinstitutional qualities and moral merit with institutional ones. I conclude that the logical error involved in trying to distinguish the self from its qualities is not avoided by the distinction between preinstitutional and institutional qualities. If the self is a pure logical subject, then the ascription of neither human worth nor moral merit is justified; and if the self is allowed to have some qualities, then the ascription of both human worth and moral merit is contingent on the possession of these qualities. In neither case can the independence of human worth from moral merit be reasonably maintained. And so egalitarians have given no good reason yet for

[16] Rawls, *A Theory of Justice*, 104.
[17] Ibid., 437.
[18] Ibid., 114–15.

rejecting the obvious point that people who habitually cause simple evil, and thus lack moral merit, have less human worth and are entitled to less protection of their freedom and welfare than people who show a long pattern of morally good conduct, and thus have moral merit.

THE GROUND OF DESERT

The second belief underlying the supposed independence of human worth from moral merit is that human worth attaches to universal qualities of humanity, while moral merit is partly due to individual qualities people have but do not deserve. The universal qualities upon which human worth depends are common human potentialities, such as the capacity for choice, rationality, altruism, self-direction, and so forth, and justice, equality, and the rights to freedom and welfare protect the conditions in which these potentialities may be realized. By contrast, moral merit depends on character. But character, in turn, depends, to a considerable extent, on natural endowments and social circumstances. Morally good character requires some intelligence, the capacity for self-control, a mental equilibrium that makes it possible to pay attention to others, the absence of brutalizing influences, and not being victimized by extreme poverty, discrimination, or exploitation. People with morally good character must have inherited some good genes, and they had to be raised in at least a minimally hospitable setting. Such advantages, however, are arbitrary grounds for moral merit. Therefore, it would be unjust to distribute rights to freedom and welfare unequally, according to moral merit. It is far more reasonable to distribute them according to human worth and human potentialities, so that the arbitrariness of natural endowments and the conditions of birth and upbringing would be minimized. As Rawls puts it: "It seems to be one of the fixed points of our considered judgments that no one deserves his place in the distribution of native endowments, any more than one deserves one's initial starting place in society. The assertion that a man deserves the superior character that enables him to cultivate his abilities is equally problematic; for his character depends in large part upon fortunate family and social circumstances for which he can claim no credit. The notion of desert seems not to apply to these cases."[19]

The first thing to notice about this argument is that it concentrates on "native endowments," "superior character," and the appropriateness of "desert" for their possession. The assumption is that the uni-

[19] Ibid., 104.

versal qualities to which equal human worth attaches are not tainted by evil. The endowments that all people are supposed to have, but have to varying degrees, are taken to be morally positive forces; and then the argument is that those who happen to have more of them, because of luck in the genetic lottery or of being born into a hospitable environment, do not deserve more moral credit than those who are less fortunate.

But this assumption ignores what tragic situations show us. All human potentialities are vulnerable to evil; contingency, indifference, and destructiveness do not cease to be corrupting influences at the point where egalitarians suppose that moral merit ends and human worth begins. All aspects of human conduct are subject to the essential conditions of life. Consequently, human worth has exactly the same status as moral merit. If one is arbitrary, and hence an unjust ground for unequal desert, then so is the other. If desert does not attach to moral merit, then it does not attach to human worth either, for whether people possess the potentialities justice, equality, and rights are meant to protect is just as arbitrary as the possession of a morally good character is said to be.

Rawls seems to be prepared to accept this. He writes: "A just scheme . . . answers to what men are entitled to; it satisfies their legitimate expectations as founded upon social institutions. But what they are entitled to is not proportional to nor dependent upon their intrinsic worth. The principles of justice . . . do not mention . . . desert, and there is no tendency for distributive shares to correspond to it."[20] Sandel's comment on this passage seems to me to be absolutely correct: "The principles of justice do not mention . . . desert because, strictly speaking, no one can be said to deserve anything. Similarly, the reason people's entitlements are not proportional to nor dependent upon their intrinsic worth is that, on Rawls's view, *people have no intrinsic worth,* no worth that is intrinsic in the sense that it is theirs prior to or independent of or apart from what institutions attribute to them."[21] And there is no doubt that this is what Rawls means, for he explicitly says: "The essential point is that the concept of moral worth [i.e. a combination of what I mean by human worth *and* moral merit] does not provide a first principle of distributive justice. This is because it cannot be introduced until after the principles of justice and of natural duty and obligation have been acknowledged. . . . [T]he concept of moral worth is secondary to those of right and justice, and it plays no role in the substantive defi-

[20] Ibid., 311.
[21] Sandel, *Liberalism and the Limits of Justice,* 88.

nition of distributive shares."[22] So, the price we have to pay for giving up the idea that desert ought to be proportional to moral merit is that we also have to give up the idea that desert ought to be based on human worth.

Why, then, should we treat people with the vices of insufficiency, expediency, and malevolence in the same way as we treat the strong, conscientious, and benevolent ones? The answer with which we began, and whose underlying assumptions we are now examining, appealed to universal and necessary human worth as a ground for desert to override differences in individual moral merit. But since this appeal can no longer be made, the question stands.

THE POTENTIALITIES OF HUMAN NATURE

This brings us to the third belief supporting the supposed independence of human worth from moral merit. It may be said that although no one deserves anything in preinstitutional settings, there is still a deep sense in which we are committed to the idea that people deserve to be able to develop their potentialities. We are human, and it is natural for us to wish well for humanity. Justice, equality, and the rights to freedom and welfare protect the conditions in which human potentialities can be developed, and this is the fundamental reason for defending them. The idea of human worth is meant to capture this commitment we have, or ought to have, to the welfare of humanity collectively. The presumption in favor of the human worth of individuals is a distributive consequence of the general idea.

The obvious difficulty with this is that human potentialities are mixed; they are benign and aggressive, altruistic and selfish, generous and envious, gentle and cruel. If the commitment to human welfare calls for the development of good human potentialities, it also calls for the suppression of evil potentialities. If human worth licensed the indiscriminate fostering of human potentialities, it would not support human welfare. But the appeal to moral merit allows us to distinguish between good and evil potentialities, and it provides a ground for encouraging the first and discouraging the second. So, human welfare is better served by fostering or suppressing human potentialities proportionally to their likely contribution to moral merit than by the egalitarian indiscriminateness that follows from human worth.

It seems that the only way to resist this argument is by denying that good and evil human potentialities have an equal status in human

---

[22] Rawls, *A Theory of Justice*, 312–13.

nature. To put it bluntly, the defense of the egalitarian belief presupposes that human nature is primarily, predominantly, or chiefly good. If this were so, then there would indeed be a reason for fostering the development of human potentialities. I think that it is widely believed that human nature is like this. Although the belief is often unstated, it is in the background, the egalitarian belief requires it, and it is a pervasive influence on our sensibility. It is part of our inheritance from the Enlightenment beliefs in the possibility of progress, the rationality of humanity, and the ascription of evil to the corruption caused by badly designed institutions. Its patron saint is Rousseau.

In reaction to it, I cannot improve on James Fitzjames Stephen's trenchant words: "It is one of the commonest beliefs of the day that the human race collectively has before it splendid destinies of various kinds, and that the road to them is to be found . . . in the recognition of a substantial equality between all human creatures. . . . These doctrines . . . are regarded not merely as truths, but as truths for which those who believe them are ready to do battle. . . . Such, stated in the most general terms, is the religion of which I take 'Liberty, Equality, Fraternity' to be the creed. I do not believe it." Stephen continues, "I believe that many men are bad, a vast majority of men are indifferent, and many good, and that the great mass of indifferent people sway this way or that according to circumstances, one of the most important of which circumstances is the predominance for the time being of the bad or good.[23]

Let us now consider how the assumption that human nature is predominantly good translates into a support for the egalitarian belief. The usual strategy for supporting human worth against moral merit is to contrast people who have greater and lesser moral merit. It is then argued that the ones with less moral merit do not get written out of morality; they are still moral agents, and they have a claim on our moral regard. The reason for this is that, although they have misused their potentialities, they still possess them. Therefore, there is hope for reform and improvement. Human worth attaches to potentialities, which cannot be easily lost. Since potentialities are prior to their use or misuse, human worth is prior to moral merit.

There goes with this thinking a particular metaphor for morality. Morality is like language, and becoming a moral agent is like learning one's mother tongue. Both are skills, both are possessed by just about everybody, both are acquired as a matter of course (and it is not their possession but rather their lack that requires explanation), both allow

---

[23] Stephen, *Liberty, Equality, Fraternity,* 52–53 and 226.

for ranking agents according to their performance, both are necessary for the welfare of individuals as well as of society, both require
conformity to rules, both can tolerate some violations of the rules,
and the rules of both can be changed either deliberately or by gradual evolution. Thinking of morality as a skill, of course, has a long
history going back at least to Plato.[24]

The suggestion implicit in this way of thinking, and the significant
one for our present purposes, is that vis-à-vis the skill, we all start, as
it were, at zero and go on from there. We become more or less good
at it, our performances have various merits, but it cannot happen, no
matter how poor our performances are, that we fall below zero. In
this realm, there cannot be negative merit. As with language learning,
so with moral development, we cannot deteriorate in the opposite direction. The zero where we start is absolute zero. The important implication is that immorality is not the opposite of morality but being
a poor moral performer. Immorality is due to the inadequate development of our moral potentialities; it is not the development of another countervailing potentiality. The worst that can happen is that
we fail to develop the potentialities at all. And the corollary is that
what needs explanation is our failure to develop or to perform well.
Since everybody has the potentialities, the explanation must be some
interference with the development of potentialities. This is behind
the egalitarian idea that human worth supports inalienable, imprescriptible, indefeasible rights to the conditions in which the potentialities can be developed without interference.

The trouble with the language metaphor is that it cannot accommodate central features of morality. It is true that one form of immorality is to fail to do what would be good, but another form is to
do evil. And often, to do evil is not to fail to act according to the
dictates of our morally good potentialities but to act according to our
morally evil potentialities. Immorality is not just a form of omission,
due to ignorance or weakness, but also an active force of evil. Selfishness, cruelty, aggression, greed, hostility, and malice are also human
potentialities; they are regular—sometimes chosen, sometimes unchosen—performers in the repertoire of human motivation.

The significance of vices, both chosen and unchosen, is that they
show the inadequacy of the metaphor suggested by egalitarianism.
People in whose characters the vices of insufficiency, expediency, and
malevolence achieved dominance do not merely have unrealized
morally good potentialities; they have realized morally evil potentialities. They do not just lack moral merit; they have moral demerit. It

[24] For the use Plato made of it, see Irwin, *Plato's Moral Theory.*

is not that they have risen only a very little above the absolute-zero point at which morality, according to the egalitarian metaphor, starts. Rather, they have sunk more than a little in the opposite direction, in the direction of immorality. Consequently, the existence of vices shows that it is a mistake to think of morality as a skill, like speaking a language, in whose acquisition we can only improve.

If we must have a metaphor for morality, it should be one that allows for both improvement and deterioration, gain and loss, perfectibility and corruptibility. One metaphor that suggests itself is that morality is like health, while immorality is like sickness. Normal human beings are born with potentialities of both, and as they live their lives, so they may develop one or the other, and often a mixture of both. Just as people can be healthy or sick, so they can be good or evil. Human life is a continuum between the extremes of perfect health and fatal illness, and different people are situated at different points on it. Moral life is similarly a continuum between moral monstrosity and sainthood.

If we think about morality and immorality on this model, then the inappropriateness of regarding human worth as necessary becomes apparent. Human worth can be lost because people may have so much moral demerit as to come to occupy a position on the moral continuum well below the point at which good and evil are equally balanced. Kant, the great defender of human worth, to whom egalitarians often turn for support, is quite clear (and clearly inconsistent) about this. Human worth can be lost through moral demerit: "Lying is the . . . obliteration of one's dignity as a human being. A man who does not himself believe what he says to another . . . has even less worth than if he were a mere thing."[25]

Critics of egalitarianism need not peg their case on Kant's being right about the seriousness of lying. But as I have been arguing, Kant's general point is correct. Human worth is proportional to moral merit, partly because the egalitarian attempt does not succeed in tying universal and necessary human worth to good potentialities that can never be lost. The problem is not that good potentialities can be lost but rather that they can be overwhelmed by evil potentialities. As evil potentialities may dominate good ones, so human worth may be replaced by its opposite. And its opposite is not less worth but the virulent growth of vice, the domination of a life by evil potentialities.

We may reflect on our moral life and on the respective prominence of good and evil in it by remaining on the level of participation, ob-

---

[25] Kant, *The Metaphysical Principles of Virtue*; the quoted passage is in chapter 2, "Concerning Lying," paragraph 9.

servation, and experience. On this level, the arguments I have offered against the belief that human nature is primarily good seem to me to be decisive. But defenders of this belief sometimes move to a different level—the metaphysical. Rawls is disinclined to do so. His aspiration is to "develop a viable Kantian conception of justice" that "must be detached from its background in transcendental idealism" and one that "satisfied the canons of a reasonable empiricism."[26] However, Kant and many of his followers regard it as necessary to move to the level of metaphysics. From that level, the considerations about evil I have advanced here appear not as counterexamples but as parts of the facts to be explained metaphysically. Kant's metaphysical argument for the essential goodness of human beings is the third and deepest assumption on which choice-morality rests, and it is the subject of the next chapter.

MORAL INEQUALITY

My conclusion here is that egalitarians do not provide an acceptable reason for rejecting the obvious and commonsensical conviction that human worth is proportional to moral merit. It is rationally and morally justified to recognize the moral inequality between people who habitually cause evil and those who habitually cause good. Correspondingly, it is likewise justified to regard desert as varying with moral merit.

The practical implication of the rejection of egalitarianism is not that we are free to declare open season on evil people. Of course we should not harm them indiscriminately. But it does seem that it is both reasonable and morally right that people who habitually cause evil should be appropriately censured. The severity of this censure varies; it may be imprisonment if the offenses are criminal, but it may take such other forms as moral contempt, social ostracism, or public dishonor. For the decision of how severe the censure should be, we can appeal to the extenuating version of the Principle that ought implies can.

I do not think that egalitarians need to disagree with this. My point is that they cannot both agree and hold that human worth is independent of moral merit. For the moral demerit of evil people undermines the claim that they have the same human worth and deserve the same treatment as benefactors of humanity. Since egalitarians are committed to such absurd consequences of their position as, for instance, that Hitler and Einstein have equal human worth, they should

---

[26] Rawls, "The Basic Structure as Subject," 165.

abandon choice-morality and the soft reaction in favor of character-morality and the hard reaction.

Furthermore, it also seems reasonable and morally right that people with long patterns of evil conduct should not receive the same protection of their rights to freedom and welfare as people who have not shown themselves to be undeserving. How could it be other than just that mafiosi should not get the same police protection as do the district attorneys who prosecute them, or that school lunches should be more nutritious than prison lunches, or that we should care more about the welfare of hostages than about the welfare of terrorists? And the same goes for freedom rights. How could it be seriously advocated that people who have shown themselves to be vicious and corrupt should have the same rights to be elected to public office, teach the young, or administer the criminal law as those who are fair and kind?

My argument has been that egalitarians cannot give the obvious answers to these questions and hold, as Rawls does, that it is wrong for "common sense to suppose that . . . the good things in life . . . should be distributed according to moral desert," or say, with Vlastos, that "the worth of all persons is equal, however unequal may be their merit."[27] It is rationally and morally justified that common sense should prevail against the ill-advised social program of egalitarianism.

To avoid misunderstanding, let me emphasize that the merit to which I believe human worth is proportional is moral, not merit based on birth, talents, membership in some social group, or inheritance. Nor do I think that we should get rid of the ideals of justice, equality, and rights. On the contrary, properly interpreted, these ideals are important moral forces. But their proper interpretation excludes the claim that justice requires treating human beings as if they had equal human worth and consequently equal rights to freedom and welfare. I am keenly aware of the abuse to which arguments based on moral merit are prone. We learn from history about the horrible things that have been perpetrated in its name. However, it seems to me that this is a danger all ideals face. The remedy is not to deny the obvious rational and moral credentials of the ideal but to prevent its abuse.

I have been endeavoring to show that human worth depends on moral merit, and since moral merit varies, human worth is unequal.[28]

---

[27] Rawls, *A Theory of Justice*, 310, and Vlastos, "Justice and Equality," 43.

[28] For a discussion that in some ways parallels my own, see Larmore, *Patterns of Moral Complexity*, 84–90. Larmore recognizes the inequality of human worth. However, he

The equality of human worth is another one of the mistaken assumptions upon which choice-morality rests. The criticism of these assumptions should undermine choice-morality and make us question the appropriateness of the soft reaction to unchosen evil. The corollary of the doubts I have been trying to engender is that character-morality and the hard reaction it prompts should appear in increasingly favorable light. Thus, our sensibility should undergo a gradual reorientation toward facing the evil that people cause and away from the unwillingness to hold habitual evil actions against their agents. This is not so much a rush to judgment as an attempt to overcome the reluctance to judge. The impetus for the reorientation is the insufficiently appreciated truism that if we care about minimizing evil, then we must be prepared to judge habitual evildoers adversely, quite independently of whether they choose the evil they do. The presence of choice should affect the severity of our judgments, but the appropriateness of our judgments depends on the evil being done.

In concluding the argument of this chapter, we may take another step toward the development of character-morality by adding an eighth thesis to the previous seven. This is *the dependence of moral desert on moral merit*. One consequence of this thesis is that since people differ in respect to their moral merit, they deserve different things. And moral merit varies among people, depending on the good and evil they cause.

---

still maintains—inconsistently, it seems to me—that we owe equal respect to everyone; see 59–66.

CHAPTER SEVEN

Good and Evil in Human Nature

EVIL AS CORRUPTION

We are engaged in making explicit and criticizing the increasingly deeper assumptions underlying the soft reaction to evil. We have seen that the soft reaction follows from a particular view of the nature of morality, a view I have dubbed choice-morality, and that the inspiration of choice-morality, and thus of the soft reaction, is Kantian. In this chapter, I shall consider the deepest of the three assumptions that support choice-morality, and this brings us directly to Kant's view of evil. As far as I know, Kant's *Religion within the Limits of Reason Alone* is the only work by a major philosopher devoted to a consideration of evil. Thus, it would be highly relevant to my interests, even if it did not provide the foundation of the reaction to evil that I find mistaken.

I have argued that the first assumption of choice-morality, that the domain of morality coincides with the domain of choice, is untenable because part of the concern of morality is with minimizing evil. Since much evil is caused by unchosen actions, therefore, if morality is to be faithful to its concern, it must attend to unchosen evil. The second assumption of choice-morality is that although human beings have different degrees of moral merit, they are equal in respect to their worth as human beings. According to this assumption, not even habitual evil actions can diminish human worth, because worth attaches to the human capacity for choice, not to the moral status of the choices actually made. Behind this assumption is the metaphor that morality is like language. All normal human beings are supposed to acquire it and become variously adept at following its rules, so immorality must be interpreted, the metaphor suggests, as deficiency in learning or using a skill. Doing evil is not to exercise a disposition contrary to morality but to fail to exercise, or to exercise poorly, the moral disposition all human beings have, and have merely in virtue of being capable of choice. As we have seen in the last two chapters, the difficulty with this assumption is that much evil is caused without choice, the worth of people who habitually cause chosen or unchosen evil is less than the worth of those who habitually benefit others, and choice itself can be put in the service of evil dispositions. The role of the third assumption of choice-morality is to counter these difficulties. It is intended to show that human nature is fundamentally good, that evil is a corruption of it, that the fundamental goodness of human nature is necessarily connected with the capacity to choose, and that human worth is thus possessed equally by all moral agents. This is the deep and influential position of Kant. It permeates substantial portions of our sensibility. Yet, I shall argue, it is mistaken.

To appreciate the complexities and richness of Kant's view, I shall begin with the simple version of the idea that goodness is basic and evil is a corruption of it. As we recognize the difficulties of the simple version, so we are driven to the complexities of Kant's position. The simple version is that the primary potential implicit in human nature is for the good. The explanation of evil is that something has gone wrong in the development of this potential. As Rousseau puts it: "God makes all things good; man meddles with them and they become evil. . . . [a]ll wickedness comes from weakness. The child is only naughty because he is weak; make him strong and he will be good; if we could do anything we should never do wrong."[1]

At the core of this simple version, there is an optimistic vision. The scheme of things is essentially good, there is a rational and moral order in reality, and we human beings, in our uncorrupted state, are part of this rational and moral order. Evil comes from our failure to conform to it. The source of this failure may be internal or external to human agents.

That the failure is predominantly internal is the implication of the Socratic ideal we discussed in chapter 1. Plato, Aristotle, the Stoics, many (but not all) Christians, and Spinoza have developed some of the notable historical accounts of it. Two contemporary versions are formulated by Norton and Midgley.[2] As Rousseau says, our weakness is the cause of the evil we do. If we do evil because we have failed to recognize the right principles or because we made a mistake in applying them, then our weakness takes the form of an intellectual failure. If we know the right principles, but some defect in our characters prevents us from acting according to them, then our weakness is a volitional failure. The implication is that if intellectual or volitional failure does not stand in the way, then moral agents will act in conformity to the requirements of morality. Evil is thus due to our interference with the natural course of events.

If this is a straight empirical thesis, then it is plainly false. As we

---

[1] Rousseau, *Emile*, 5 and 33.

[2] Norton advances an updated version of eudaimonism in *Personal Destinies*. Midgley defends what she calls the negative view of evil in *Wickedness*.

have seen, there are moral monsters who habitually choose to cause evil, knowing perfectly well that they are violating moral principles and showing considerable strength of will in performing their evil actions. But defenders of this view would not accept moral monsters as counterexamples to their thesis. And this shows that they are not making a simple empirical claim. Their argument is that the intellectual or volitional weakness responsible for these evil actions may not be obvious; nevertheless, one or the other must be there. If it were not, the performance of evil actions would be incomprehensible. If evildoers understood the rational order of reality and if they were not deterred by some sickness in their souls from acting accordingly, then they would not do evil. In the absence of weakness, evil agents would understand that they themselves are more fundamentally harmed than their victims. For evil actions tend to increase the agents' separation from the rational and moral order, while living according to it is essential for the agents' welfare. The good life is the rational life because the moral principles to which good lives conform are applications of the laws implicit in the rational order to human affairs.

There are two reasons for rejecting the metaphysical argument advanced in support of the simple version of the view that evil is the corruption of our primarily good nature. It does not account for the relevant facts, and it is inconsistent. To begin with the factual issue: why should we think that, contrary to common human experience, it is always intellectual or volitional failure rather than such active and positive spurs to action as the vices of selfishness, greed, malice, envy, or cruelty that are responsible for evil actions? The only answer defenders of the simple version give is that it must be so because there are no other explanations available of evil than that it is a falling away from the rational and moral order of reality. But there are other explanations. One is that reality is neutral about moral questions and that such order as there is implies no moral conclusions. Morality is a human invention, much like art, language, and politics are, so there is no reason to think that knowledge of the scheme of things or actions conforming to it can lead to moral improvement. Another explanation is that while reality does imply moral conclusions, the scheme of things is evil, or it is a mixture of good and evil. Thus, living according to it may actually increase the amount of evil in the world. My point is not that one of these competing explanations is true but that the simple version has not excluded them, and it has not established that its explanation is preferable to them. Hence, the claim that we must view the significance of the facts in the way it suggests is devoid of the persuasive force defenders of the simple version claim for it.

The second difficulty is that the simple version is inconsistent. Human beings are either part of the natural order or not. If they are, then the evil actions they perform are also part of the natural order. But if evil actions are irrational and immoral, then the natural order of which they are parts must also be at least partly irrational and immoral, and thus evil. And this, of course, is precisely what the underlying metaphysics denies. On the other hand, if human beings are not part of the natural order, because, for instance, free will enables us to transcend it, then there is no longer any reason to suppose that principles inferred from the natural order could or should guide human conduct in its transcendent aspects. Once again, the argument is not that the simple version is committed to a false metaphysical belief but rather that regardless of which of two possible metaphysical beliefs it accepts, it cannot consistently hold both it and the belief that evil is due to the weakness that corrupts our primarily good nature. I conclude, therefore, that the simple version of the attempt to attribute evil to internal corruption fails.

Another alternative is to attribute evil to external factors. The usual explanation is to blame civilization or some aspect of it for obstructing or interfering with our primary potential for the good. Just what aspect of civilization is the culprit is a matter of disagreement. It may be the division of labor and exploitation, competition for scarce resources, growth in population and the consequent increase in impersonal relationships, repression by rulers, and so on. In its more sophisticated versions, inevitable structural features of social life are held to be corrupting, rather than such specific and local causes as, for instance, industrialization, capitalism, or the dissolution of extended families. The common metaphor representing the different versions of this view is that there was a Garden of Eden and that the snake was responsible for our expulsion. This is the view of those countless millenarian movements that aim to make us good and pure and simple again by returning to a legendary haven supposed to have existed in the misty past.

The first thing to notice is how very tenuous is the connection between this view and the evidence that could be adduced for or against it. The state of nature in which the savage was noble is necessarily elusive. We have two kinds of evidence about preliterate forms of life: the extant bones of the beings and the artifacts they produced. The bones are uninformative about the primary moral dispositions of the agents who were once wrapped around them. The testimony of the artifacts, on the other hand, is bound to be suspect because they are products of civilization. Since it is to civilization that corruption is supposed to be due, we must look for a state prior to it. But in that state artifacts will not have been produced yet. If, forced by necessity, we look at the earliest artifacts, then testimony adverse to the present theory can always be attributed to the corruption that has already set in, while favorable evidence can always be dismissed by critics on account of its anachronism.

However, defenders of this view are not given to historical or archaeological argumentation. They tend to appeal to our observation of human beings, supported by sociological and anthropological evidence. They call our attention to isolated primitive tribes who live peaceful lives until the corrosive effects of contact with the outside world corrupt them, and they reflect on the causes of evil in our own context. They show how poverty, boredom, soul-destroying work, war, exploitation, and other social ills breed crime, vices, brutality, cynicism, and despair. What are we to say in response to this?

I think that it is obviously true that external influences may corrupt people. But the question is whether all corruption is due to external influences. To this question the above argument does not address itself. If it did, it should notice that identical external causes have different effects on people living in the same context; that evil actions are often done by people who have enjoyed the benefits that are the other side of social ills; that some vices recur in vastly different social contexts, so that aggression, greed, selfishness, malice, and hostility seem not to vary with vastly differing external circumstances; and that for each idyllic primitive tribe, there are countless others cultivating indigenous brutality. What observation in our own and other contexts tends to suggest is that corrupting external influences are neither necessary nor sufficient for very many evil actions. People sometimes do evil in the absence of specific external influences, and they sometimes refrain from doing evil in their presence. It is, therefore, reasonable to look for an internal propensity that makes us receptive or resistant to specific external influences. Thus, so far we have found no good reason either to believe that our primary potential is for the good or to accept the explanation of evil as corruption due to external or internal causes. Obviously, external and internal factors have something to do with evil actions, but we have to look further to find out what that is.

THE THIRD ASSUMPTION OF CHOICE-MORALITY: THE BASIC GOODNESS OF HUMAN NATURE

This brings us to Kant. His view is in agreement with the simple version in regarding evil as the corruption of our primarily good nature, but Kant offers considerably more sophisticated arguments in support of it. He concedes the existence of evil motives, so he cannot be faulted for ignoring the facts the simple version overlooked. Nor does Kant intend to appeal to unsupported metaphysical beliefs about the existence of a rational and moral order in reality. It seems, therefore, that his position is not vulnerable to the objections that I advanced against the simple version. Yet, appearances are misleading; in fact, Kant has not accounted for all the relevant facts, and he has not freed himself from unjustifiable metaphysical assumptions. But let us begin by understanding his view.

Under the heading "Original Predisposition to Good in Human Nature" (21), Kant divides this predisposition into three.[3] Roughly, the first is the predisposition to satisfy basic physical and psychological needs dictated by the preservation of the individual and the species. The second is to evaluate rationally the satisfaction of basic and culturally conditioned needs in the light of our conception of happiness. The third is to submit our will to the command of the moral law, and thus to universalize the principles on which we act. Much more needs to be said about the last, but for the moment let us concentrate on Kant's fundamental claim: "All of these predispositions are not only *good* in negative fashion (in that they do not contradict the moral law); they are also predispositions *toward good* (they enjoin the observance of the law). They are *original*, for they are bound up with the possibility of human nature. Man can indeed use the first two contrary to their ends, but he can extirpate none of them" (23). Thus, the fundamental predispositions of human nature are good, and although they can be misused, they cannot be lost. There is no doubt that Kant holds this, for he repeats it: "Natural inclinations, *considered in themselves*, are *good*, that is, not a matter of reproach, and it is not only futile to want to extirpate them but to do so would also be harmful and blameworthy" (51).

If our predispositions are good, then how does it happen that we perform evil actions? Kant's answer is that there is also "the Propensity to Evil in Human Nature" (23). "This propensity can be considered as belonging universally to mankind (and hence as part of the character of the race), it may be called a *natural* propensity in man to evil" (24). So, we have a predisposition to the good and a propensity to evil. What is the difference between the two? "A propensity is distinguished from a predisposition by the fact that . . . [it has] been *acquired* (if it is good), or *brought* by man *upon himself* (if it is evil)" (24). Thus, our predisposition to the good is "original," while our propen-

---

[3] Numbers in parentheses refer to the pages of Kant's *Religion within the Limits of Reason Alone.*

sity to evil is "brought by man upon himself." How do we bring the propensity to evil upon ourselves? "Evil is possible only as a determination of the free will, and since the will can be appraised as good or evil only by means of its maxims, this propensity to evil must consist in the subjective ground of the possibility of the deviation of the maxims from the moral law" (24). I take Kant to mean that we start with a predisposition to the good, then we exercise our free will and choose to act according to some inclination or another. If the inclination on which we choose to act deviates from the moral law, then by our action we exemplify an evil maxim.

This deviation can be caused by "the *frailty* of human nature" (24): we adopt a good maxim but fail to act on it due to weakness; or it may be caused by "the *impurity* . . . of the human heart" (25): we adopt a good maxim, but we act on mixed motives, and so our actions "are not done purely for duty's sake" (25). Last, we may deviate from the moral law because of "the *corruption* of the human heart" (25), which "is the propensity of the will to . . . neglect the incentives springing from the moral law in favor of others which are not moral" (25). "The propensity to evil in mankind is universal, or, what comes to the same thing, . . . it is woven into human nature" (25).

But the predisposition to the good and the propensity to evil are not "woven into human nature" in the same way. "Man (even the most wicked) does not, under any maxim whatsoever, repudiate the moral law in the manner of a rebel (renouncing obedience to it). The law, rather, forces itself upon him irresistibly by virtue of his moral predisposition; and were no other incentive working in opposition . . . he would be morally good" (31). The moral law is necessary; the predisposition to the good cannot be extirpated. Evil maxims, by contrast, are contingent; all human beings have a propensity to deviate from the moral law; yet the deviation is due not to the repudiation of the moral law but to frailty, impurity, or corruption, which prevent us from acting according to it.

"Hence the distinction between a good man and one who is evil . . . must depend upon *subordination*, . . . i.e. *which of the two incentives he makes the condition of the other*. Consequently man . . . is evil only in that he reverses the moral order of incentives when he adopts them into his maxim. He adopts, indeed, the moral law along with the law of self-love; yet when he becomes aware that they cannot remain on a par with each other but that one must be subordinated to the other . . . he makes the incentive of self-love and its inclinations the condition of obedience to the moral law" (31–32). So, Kant's view is that evil is due to a reversal of the priorities morality commands. All our predispositions are good, but we should subordinate our other predispositions to the moral one; that is, we should be guided in the satisfaction of our needs and in the pursuit of happiness by the moral law. Evil occurs when we are not so guided, when our self-love is allowed to take precedence over doing our duty. This is not to say that self-love, motivating the satisfaction of needs and the pursuit of happiness, is evil—on the contrary, it is good. What is evil is to deviate from the moral law in the name of self-love. We all have a tendency thus to deviate, but "we are not to call the depravity of human nature *wickedness* taking the word in its strict sense as a disposition . . . to adopt evil *as evil* . . . we should rather term it the *perversity* of the heart. . . . Such a heart may coexist with a will which in general is good: it arises from the frailty of human nature, the lack of sufficient strength to follow out the principles it has chosen for itself, joined with its impurity, the failure to distinguish incentives . . . from each other by the gauge of morality" (32–33).

To sum up, Kant believes that human nature is basically good. Evil arises because we choose to subordinate our moral predisposition to that of self-love. We act to satisfy our needs and to pursue happiness, and we deviate from the requirements of morality. The deviation does not consist in the satisfaction of needs and the pursuit of happiness, for these, in themselves, are good. The deviation consists in acting to achieve these good ends in violation of the moral law. And we violate it because we are weak, our motives are impure, and our will has been corrupted. Moral progress consists in trying to overcome these defects. Thus, man is *"not basically* corrupt (even as regards his original predisposition to good), but rather . . . still capable of improvement. . . . For man, therefore, who despite a corrupted heart yet possesses a good will, there remains hope of a return to the good from which he has strayed" (39).

EVIL AND CHOICE

One of the objections to the simple version of the view that evil is corruption was that it cannot account for moral monsters. Since there are people with sharp intellect and strong will who habitually choose to do evil, it is a mistake to suppose that evil must be due to some cognitive or volitional weakness that corrupts our essential goodness. Part of the strength of Kant's position is that it is not vulnerable to this objection. It recognizes that there are people who habitually subordinate the moral law to self-love. Kant, therefore, has a way of accounting for even the most horrendous cases of evildoing. He begins with the obvious fact of moral psychology that people may and do choose to live evil lives. His concern is with providing an explanation of the significance of this fact. Thus, he can readily accept that the existence of evil is presupposed by the view that evil is corruption of the good. So, it is a misunderstanding to object to Kant's position on the grounds that he takes insufficient notice of our native propensity to choose evil.[4] Rousseau may have been guilty of this mistake, but Kant is not.

But there *is* a sense in which Kant denies that there are moral monsters. If being a moral monster is taken to mean that people may become so corrupt as to extinguish in themselves the predisposition to obey the moral law, then Kant denies its possibility. We cannot lose that predisposition, no matter how evil we may become, because the predisposition is necessarily connected to the capacity to choose, and that capacity is a necessary condition of performing evil actions. Kant is making a logical point here; he is not advancing a moral argument. And this logical point, of course, is the distinctive feature of his thinking about morality. He begins with the common and obvious facts of moral life and works backward from them. His aim is to discover what must in general be true of human beings and the world so that these common and obvious facts could be as they are.

To appreciate the full force of this argument, I shall begin with another factual objection. We have seen that Kant has a way of handling cases of chosen evil, but what about unchosen evil? What about, not moral monsters, but those dominated by the vices of insufficiency, expediency, and malevolence, yet through no choice of their own? Let us postulate for the sake of clarity that the evil such people do is *purely* unchosen. They habitually act the way they do, because they have been indoctrinated by a pernicious morality, or because they make an understandable mistake in their moral commitments, or because their character defects make them incapable of acting otherwise, or because they are distracted, inattentive, or lethargic due to physiological or psychological causes they are powerless to alter. Now if there were such people, as there obviously are, they would seem to present counterexamples to Kant's thesis. For the agents of habitual unchosen evil have not chosen to subordinate the moral law to self-love. They are habitually performing evil actions, but not by choice. Consequently, Kant's analysis of evil as necessarily presupposing choice seems to fail.

Kant's reply is that the idea of unchosen evil is incoherent. To be sure, he does not deny that people may habitually cause undeserved harm to others without choosing to do so. What he denies is that such

---

[4] Silber argues in this way against Kant's view in "The Ethical Significance of Kant's *Religion*." Wood's reply to Silber in *Kant's Moral Religion* seems to me to be correct.

people can be justifiably described as evil. For evil presupposes choice, and these people had no choice. He says, "Duty demands nothing which we cannot do" (43), and "when the moral law commands that we *ought* now to be better men, it follows inevitably that we must *be able* to be better men" (46), and "we *ought* to conform to . . . [our morally legislative reason]; consequently we must *be able* to do so" (55). Agents of unchosen evil do not come under the command of duty; they are not subject to the moral law, and morally legislative reason does not apply to them, because they are not able to be otherwise. So, the first step in the transcendental argument is the familiar Principle discussed in chapter 5, "ought implies can." But whereas there it was considered in its own right, here it is part of a larger argument.

Let us, then, inquire why Kant supposes that evil implies choice, or that unchosen evil is an incoherent notion. The answer depends on what Kant means by will, freedom, and reason and on how these three are taken by Kant to be connected with morality. Perhaps the most important distinguishing feature of Kant's moral philosophy is that he sees will, freedom, reason, and morality as necessarily connected. So, in trying to come to grips with any of these notions in Kant's thought, we inevitably encounter the others.

Kant says that "will is a kind of causality belonging to living beings so far as they are rational. *Freedom* would then be a property this causality has of being able to work independently of determination by alien causes."[5] The will is a kind of power to produce changes in ourselves and the world. This power may be heteronomous or autonomous. In the first case, its exercise is determined by causes outside of itself; we will something because we have been made to will it by natural necessity or coercion. In the second case, nothing from outside impels the will. It moves, as it were, by itself; we will something because, and only because, we ourselves have decided it. When the will is autonomous, it is free. The freedom of the will thus means, negatively, that it is not determined "by alien causes" and, positively, that it is subject only to its own law. The "freedom of the will, although it is not the property of conforming to laws of nature, is not for this reason lawless. . . . What else then can freedom of the will be but autonomy—that is, the property which the will has of being a law to itself?"[6]

But Kant claims not only that the autonomous will is free but also that it is rational. Rationality is connected with the freedom of the

[5] Kant, *Groundwork*, 107.
[6] Ibid.

will through the nature of the law that the autonomous will is to itself. What is this law? Kant gives several formulations of it, and the relation among them is an exceedingly complicated matter.[7] But since these complications are irrelevant to my purposes, I shall consider only the first formulation: "Act only on that maxim through which you can at the same time will that it should become a universal law."[8] Paton says that this is an "unconditioned objective principle . . . one which every rational agent irrespective of his desires for particular ends would necessarily obey if reason had complete control over his passions."[9] Let us try to understand the reasons for this claim.

The law a perfectly free and rational will would choose is unconditioned because if its acceptance depended on any condition outside of itself, then the will would be, to the extent of its dependence, heteronomous, and hence unfree. Furthermore, the law is objective because it is independent of the subjective situation of particular agents. It is a law that would recommend itself to all agents, regardless of the circumstances, provided only that they were totally free and rational. So, its objectivity means that all such agents would choose it, and hence that it is a universal, impartial, and impersonal law.

Guided by this law, all free and rational agents would proceed in the same manner. Whenever they face a situation in which they have to act, they would choose the action that other free and rational agents would choose if they were in that situation. The failure to proceed in this manner is a sign of diminished freedom and rationality. If they are guided by their own desires or by circumstances peculiar to them, then "alien causes" determine their actions, and so they act heteronomously, and thus unfreely. If alien causes are absent and yet the agents do not act according to the universalizable principle, then they are bound to be inconsistent, and hence irrational.

The nature of the inconsistency involved in acting according to a nonuniversalizable principle is a controversial matter. Kant says that the inconsistency is one of contradiction, but this is to explain the obscure by the equally obscure, for he leaves it unclear what contradicts what, and whether the contradiction is logical, physical, psychological, or of some other kind. I shall follow Korsgaard's interpretation:[10] "The contradiction in question is a 'practical' one: the universalized maxim contradicts itself when the efficacy of the action as a

---

[7] For a standard discussion, see Paton's *The Categorical Imperative*, book 3.

[8] Kant, *Groundwork*, 52.

[9] Paton, *The Categorical Imperative*, 123.

[10] See Korsgaard, "Kant's Formula of Universal Law" and "The Right to Lie: Kant on Dealing with Evil."

method for achieving its purpose would be undermined by its universal practice."[11]

Let us make this concrete by considering first a case of acting according to the moral law and then acting in violation of it. Take truthfulness as an example. It is an indispensable part of communication, for if people in general did not tell the truth in situations where it is reasonable to expect them to do so, then communication would be impossible. People would not, then, believe what others tell them. Consequently, they would not know how to take what has been communicated to them. Perfectly free and rational agents would realize that this is so and they would always tell the truth in appropriate situations, since to fail to do so would undermine the possibility of the very activity—communication—in which they are engaged. These exemplary agents would, therefore, always act in conformity with the law they want universally observed, namely, to tell the truth in appropriate situations. The corollary is that lying, that is, intentionally deceiving others, is inconsistent and hence irrational. Rational agents would not want to jeopardize the activity in which they freely and reasonably participate. Since lying weakens communication, it is inconsistent both to want to communicate and to sabotage it. Analogous arguments can be constructed for paying debts, keeping promises, honoring contracts, helping others, respecting property, according dignity to others, and so on.

However, the fact is that we are not perfectly free and rational. Consequently, the law "Act only on that maxim through which you can at the same time will that it should become a universal law" is not a *description* of how we actually act but a *prescription* of how we ought to act. Hence, the name Kant has given to the law is *the categorical imperative*. It is categorical because it is not conditional on particular circumstances, and since it is the law for autonomous agents, it is not conditioned by alien causes either. It is also an imperative because it is action guiding. The force of it is that provided only that agents were perfectly free and rational, they would act according to it. Contrariwise, the failure to act according to it is attributable either to being driven by causes beyond our control or to irrationality.

The remarkable feature of Kant's argument is that it begins with the question of how free and rational agents would act and ends with the conclusion that they would act in accordance with the moral law. For the categorical imperative is meant to combine the requirements of rationality and morality, and it is intended to establish that they are the same.

[11] Korsgaard, "The Right to Lie," 522.

To see that this is so, let us recall the contrast between self-love and the moral law. When we are moved by self-love, we seek to satisfy our needs and pursue our happiness. The predispositions to act in these ways, it will be remembered, are good. But in acting according to self-love, we may or may not be guided by the moral law. Evil arises when we fail to subordinate self-love to the moral law. Since the moral law is the categorical imperative, the satisfaction of needs and the pursuit of happiness are morally good, provided they proceed on a universalizable maxim. Accordingly, in acting out of self-love, we ought not to make exceptions either for ourselves or for others. We ought to rise above the claims of individuality, even if they happen to be our own or of those we love, and we ought not to be distracted by the peculiarities of particular contexts. Rationality and morality require that when we are faced with a choice of action, we should ask ourselves: what would any free and rational agent do in my situation? and act accordingly. Or we should ask what is the same question: would I find the principle on which I act acceptable as a principle on which everyone else also acts? Rationality and morality require us to understand that we are not only agents but also legislators, because through our actions we strengthen or weaken the principles to which we are committed. Immorality or evil is irrational because it weakens the principles to which we would be committed were we fully free and rational.

Having tiptoed across the minefield of Kantian exegesis, we can now come back to the question of why Kant finds the idea of unchosen evil incoherent. The short answer is that morality necessarily involves choice, so that an action cannot be both unchosen and evil. The point of my exegesis was to articulate the assumptions upon which the short answer rests. These assumptions are that choice depends on the will being free; the freedom of the will is to be understood as autonomy; autonomy is the will being a law to itself; the law is the categorical imperative; and the categorical imperative formulates the requirements of both morality and rationality, which come to the same thing.

THE FAILURE OF KANT'S ARGUMENT

Thus, Kant arrives at the same conclusion as the one upon which the Socratic ideal rests. There is a rational and moral order, and evil is a departure from it. If we understood this order and conformed in our actions to it, we would not cause evil. But there is also a considerable difference between the Socratic and the Kantian ideals. The former locates the order in reality, the latter in human beings. According to the former, rationality and morality require that we should conform to something outside of ourselves. According to the latter, the source of rationality and morality is in ourselves, in the autonomous will. *We* legislate rationality and morality into existence by acting as the categorical imperative commands. We are free to choose the principled mode of life, and if we choose it, we have chosen the categorical imperative. It is only deficiency in our understanding or will, causing a self-defeating inconsistency, that stands between having made the choice for the principled mode of life and the recognition that we have committed ourselves to the categorial imperative. Kant's achievement in moral philosophy rests on the success of his attempt to show the ncessary connection between that basic choice and the categorical imperative.

The difference between the Socratic and the Kantian ideals influences the kind of justification that may be offered for them. The justification of the Socratic ideal must be metaphysical. The ideal is essentially committed to the claim that, behind the messy world of appearances in which evil is rampant, there is a good and rational world with which evil is incompatible. It is one of Kant's epistemological achievements to have shown the impossibility of the metaphysical justification that the Socratic ideal requires. But what about the justification of the Kantian ideal itself?

Let us begin by noting its considerable attraction. It is not an exaggeration to say that large portions of our sensibility are Kantian. We regard ourselves as self-legislating autonomous agents. We believe that we are free to choose between good and evil and that we are responsible for our choices. Thus, we are predisposed to accept the first assumption of choice-morality, the strong version of the Principle that "ought implies can." If morality has to do with choice, then unchosen actions fall outside of the jurisdiction of morality. We also believe that in respect to autonomy, the capacity for choice, we are equal, for we all possess it. Our humanity is inseparable from that capacity, and we all have a predisposition to use it in a morally good rather than evil way. Consequently, we find that the second assumption of choice-morality, the equality of human worth, expresses one of our deep moral convictions.

Kant's influence affects not so much the formulation and acceptance of these beliefs but rather their justification. We turn to him not for guidance about what we ought to do but for the justification of the principles that guide us in doing what we feel we ought to do. His influence is due to having methodically and relentlessly pushed these assumptions back to their source in human freedom. And there he located not only the ultimate justification for them but also ground for hope. For we cannot lose our freedom, and as long as we have it "there is hope of return to the good from which ... [we have] strayed" (39). Nevertheless, Kant's hope is false hope; the magnificent edifice he has erected is a castle in the air. The idea of human freedom is exactly the same sort of metaphysical fiction as the Socratic belief in a rational and moral order.

Freedom is the autonomy of the will. But how is it possible for the will to be autonomous? How can it be a law to itself and escape the influence of causes outside of itself? The will is the power to choose among alternatives. Ordinarily, we think that this power is influenced by many factors over which the choosing agents have no control, such as past experiences, the circumstances in which the choice has to be made, the likely consequences, the native abilities agents bring to their choices, the presence or absence of threats, bribes, temptations, and so on. The freedom of the will, however, means that choices are and must be made independently of all these influences. But how could that be? How could it happen that particular actions performed by particular agents are both subject to external influences and not subject to them? Kant's answer is that "there is not the slightest contradiction in holding that a *thing as an appearance* (as belonging to the sensible world) is subject to certain laws of which it is independent *as a thing* or a being *in itself*."[12] Thus, freedom is possible because external influences belong to the world of appearances, while the law that the will is to itself belongs to another world, the world of things in themselves. The laws of nature determine what happens in the world of appearances, but self-legislating agents determine what choices they make in the world of things in themselves. So, we are driven to postulate the existence of a world, transcending the world we know, in order to show that freedom is possible. Of that world, however, we know and can know nothing, except that it must exist. We can have no knowledge of it because we can know only what we can experience, and that necessarily restricts us to appearances. Yet we know that there is a world transcending experience; if there were not, freedom would not be possible.

It is generally conceded that this is an indefensible argument.[13] In the first place, it does not explain how freedom is possible. To say that its possibility rests on something about which we cannot know anything is merely to give another name to the inability to provide the required explanation. This, as Kant says in another context,

---

[12] Kant, *Groundwork*, 117.

[13] See e.g. Paton, *The Categorical Imperative*, chapter 26; Silber, "The Ethical Significance of Kant's *Religion*," xcvii–ciii; Hill, "Kant's Argument for the Rationality of Moral Conduct."

"would be to explain something, which in terms of known empirical principles we do not understand sufficiently, by something which we do not understand at all."[14] Curiously enough, Kant himself realized that this is what he was doing: "Freedom . . . is a mere Idea: its objective validity can in no way be exhibited by reference to nature and consequently cannot be exhibited in any possible experience. Thus the Idea of freedom can never admit of full comprehension."[15] So, at the foundation of his system, the foundation upon which choice-morality, the acquitting version of the Principle, and the equality of human worth rest, there is "a mere Idea . . . [whose] objective validity can in no way be exhibited."

Second, if we overlook the arbitrariness of Kant's postulation of freedom, we encounter its inconsistency with the rest of his thought. In his epistemological work, Kant's aim was to show the illegitimacy of the kind of metaphysical speculation that underlies the Socratic ideal and much else. "The dictum of all genuine idealists . . . is contained in this formula: 'All knowledge through the senses and experience is nothing but sheer illusion, and only in the ideas of the pure understanding and reason is there truth.' The principle that dominates and determines my idealism, is on the contrary: 'All knowledge of things merely from pure understanding or pure reason is nothing but sheer illusion, and only in experience is there truth.' "[16] Since freedom "cannot be exhibited in any possible experience," we must suppose that it is "sheer illusion."

Third, if we are not deterred by the arbitrariness and inconsistency of Kant's view, we have to contend with its extreme implausibility. Assuming that the actions we perform are subject to the natural necessity operating in the world of appearances and that our choices to perform them are based on the law the will is to itself in the world of things in themselves, we must ask how these two sets of causes are related to each other. Neither set is dispensable. Without natural causes, our senses could not acquire the information upon which our choices are based; while without freedom, we could not make choices. So, we must have two sets of causes, and they must be independent of each other, since the two worlds in which they operate are independent. One is capable of being experienced and exists in time; the other is beyond the possibility of experience and exists timelessly. Thus, we are driven to the supposition that two sets of causes determine our choices; that although they are of radically different nature,

---

[14] Kant, *Critique of Pure Reason*, A772.
[15] Kant, *Groundwork*, 119.
[16] Kant, *Prolegomena*, 123.

they just happen invariably to produce the same effect; that one set makes it impossible for us to act otherwise than we do, while the other set necessarily allows that we do not have to do what we do. One set of causes has its place in the world of appearances, the other in the world of things in themselves, and these two worlds, as it were, run on parallel tracks, so that they felicitously coincide every time human beings make a choice. The only reason for accepting this incredible idea is that it is a consequence of Kant's argument. However, a more attractive alternative is to reject the argument from which such consequences follow.

In closing, I want to guard against a possible misunderstanding of my criticism of Kant. I have been objecting to his analysis of freedom. This should not be taken as a denial of freedom itself or of the obvious connection between freedom and morality. It is the Kantian analysis of freedom I have denied. Freedom is a perfectly acceptable notion, and we should continue to use it to describe an important part of our moral experience. But I do not think that we need a metaphysical theory of freedom; what we need is to recognize the defects of arguments advanced against the possibility of freedom. And in this respect, help is readily available.[17]

THE REJECTION OF CHOICE-MORALITY AND THE SOFT REACTION

My argument in this chapter is intended to show the failure of Kant's attempt to establish a necessary connection between morality, rationality, and freedom. Kant's notion of freedom is untenable; consequently his analysis of morality as the exercise of free will and of rationality as the free choice of the categorical imperative must be seen as equally flawed. Whether an action is good or evil cannot depend on the Kantian analysis of freedom. Yet this analysis is the underpinning of Kant's rejection of the possibility of unchosen evil. If freedom does not derive from our membership in the world of things in themselves, if freedom is not the power to choose independently of natural causes, including our needs, inclinations, and conceptions of happiness, then we must conceive of human nature otherwise than Kant did. It cannot be that freedom, rationality, and morality are joint forces fostering the development of our primary potential for goodness. These forces must be understood in the context of the only world we know and can know. They do not influence us in competition with natural causes; they are among the natural causes influenc-

---

[17] See e.g. Frankfurt, "Freedom of the Will and the Concept of a Person"; Matson, *Sentience*, 162–83; Strawson, *Freedom and Resentment*, 1–25; Taylor, "Responsibility for Self"; and my own "Freedom."

ing us. Since the connection among natural causes is contingent, freely chosen actions can be rational or irrational, good or evil. And, most pertinently for my present purposes, evil actions can be chosen or unchosen.

As Kant saw, good and evil potentialities exist in us side by side, and it is the task of morality to foster the first and curb the second. But as Kant did not see, rationality and free choice need not inform the development of these potentialities. For we can be pushed in one direction or the other by circumstances over which we have no control, and it is false hope to suppose that as we enlarge the area of rational control, so we are bound to foster our good potentialities. The hope is false because it ignores our evil potentialities. Evil need not be the corruption of the good; it may be its rival—and, depending on circumstances, its dominant rival. "To say that altruism and morality are possible in virtue of something basic to human nature is not to say that men are basically good. Men are basically complicated; how good they are depends on whether certain conceptions and ways of thinking have achieved dominance, a dominance which is precarious in any case."[18]

If human nature is a mixture of good and evil potentialities, and if either may achieve dominance over the other in suitable circumstances, then the three assumptions of choice-morality are further weakened, and so is the justification for the soft reaction to unchosen evil. The logic of my argument against accepting the acquitting version of "ought implies can," the equality of human worth, and the fundamental goodness of human nature is to show how each of these assumptions is incompatible with some common and undeniable facts of our moral lives. This argument is intended to force defenders of choice-morality either to concede the inadquency of their view or to give some reason for rejecting the facts to which I have appealed. Kant's moral philosphy is such a reason, although, as we have seen, flawed.

The acquitting version of "ought implies can" denies the moral relevance of habitual unchosen evil on the ground that the appropriateness of moral judgments is necessarily connected with choice. But we have seen that Kant's argument for their necessary connection fails. Thus, nothing stops us from claiming the obvious, namely, that vices like insufficiency, expediency, and malevolence often dominate human lives and result in underserved harm, and when they do, their agents are evil, even if they have not chosen their actions.

The equality of human worth is incompatible with regarding the

[18] Nagel, *The Possibility of Altruism*, 146.

agents ruled by vices as having less worth than habitual benefactors of humanity, because human worth is assumed to depend on the capacity for choice, which everyone has equally. That assumption, however, is supported only by the metaphysical fiction that we are self-legislating members of the world of things in themselves and by the false hope that if we choose freely and rationally, then we shall choose the good. It is one of the most glaring and disheartening facts of moral life that countless people are brutal, cruel, selfish, and malicious and that these vices are so deeply and enduringly entrenched in their characters that there is no reason to suppose that they will change. To make it a cornerstone of our morality that such people have as much worth as their kind, gentle, altruistic, and benevolent counterparts is a dangerous folly.

The explanation of widespread evil in terms of such unchosen vices as insufficiency, expediency, and malevolence was rejected by Kant on the grounds that unchosen evil is an incoherent notion. Evil is assumed to be due to the freely chosen subordination of the moral law our goodness predisposes us to accept to self-love. But since our goodness was taken to be the tendency to choose the moral law freely, as the Kantian analysis of freedom collapses, so also does this heroic insistence on our primary potential for goodness in the face of the prevalence of the evil we cause.

Thus, given the failure of the Kantian defense of these three assumptions and the fact that they contradict plain facts we encounter daily, we should reject them. And as we do so, we should do likewise with choice-morality and the soft reaction to unchosen evil.

The Mixed View of Human Nature

I have argued that the explanation of evil in terms of the corruption of our native dispositions for goodness fails. We have no reason to think that human nature is primarily good. Unbiased observation of our conduct suggests that human nature contains a mixture of good and evil potentialities. We naturally and spontaneously tend to act both to benefit and to harm others and ourselves. Expediency and conscientiousness, insufficiency and strength, malevolence and benevolence coexist in us. They are not idiosyncratic products of particular cultures but commonplaces of all forms of life. The reasonable question to ask about them is why they are so deeply entrenched in such a variety of historically, climatically, religiously, economically, and socially different contexts. And the answer that suggests itself is that these virtues and vices are ubiquitous because they derive from culturally invariant human propensities. Thus, we come to the ninth thesis of character-morality—*the mixed view of human nature*—which accepts as true both that our evil inclinations often break out of the constraints of civilization by which we aim to control them and that we also have a natural tendency to goodness.

However, the characterization of our native propensities is more complicated than this thesis may at first sight suggest. We cannot simply identify evil actions with those promoting the agents' welfare and good actions with those promoting the welfare of others. Promoting our welfare by attempting to develop virtues and suppress vices is a precondition of benefiting others. And there are many instances of evil conduct in which we forget about ourselves and care single-mindedly about injuring other people; revenge, malice, and fanaticism often take these forms. So, distinguishing between self-regarding and other-regarding conduct is neither necessary nor sufficient for drawing the distinction between good and evil conduct.

This is not exactly a revolutionary observation, but it is worth making because the very obviousness of the mixed view may raise doubts about its significance. These doubts may be allayed if it is realized that many widely held moral theories are actually committed to the rejection of this obvious position. We have seen how this is true of Socratic eudaimonism, Christianity, Rousseau and his millenarian followers, and Kant. We can now add to this list the numerous metaethical theories that identify the domain of morality with the domain of other-regarding conduct or deny that self-regarding conduct can qualify as moral.[19]

The mixed view of human nature has a further consequence. The way in which we understand evil is crucial to our conception of morality, and if we misconstrue evil, as I have argued these alternatives to the mixed view do, we shall advocate an unsatisfactory conception of morality. If we see evil as the natural human response to an inhospitable world, then we shall be disposed to look to morality as a device for curbing it. If our view is that "human beings have some natural tendency to be more concerned about the satisfaction of their wants . . . than those of others . . . [and] beside complete or comparative indifference, [there is also] active malevolence," then we shall think that "the 'general object' of morality . . . is to contribute to the betterment . . . of [this] human predicament, primarily and essentially by

---

[19] E.g. "[Morality involves] judgments . . . that pronounce actions and agents to be right, wrong, good, bad, etc., simply because of the effect they have on . . . *other* persons" (Frankena, *Perspectives on Morality*, 126). Also, "If human beings did not care about one another there could not be what we speak of as morality, for the reason that morality is a manifestation of that caring" (Beehler, *Moral Life*, 1). For a critical survey of the literature and further references, see Louden, "Can We Be Too Moral?"

seeking to countervail 'limited sympathies' and their potentially most damaging effects."[20] If to cause evil is our natural and dominant tendency, then we need morality to regulate our conduct, so as to enable decently organized social life to go on. The justification of morality, then, is that, since stable social life is a condition of human welfare, all reasonable people should act as morality requires, and that involves curbing their propensities to evil. This is the view of Hobbes and of some psychoanalytic theorists.[21]

There are two widely noted and very serious difficulties with this way of thinking about morality. The first is that since it justifies morality in terms of self-interest, the dictates of morality will not go beyond the dictates of self-interest. The test reasonable moral agents will apply to their conduct is whether or not it will jeopardize the conditions required for decent social life. And then they will rightly conclude that occasional violations will not cause a general collapse. They will, therefore, be led by this view of morality to violate its own requirements whenever it serves their interests, provided they can do so surreptitiously to avoid getting caught and to prevent others from imitating them. Neither the conduct nor the character traits it encourages can be said to further the aims of morality.

The second difficulty is that we look to morality to help us to live good lives, yet even if we did all that this conception of morality demands, we would still be very far from having good lives. For successfully curbing evil in ourselves and others is perfectly compatible with bored, frustrated, or miserable lives. The minimization of evil is clearly a necessary condition of good lives, but equally clearly, it is not sufficient for it. If morality merely overcame our limited sympathies and their most dangerous effects, we would still have nothing to live *for*. A morality concerned only with avoiding evil is an inadequate morality. Of course, utilitarians and contractarians can go beyond this limited concern. But in doing so, they must appeal to propensities in human nature whose realization may make life good. And as they make this appeal, so they must leave behind the supposition that evil is our dominant propensity.

The view that evil is the corruption of our essentially good nature avoids both these problems. It accepts that one task of morality is to curb evil, but since evil stands in the way of developing our native goodness, morality is not a system of prohibitions but a liberating force. It removes impediments from the way of good lives. Hence,

---

[20] Warnock, *The Object of Morality*, 21 and 26.

[21] For a recent account of Hobbes's position, see Kavka, *Hobbesian Moral and Political Theory*. The psychoanalytic literature is vast. For a recent philosophically informed approach, see Wollheim, *The Thread of Life*.

there cannot be a conflict between morality and self-interest, for they have identical aims: to enable each of us to develop our potentialities and thus to make good lives for ourselves. Nor is it a mystery of what we should do with our lives, once evil does not threaten them. Each of us should proceed by "progressively actualizing the excellence that is his innately and potentially" and "become the person he potentially is and . . . cultivate the conditions by which others may do likewise."[22] This is the view of those Platonists and Aristotelians who follow in the tradition of Socratic eudaimonism.

The great problem for this conception of morality is the existence and frequency of evil. For evil shows that alongside our potential excellences, there also exist potentialities for depravity. Neither is logically or psychologically prior to the other. So, a morality that will remove impediments from the way of developing our potentialities will actually encourage evil. We cannot afford the kind of liberation eudaimonists hope for and advocate, because we need the civilizing restraints of morality to curb and channel our native propensities toward insufficiency, expediency, malevolence, and other vices. If eudaimonists accept this—and I see no reason why they could not or would not—then they can no longer hold that human nature is primarily good and that evil is a corruption of it.

The conception of morality—character-morality—suggested by the mixed view of human nature naturally embraces the points to which its rivals may arrive after criticism. Character-morality is concerned with how we can live good lives. It requres both curbing evil, which makes good lives possible, and the pursuit of goods, which gives good lives their content. Thus, it has an evil-avoiding and a good-producing aspect. I shall argue that the nature and justification of these two aspects are different, that they are asymmetrical, and that the recognition that they are so will point the way toward a strategy for coping with evil.

[22] Norton, *Personal Destinies*, ix and 358.

CHAPTER EIGHT

Character-Morality: Taking Stock

CHARACTER-MORALITY AND THE ESSENTIAL CONDITIONS OF LIFE

The secular problem of evil arises for those who are committed to morality, and thus to advancing the cause of human welfare, but who also believe that we cannot reasonably look for solutions, if there are any, outside of humanity. A large part of the problem is that much evil is caused by evil agents who do not choose to cause it. The significance of unchosen evil is not merely the difficulty it presents about the reasonable moral reaction to agents who cause it but the deeper one that if much evil is unchosen, then the prospects of doing anything about it appear to be dim. For choice makes control at least possible, but if much evil is unchosen, then it is hard to see how we could even attempt to control it. This is one main question character-morality struggles with, and to do so with some hope of success, we must try to understand the conditions responsible for the state of affairs diagnosed as the secular problem of evil.

In this context the tragic view of life proves to be especially illuminating, for it brings us face to face with the tension in our lives, of which the secular problem of evil is a symptom. The tension, it will be remembered, is between our aspiration to live good lives and the essential conditions of life. Contingency, indifference, and destructiveness permeate all aspects of our lives, including our attempts to live in a morally meritorious and personally satisfying way. And as the tragic view shows, the most daunting obstacle is that contingency, indifference, and destructiveness are not hostile external influences against which we may pit ourselves but forces that exist in us. They are part of our motivation; they inform our beliefs, emotions, and efforts; and thus they strongly influence our actions. That they have this formative role in our lives is a consequence of the essential conditions of life prevailing in the part of nature we identify as ourselves. Thus, we are moved by forces whose sources are in us, and they propel us in both beneficial and harmful directions.

Much evil occurs when the essential conditions of life find expression through our actions. Some of these actions are chosen, but many are not. For the expression of our nature does not require us to deliberate, to decide, to make an effort—all it takes for us is to act naturally and spontaneously. Nor is it that through choice we can control the evil-producing forces within us, for these forces influence both our attempts to control them and the extent to which we are capable even of making the attempt to achieve control. In seeing life thus, the tragic view does not deny that choices are possible and that they play a role in our lives. Rather, it shows how attenuated that role is and how formidable are the obstacles in the way of enlarging it by provoking us to reflect on the tragic situations in which such representatives of humanity as Oedipus, Lear, and Kurtz found themselves. These tragic figures had choices, and they busily made them; reflection brings us to understand, however, how little that exercise helped.

So, the secular problem of evil has its source in us, and we cause evil because the essential conditions of life are part of our nature. This is what makes the Socratic ideal questionable, this is what the tragic view conveys, and it is to this that the soft reaction, prompted by choice-morality, and the hard reaction, suggested by character-morality, are attempted responses. I have been concerned with showing that the soft reaction is a poor response, for it ultimately amounts to the denial of the truth we learn from the tragic view of life. We cannot but find choice-morality and the soft reaction shallow if we examine their assumptions against the background formed by the tragic view.

In the vast sea of forces to which we are subject, there is a small island formed by our choices. Choice-morality regards that island as the territory over which morality is sovereign. Everything on it and nothing beyond it is accepted as morally relevant. The consequence is that we are deprived of moral responses to much of the evil besetting us—in particular, to the evil we cause, although not by choice. Thus, morality is emasculated by the specious belief that the appropriateness of judging that something is morally evil depends on our capacity to alter it. The tragic view forces us to ask why we should suppose that it is in our power to control the undeserved harm we cause each other and ourselves. The soft reaction responds by denying that undeserved harm qualifies as evil, unless we cause it by choice. Thus, its strategy for coping with evil is to withhold the title from those instances of it that we seem to be unable to control.

Another shibboleth maintained by the soft reaction is the equal worth of all moral agents. We are enjoined to regard everyone as equally deserving, and equal desert translates into the protection of rights everyone is said to have to freedom and well-being. These rights are supposed not to vary with the moral standing of the agents. They are attributed to people merely in virtue of their humanity. If all of us were embarked on the secular equivalent of a pilgrim's progress, and if the only relevant difference among us depended on how far we have come on the road, then we would indeed have a good reason for guaranteeing equal rights to all travelers slouching, so benignly, toward Bethlehem. However, the tragic view reminds us of the naïveté of this picture. We are not moved only in morally praiseworthy directions. We are also moved in deplorable ones because contingency, indifference, and destructiveness are part of our motivation. In some people, they become the dominant part. Such people are evil, and they cause evil regularly, predictably, over a long period of time. To insist on regarding people as equally deserving, as the soft reaction does, is to ignore a substantial segment of our common moral experience. The dangerous consequence of this self-inflicted blindness is that the spread of evil is fostered by the prescription of choice-morality that we should guarantee to evil agents the opportunity to act on their vices.

Behind these misguided assumptions, and lending persuasive force to them, lies the illusion about the fundamental goodness of human nature. Evil is seen not as one of our competing motivational forces but as an obstruction of the primarily good potential we all have to live and act in accordance with the requirements of morality. It is supposed that if the obstruction were not there, we would all act reasonably and decently. Against this, we have the forceful demonstration provided by the tragic view that strong and intelligent people, acting as reasonably and decently as they can, come to cause great evil. And they do so because they are moved by internal forces in a direction contrary to human welfare. Choice-morality and the soft reaction systematically underplay the influence of contingency, indifference, and destructiveness on our actions. Hence, they are obstacles to facing evil.

As I have argued, the basic trouble with choice-morality and the soft reaction is that they ignore central facts of our moral lives, and they lead us to regard as central what is only part of the truth. The key to their hold on us is that they have seized upon part of the truth. No one can reasonably deny that choice is important to morality, that there is a sense in which human worth is a highly desirable ideal, and that there is good in human nature. But these truths should be held in conjunction with the recognition that unchosen evil is also important to morality, that human worth is proportionate to moral merit, and that there is evil in human nature.

Character-morality and the hard reaction aim to respond to the secular problem of evil by taking account of both the truths choice-morality and the soft reaction recognize and the truths they miss. The value of the tragic view is not that it accurately depicts our situation but that it emphasizes just those features of it that choice-morality overlooks and that no acceptable view can neglect. I shall now proceed to develop character-morality by showing how it can incorporate the true portions of the half-truths upon which choice-morality is based and the half-truths the tragic view embodies.

THE IDEAL OF CHARACTER-MORALITY

If we understand by "institution" an established custom, practice, system, or set of rules and principles, then we can say that morality is an institution. It is public and familiar, and knowledge of it is inescapable for normal people living in a civilized society. Of course, morality is also a controversial institution because there is much disagreement about what many of its requirements actually are and what they ought to be. But even if moral requirements were not controversial, adherence to them would by no means follow, because they are often hard and demanding and conflict with the requirements of self-interest, politics, personal loyalty, and efficiency. In trying to develop and defend character-morality, my aim is to advocate that morality should be a particular kind of institution. To make clear what that kind is, I shall begin by describing the ideal character-morality aims at. I concede right away both that morality as it now is falls very far short of this ideal and that if existing morality were miraculously transformed into the best possible character-morality, it would still fall short of the ideal. The ideal is an ideal; it is not a description but a desirable goal that should guide the criticism and reform of the institution of morality.

The ideal of character-morality may be approached by considering the nadir illustrated by the tragic situations in which Oedipus, Lear, and Kurtz found themselves. In each case, the protagonist's aspiration to live a morally meritorious and personally satisfying life was defeated by the essential conditions of life. The agents' contributions to this defeat were different in the three cases, Oedipus being the least involved, Lear next, and Kurtz the most. But even in Kurtz's case, the evil he suffered was greater than his offense actually merited, all things considered. None of them got what he deserved, and neither did their hapless victims. Thus, the tragic situations suggest, the essential conditions of life take no account of moral merit. We are both the agents and victims of contingency, indifference, and destructiveness, and these conditions may affect us in fundamental ways, regardless of our credentials as rational and moral agents. Evil people may flourish and good ones may suffer because the order of nature is not a moral order.

The ideal of character-morality is that human life ought to be such that we get what we deserve. The order to aim at is one in which benefits are consequent to merit and harm to demerit. Furthermore, in this desirable order, the greater is the merit, the greater would be the benefit; and similarly, the more serious is the demerit, the more severe would the harm be. If such an order prevailed, tragic situations would not occur, tragedy would be a genre of dystopian literature and not a profound treatment of the human condition, and belief in the inevitable triumph of truth and goodness would not be a symptom of sentimentalism or naïveté.

In our world there is no such order. That is why character-morality is an ideal, rather than the description of a trend. Yet to understand the ideal it is, we need to understand why our world has fallen short of it and, as we shall see, why it is bound always to do so. The old and influential Socratic explanation (of which Jewish and Christian teachings and the metaphysics of Plato, Leibniz, Spinoza, Hegel, and Marx are some examples) for the gap between what we deserve and what we get is that it is created by our perhaps unavoidable failures. The world is permeated by a rational and moral order; it actually embodies the moral ideal, and our own irrationality and immorality are responsible for the gap. If we were rationally and morally better, we would live in closer conformity with the order of the world, and then the discrepancy between merit and desert would be smaller.

There are two fundamental difficulties with the Socratic explanation. The first is that there is no good reason for believing that behind the world we know there exists a moral order. The only kind of evidence we have, and can have, comes from the world we know, and in that world irrationality and immorality are rampant. The second is that humanity is part of the world, and if this explanation were correct in diagnosing us as the sources of irrationality and immorality, then it would have adduced conclusive evidence against itself, since we, and thus part of the world, fail to reflect the postulated moral order. At best, we have reason to claim only that in the world rationality and morality coexist with irrationality and immorality.

Any adequate explanation of the gap between what we deserve and what we get must begin with this lamentable fact. If we do begin there, we shall see the ideal of character-morality as part of the bulwark we erect against irrationality and immorality. Its aim is to order our lives so that in them desert is proportional to merit. But in this endeavor, we cannot count on outside help. There is no blueprint implicit in the scheme of things that we might discover and one to which we might train ourselves to conform. There is only trial and error. One chief reason why people are not getting what they deserve is that there is much error. This is the type of explanation favored by Aristotle, Hobbes, Hume, and Mill, and this is what I also accept.

There is agreement between the two explanations that one rich source of the discrepancy between desert and moral merit is human agency. But the first sees our contribution as the failure to live according to a cosmic blueprint, while according to the second, our contribution is due to the adversity caused by the essential conditions of life. The ideal of character-morality is to create a human institution for coping with this adversity so that all human beings get what they deserve. And what they deserve is that the benefit and harm they receive should be proportional to their merits and demerits.

However, the attainment of this ideal is impossible because we cannot overcome the obstacles in the way. If we understand the reasons why the obstacles are so formidable, we shall also come to understand what we need to do in order to cope with them. Of course, coping does not mean that we shall do the impossible; it means that we shall approximate the ideal more closely by participating in the institution of character-morality—a participation that involves, among other things, adopting ways of life in which desert is made as proportional to merit as the obstacles allow. Thus, the ideal guides our attempt to cope with the human situation, and not the doomed aspiration to alter it.

There are three obstacles in the way of achieving the ideal of character-morality. I shall say very little about the first, comprising the essential conditions of life, since it has already received ample attention. Part of its significance is that benefits and harms are often not within human control. They may not be produced by human agency, and even if they are, the control we can exercise is itself subject to the conditions it is designed to regulate. Health and illness, talents and handicaps, fortunate and unfortunate accidents, unplanned presences and absences at crucial times and places, and physical attractiveness and repulsiveness are often nonhuman sources of benefits and harms. And when the benefits and harms are produced by human agents, they may be undeserved because the agents are moved by unchosen vices, and so, once again, the possibility of their controlling what they do is lacking. Thus, it often happens that people do not deserve what they get and do not get what they deserve. Although the ideal of character-morality is that it should aim to redress the imbalance between merit and desert created by the essential conditions of life, we are bound to fall seriously short of it because of the other two obstacles I am about to discuss.

The second obstacle is created by the scarcity of our resources.[1] By

---

[1] See the undeservedly neglected book by Walsh, *Scarcity and Evil.*

"resources" I do not just mean material ones, but something much broader, including institutional and psychological resources as well. The scarcity of material resources is by far the simplest. There is a famine or an epidemic because there is not enough food or medicine. But even if there is a surplus, there may not be available an effective delivery system to get what is needed from one location to another. A further complication is that scarcity may affect not only the supply or delivery of the goods but the expertise needed for using them appropriately. There just may not be enough nutritionists, nurses, and physicians to make intelligent use of available material goods. And then we soon arrive at the larger context in which policymakers have to weigh the conflicting claims on chronically insufficient funds obtained through taxation. There are legitimate needs both close to and far away from home; some are more dire than others, but the less dire ones have often better claim on relief because they are suffered by citizens and taxpayers, while the more serious emergency is in another country. Nor is it a matter of course that the shortage of funds can be remedied by higher taxation, for taxation tends to slow down the economy and thus diminish the funds available for future emergencies. So, the institutional dimension of scarcity is that the conflicting claims of long-term and immediate needs, resources used to generate future resources and to alleviate present misfortune, harm to one's constituency as opposed to foreigners, and serious but qualitatively different types of simultaneous problems need to be balanced, and not all legitimate ones can be satisfied.

But scarcity goes beyond the facts of institutional constraints and affects moral agents themselves, because our psychological resources are limited. There is only so much attention we can pay to the requirements of morality without incapacitating ourselves. We have limited capacities for self-examination, sympathy, patience, objectivity, being alert to suffering, or doing our duty. Thus, in addition to the essential conditions of life, scarcity also presents an insurmountable obstacle to achieving the ideal that desert should be proportional to merit.

The third obstacle would remain in the way even if the difficulties presented by the essential conditions of life and the scarcity of resources were, per impossibile, overcome. Establishing proportionality is by no means simple. The root idea is that of making benefits and harms fit the moral merits of their recipients, much as a scratch fits an itch. But unlike an itch, moral merit is unspecific, and unlike a scratch, there is an endless variety of ways in which people can be benefited or harmed. No doubt there are some things that all human beings would, in normal circumstances, regard as benefits and harms.

Conditions would have to be extraordinary for prolonged pain, dismemberment, loss of freedom, or blindness not to count as harms, and similarly, for health, security, and opportunity not to count as benefits. Yet the acknowledgment of these truisms does not even begin to help to surmount the obstacle.

First, proportionality calls for an unobtainable quantitative fit. Just how much pain, discomfort, or obloquy does, say, cowardice deserve? And does cowardice deserve more or less than lifelong self-indulgence? Who could reasonably judge in these matters, and how could disagreements be settled without arbitrariness? Second, proportionality also depends on qualitative appropriateness. It is perhaps fitting that a dishonest merchant should go bankrupt. But what is the fitting desert for moral obtuseness, false humility, sentimentality, or habitually crushing other people's enthusiasms? Third, beyond obvious instances of good and evil, which present the best candidates for fittingness, there are countless benefits and harms regarded as such only in particular contexts by particular people. Becoming a dean, receiving a golden ring for one's nose, acquiring a cat, or having one's book put on the Vatican's index count as benefits for some, harms for others, and matters of indifference to many more.

These difficulties about the quantity, quality, and identity of benefits and harms are due to there being no common measure in terms of which they could be compared. Money or the lack of it, comfort and insecurity, pleasure and pain, love and hate, and respect and obloquy each capture only some limited kinds of benefit and harm. As a result, establishing proportionality between desert and merit is often impossibly difficult.

A further problem about proportionality is caused by a different kind of impossibility involved in achieving the ideal that motivates the search. The ideal is to reestablish the moral balance that the imperfections of the world, including those of our own, have created. But there are many cases in which this cannot be done.[2] Victims of theft and fraud can be compensated for because the undeserved harm they suffer can be undone. But what would undo the damage caused by rape, torture, dismemberment, or brutalized childhood? The very idea of compensation is morally suspect in some contexts, as readers of the curious fable of Job may discover. God could take Job's cattle and sheep, and he could return them manifold after Job has proved his faith. But God also took his wife and children, and although Job found a new wife and had other children, it would be callous to sup-

---

[2] Wolgast, *The Grammar of Justice*, chapters 6–7, contain an interesting discussion of this problem.

pose, to put it mildly, that gaining a new family undid the loss of the old. If it had, we would not think well of Job.

The ideal of character-morality, then, is unattainable because the essential conditions of life, the scarcity of our resources, and the difficulty of establishing proportionality between merit and desert constitute insurmountable obstacles in the way. Although these obstacles cannot be overcome, I shall argue that the difficulties they present may be reduced. So, the ideal of character-morality may guide us in two different but connected ways.

One is the way in which we try to order our day-to-day lives. As practitioners, we are one of the sources of benefits and harms, and the ideal is that we should act so as to distribute benefits and harms according to merit. As theoreticians, we are legislators, judges, teachers, critics, and reformers, and our aim is to improve the institution of character-morality so that when practitioners are guided by its customs, principles, conventions, and traditions, then they make desert as proportional to merit as possible. But both practitioners and theoreticians move within character-morality. If what I have said about the obstacles in the way is correct, then reasonable and morally motivated people are bound to recognize that character-morality is imperfect because people frequently fail to get what they deserve. And this is so not merely because we are often irrational and immoral but because the imperfections are intrinsic to the institution.

If we allow the significance of this subversive truth to sink in, we are likely to be pushed to philosophical reflection—no longer within the institution of character-morality but about it. We move from internal to external questions. We ask not about what piecemeal tinkering would improve the institution but about loyalty to an intrinsically imperfect institution, one that can only be improved so as to be less imperfect. At this point we move to the second way in which the ideal of character-morality guides us. For if we understand why character-morality is bound to fall short of the ideal, that is, if we understand why evil is an unavoidable feature of our lives, then we shall have understood that the only chance there is for succeeding in our aspirations to live good lives is to do what we can to reduce the amount of evil that stands in the way. And that requires supporting the institution of character-morality, one of whose chief goals is to do just that.

Nine Theses of Character-Morality

The nine theses of character-morality that have emerged from our previous discussion may be regarded as the principles according to which the institution of character-morality ought to function. I shall now assemble and briefly summarize these theses.

The first thesis is *the objectivity of simple evil.* Evil is undeserved harm. Simple evil is undeserved harm that deprives people of some minimum requirement of their welfare. These requirements derive from physiological, psychological, and social conditions that characterize all normal members of our species. Harming people by depriving them of these requirements is undeserved if there is no acceptable moral justification for it. And the only acceptable justification is that human welfare requires that they be harmed. Simple evil is objective because its status as evil is determined solely by the fact of whether undeserved simple harm has been caused.

The second thesis is *the irrelevance of choice to simple evil.* It is a consequence of the objectivity of simple evil that the mental states of the agents causing it cannot alter the fact that undeserved harm has been caused. Evil consists in undeserved harm and not in the nature of the motivation that has led to its occurrence. Whether agents choose to cause evil has a bearing on our judgments of the agents, but not on whether simple evil has been caused.

The third thesis is *the reflexivity of simple evil.* Vices are character traits that regularly issue in evil actions. In evil people, vices are dominant character traits resulting in enduring patterns of evil-causing actions. Therefore, patterns of simple evil caused by actions are evidence for vices, and the vices of agents may result in their agents' themselves being evil. It follows from the irrelevance of choice to simple evil that the judgment of evil carries from actions to vices and from there to agents, depending on the evil caused and not on the presence or absence of choice.

The fourth thesis is *the importance of character to moral judgment.* As a matter of logic, not of psychology, most of the time people perform characteristic actions. Actions reflect enduring dispositions, and dispositions constitute character. Thus, actions are normally signs of character. Most actions are spontaneous responses to routine situations and not the results of choice. Choices need to be made only when the everyday predictable situations are transformed. But in civilized societies this happens only rarely. If our interest is in minimizing evil, it is far more important to concentrate on the characters of evil-causing agents than on their choices. The best way to prevent evil is by changing the characters from which most evil actions routinely follow, rather than focusing on choices, which are bound to be the exceptions, not the rule.

The fifth thesis is *the unavoidability of moral agency.* Moral agency is a consequence of the capacity of normal human beings to cause good and evil. It is not the result of choice, contract, good will, commitment, or deliberation. We cannot opt out of morality, because we are one of the sources of good and evil; our characters and actions affect human welfare. Thus, the question is not whether we are moral agents but what kind of moral agents we are to be. The answer depends, not on our chosen actions, but on our characters, from which the vast majority of our chosen and unchosen actions follow.

The sixth thesis is *the significance of moral achievement*. Our moral achievement ought to be judged by the good and evil we cause. This is what should determine our moral standing. Moral improvement has a bearing on moral achievement only because it tends to shift the balance of the good and evil we cause in a direction more favorable, or less unfavorable, to human welfare. The moral improvement of agents influences our judgment of their moral standing only by counting as an extenuating factor. The decisive consideration is the good and evil actually caused and not the difficulties encountered in the process.

The seventh thesis is *the centrality of moral desert*. One aim of moral judgment is to ascertain what particular agents deserve. And they deserve benefit or harm proportional to the good and evil they have caused. Being committed to human welfare establishes a presumption in favor of people deserving the benefits and not deserving harms. But this presumption can be overruled by the very same commitment that establishes it, for the general aim of promoting human welfare may well require depriving people of benefits and inflicting harm on them.

The eighth thesis is *the dependence of moral desert on moral merit*. Moral merit depends on moral achievement. Moral agents are of unequal merit because they differ in their moral achievements. This difference consists not merely in varying degrees of moral excellence; there are also varying degrees of moral baseness. Good and evil are both dimensions of moral achievement, and people who excel in the dimension of evil do not merely lack moral merit but acquire moral demerit. Consequently, it follows from unequal moral merit that it is morally justified to treat people with unequal merit unequally.

The ninth thesis is *the mixed view of human nature*. Human nature is neither primarily good nor primarily evil. It is a mixture of good and evil dispositions. Evil occurs because evil dispositions are expressed in action. How much evil there is depends on the balance of good and evil dispositions. Their balance shifts historically, culturally, socially, and individually. The function of character-morality is to influence this shift in a direction favorable to human welfare.

Two Aspects of Character-Morality

Character-morality can promote human welfare either by aiming to prevent undeserved harm or by encouraging the production of deserved benefit. Thus, character-morality can be said to have an evil-avoiding and a good-producing aspect. The significance of these two aspects is that corresponding to them character-morality has two sets of goals, two sets of requirements, two sets of justifications for conforming to the requirements, and thus two different tasks.

The good-producing aspect is the smiling, yea-saying face of character-morality. It has to do with the ideal of living lives in which personal satisfaction and moral merit coincide, with the development of virtues, the establishment of free, just, law-governed societies, the encouragement of people to conduct various experiments in living, the pursuit of happiness, the protection of rights, and the realization of life plans. But for these immensely desirable activities to go on, certain conditions must obtain. These include the protection of the minimum requirements of human welfare, requirements whose violation causes simple evils. The evil-avoiding aspect of character-morality is concerned with providing this protection. It is a nay-saying, severe, repressive, coercive force. Its main task is to prohibit moral agents from acting on their evil impulses. It is a demanding, stern censor, often forbidding us to do what we want to do.

The justification of the requirements of the evil-avoiding aspect of character-morality is that unless we conform to them, good lives are impossible. But conformity is insufficient for good lives. The justification of the good-producing aspect of character-morality is that conformity to it is constitutive of good lives. The evil-avoiding aspect aims to establish the conditions in which good lives can be lived. The good-producing aspect aims to show how we can live them. One central task of the evil-avoiding aspect is to discourage our potentialities for evil; a chief aim of the good-producing aspect is to encourage the development of our potentialities for the good. One aims to suppress vices, the other to foster virtues.

Our sensibility, influenced by choice-morality and the soft reaction, tends to concentrate on the good-producing aspect. The majority of current debates are about strategies for pursuing the good. This is what utilitarians, Kantians, contractarians, and eudaimonists largely argue about. But underlying their often substantial disagreements is the assumption that insofar as moral agents are rational, they are motivated to pursue the good. Part of the significance of the tragic view of life is that it shows the inadequacy of this assumption. The rational pursuit of evil is likely, not merely possible, because of the motivational forces of contingency, indifference, and destructiveness that move us toward it. The great question is how to avoid evil, given that its avoidance depends on agents who are, at least to some extent, moved by it.

In struggling to answer this question, I argued—against the deliverances of our sensibility—for the need to concentrate on the evil-avoiding aspect of character-morality. My argument presupposes that character-morality does indeed have two aspects, but it may appear that the difference between them is merely verbal. One and the same person or action can be described both as withholding a deserved benefit and as inflicting an undeserved harm. If there is a clearly formulated requirement for a particular conception of a good life, then it is either violated or observed. A violation can be said to be a nonobservance, and an observance is characterizable as a nonviolation. Thus, harming people by depriving them of life, liberty, or property may be supposed to be the same as failing to observe their rights. And contrariwise, to refrain from interfering with people's life, liberty, or property is but to recognize their title to these benefits.[3]

Yet this initial appearance is misleading. Its plausibility derives from vagueness about who is to observe or refrain from violating the requirements. Although many of the requirements of character-morality are general and impersonal, they are, nevertheless, encountered by particular individuals in particular situations. But it is not true of such agents in such situations that by not causing evil they are bound to produce good, or that by failing to produce good, they will necessarily cause evil. My not murdering you does not mean that you will live, for you may die of natural causes or by another hand. Similarly, I may not feed you when you are hungry, but that need not condemn you to starvation, for you or someone else may provide. If it is understood that the requirements of character-morality are particularized, then the option of causing good or causing evil appears not as an exclusive alternative but as allowing for other possibilities. Thus, vis-à-vis individual agents, the production of good and evil are contraries, not contradictories. This does not show that our evil-avoiding and good-producing efforts are asymmetrical, but it does allow for the possibility.

To show that the asymmetry between our evil-avoiding and good-producing activities is not merely possible but actual, we need to consider it from the point of view of individual agents acting in particular contexts. The first thing to notice is that moral agents need to

[3] For an exploration of this issue in respect to life and death, see Steinbock, *Killing and Letting Die.*

make a different kind of effort when they are engaged in avoiding evil from the one they are called upon to make in trying to produce good. The effort required for avoiding evil is to refrain from doing something, while for producing good it is to direct their actions in a particular way. One is negative, and its symptom is the lack of overt action; the other is positive, and it is shown by the agents' doing something readily observable. In the first case, the agents leave the external world as it was before their efforts, and if there is a change, it takes place inside themselves. In the second case, the agents alter the external world by producing in it a change for the better. In both cases, the agents may be motivated by the moral requirement to give others their due; in both cases the requirement may be internalized and give rise to such virtues as justice, conscientiousness, or benevolence. But both the requirements and the virtues express themselves in two different ways: providing what is deserved, and not providing what is not deserved. The good-producing aspect of character-morality is concerned with the former, while its evil-avoiding aspect is concerned with the latter.

It is important to avoid a way of misunderstanding the asymmetry I am arguing for. Providing what is deserved does not only mean producing deserved benefits; it also means producing deserved harms. And analogously, not providing what is not deserved includes refraining both from causing undeserved harm and from causing undeserved benefit. Thus, the requirements of the evil-avoiding and the good-producing aspects of character-morality can each be violated either by undeserved harms or by undeserved benefits. The difference is that the requirements in the case of avoiding evil is to refrain from causing evil, while in the case of producing good it is actively to cause good. But the failure to refrain from causing evil may involve causing undeserved harm or failing to produce deserved benefit. Likewise, the failure to produce good may take the form either of producing undeserved benefit or of not producing deserved harm.

I stress this point because it is sometimes erroneously supposed that morality requires us not to cause harm. What morality requires, among other things, is that we do not cause *undeserved* harm. Morality often requires us to cause deserved harm. Punishing criminals, holding evildoers in contempt, showing distaste, expressing disapproval, refusing to associate with vicious people, and demanding that people dominated by the vices of insufficiency, expediency, and malevolence be held accountable for the undeserved harm they cause may all be perfectly justified moral reactions. The obverse of the error of denying that this is so is to suppose that morality requires us to produce benefits. The requirement is to produce *deserved* benefits. Undeservedly benefiting others may take the form of nepotism, discrimination, bribery, paternalism, or intrusive meddling. And none of these is required by morality.

I hasten to add that the moral requirement not to cause undeserved harm does not mean that we must always inflict deserved harm. Considerations of mercy or forgiveness may reasonably override this requirement. Nor does the obligation to produce deserved benefit invariably compel us not to produce undeserved benefit. In particular cases, the benefits produced by mercy or generosity can outweigh the general presumption against the likely harm caused by giving people undeserved benefits.[4] Whether or not a particular moral requirement is justifiably overruled depends on how doing so would affect the general aims of character-morality: the maximization of good and the minimization of evil.

The second consideration relevant to the asymmetry between the good-producing and the evil-avoiding aspects of character-morality derives from the different degrees of undeserved harm that are likely to follow from the violation of their respective requirements. There is a directness and immediacy involved in causing evil that is normally absent from the failure to produce good. Causing harm damages its victims, but the failure to produce benefit need cause no damage. If I violate the prohibition against undeservedly depriving people of life, liberty, or property, then I injure them. But my violation of the prescription to protect people's lives, liberty, or property need not injure them, for the absence of my protection does not mean that they will be deprived of these benefits.

This general point is not vitiated by cases in which particular moral agents are the sole sources of benefit for some who depend on them. In such cases, if they do not provide the benefits their dependents' welfare requires, then no one else will. So, if they fail to do so, they will cause harm just as surely as if they had inflicted it. Mothers, nurses, or people chancing on the scene of an accident may be in the position of having sole control over the welfare of others. But even in these cases, there is a distinction between causing undeserved harm and allowing it to happen. It is true that the practical consequences of the act and its omission are identical. However, the ways in which the consequences are produced and the ways in which agents may be motivated to avoid producing them are still different. In causing harm, the agents are active in bringing about the consequences, while in allowing harm to happen, they are passive observ-

---

[4] The distinction I draw here is similar to the distinction between what reason requires and what it allows; see Gert, *The Moral Rules*, chapter 2.

ers. It may be that we would wish to hold passive agents as accountable as active ones. Yet we would hold them accountable for different things. Moreover, the situations in which particular agents are the only possible suppliers of required benefits are rare. Normally, the harm that follows from causing evil is certain and swift, while the consequences of failing to produce good are more remote. This being so does not excuse the latter, but the asymmetry between the two cases leaves open the question of comparative accountability. What the asymmetry does establish is that the motivational sources of causing evil are different from those involved in failing to produce good. Consequently, what we need to do to avoid these different kinds of failings are also different.

The asymmetry between causing evil and failing to produce good supports the claim that character-morality has an evil-avoiding and a good-producing aspect. From now on, my procedure will be largely to ignore the good-producing aspect of character-morality[5] and to concentrate on the evil-avoiding one. Thus, in the next chapter, I shall consider what kind of institution character-morality should be so that it would best foster the avoidance of simple evil. And in subsequent chapters, I shall discuss what individual moral agents can do in their own lives to minimize simple evil.

THE STATE OF THE ARGUMENT

I have been endeavoring in this chapter to formulate a conception of character-morality. This involved describing the ideal that character-morality aims at and understanding why it is bound to fall short of achieving it. The ideal motivates the attempt to face evil, but not by pursuing the impossible goal of overcoming the essential conditions of life, the scarcity of resources, and the establishment of proportionality between merit and desert. The ideal is to maintain an intrinsically imperfect human institution whose purpose it is to come as close as possible to assuring that people get what they deserve. Evil is the most formidable obstacle in the way because much of it is caused by the unchosen vices of human agents who alone can provide the sought-for assurance.

Character-morality prompts us to face evil, and the hard reaction is the manner in which we can face it reasonably. The hard reaction is supported by the nine theses of character-morality. Given these theses, the hard reaction is to hold moral agents accountable for their

[5] This is the subject of my *Moral Tradition and Individuality* and *The Examined Life*.

vices, even if they are not chosen. The justification of the hard reaction is that it is the most reasonable way of coping with evil.

The hard reaction is intended to replace the illusions of the soft reaction and the hopelessness created by the tragic view of life without succumbing to the transcendental temptation. To show that the hard reaction is a more reasonable response to the secular problem of evil than its rivals, I have been advancing a three-stage argument. The first stage was intended to clarify the nature and seriousness of the secular problem of evil. The second stage involved showing the inadequacies of competing approaches. This was a complex matter because both the tragic view and choice-morality contain much that is of value. In this chapter, we have embarked on the third stage: on the attempt to develop character-morality and the hard reaction by giving them content. This content comes from salvaging from its rivals what is left intact after criticisms of them, from the nine theses, and, what is yet to be added, from working out the institutional and personal implications of character-morality and the hard reaction.

CHAPTER NINE

The Institutional Dimension of Character-Morality

WHAT KIND OF INSTITUTION SHOULD CHARACTER-MORALITY BE?

Character-morality presents itself to moral agents both as a set of external requirements, comprising various rules, principles, values, customs, practices, and ideals, and as an internal impetus that includes the motivation to live and to act in conformity with these requirements. The first is part of the institutional dimension of character-morality; the second is part of the personal. If, morally speaking, things are going well, moral agents can justifiably regard the external requirements and the internal impetus as having the shared goal of fostering good lives. Thus, the external requirements become internal motivational forces. As a result, morality does not appear as a restriction on the ways reasonable moral agents want to live, but as a means of providing possible ways of living well. In this ideal state, the question of why one should be moral has the obvious answer that living morally is the best way of living. Personal satisfaction and moral merit coincide in moral lives, and they are seen as coinciding because what reasonable agents find satisfying is identical with what possesses moral merit.

As we have seen, however, character-morality is bound to be imperfectly realized, so this ideal state will not be achieved. There will always be a discrepancy between the institutional and personal dimensions of character-morality because personal satisfaction and moral merit will never coincide perfectly. One deep reason for this discrepancy is that, since human nature is mixed and the essential conditions of life inform it, we often cause evil by being and acting in ways that fail to make desert proportional to moral merit. The scarcity of resources and the difficulties in the way of establishing proportionality between merit and desert also contribute to making matters worse. The ideal of character-morality is to minimize the discrepancy between merit and desert, and this can be done either from the institutional or the personal direction. In this chapter, I shall concentrate on the first.

In the light of our previous discussion, it is possible to focus the question quite sharply. We want to know what kind of institution character-morality should be, given some self-imposed limitations and conclusions I regard as having established. To begin with limitations, the question is restricted, first, to the evil-avoiding aspect of character-morality, and it leaves aside the good-producing aspect. Second, even within the evil-avoiding aspect, our concern is only with simple, not with complex, evil. Thus, the kind of answer we are looking for should tell us what external requirements character-morality should prescribe so as to minimize the amount of simple evil in our lives. But the conclusions incorporated in the nine theses of character-morality enable us to sharpen the question even further. We know that much evil is unchosen, so that the way in which evil may be minimized does not primarily involve influencing the choices moral agents make, but rather influencing their actions regardless of whether they are chosen. We also know that most actions follow from the characters of their agents. Our policy, therefore, must be to influence actions by looking for institutional ways of shaping characters. Furthermore, given the objectivity and reflexivity of simple evil, we know as well that certain character traits—namely, vices—predictably result in simple evil, so we can specify some particular ways in which character-morality ought to aim at shaping characters. The ideal guiding this attempt is to instill in moral agents the disposition to act naturally and spontaneously so as to make desert approximate merit as closely as circumstances allow. What kind of institution will conform to these requirements?

It will be an institution to which allegiance is part of the sensibility of a society. People who consciously or unconsciously regard themselves as members of their society are likely, for that reason, also to share its sensibility. In the vast majority of cases, sensibility originates not from choice but from being born into a context composed of family, social stratum, society, and historical period. The sensibility pervades the attitudes of people living together. The ways in which they conduct themselves in a wide variety of situations, the judgments they make of their own and of other people's conduct, their expectations, their contempt and admiration, their delight and outrage, their surprise and disillusionment, what they take for granted and what they are prepared to recognize as special cases, and what counts as excuse and what adds condemnatory force all derive from the sensibility in the background. Into this sensibility they were born, and in it they were educated from their earliest days.

The education does not come to them merely as parental precepts and admonitions, it is not conveyed only by the voice of some recognized authority, it is not just a set of rules that has been articulated, learned, and practiced through trial and error—the education is largely unconscious, inarticulate, and unintentional on the part of both the teachers and the pupils. For the education is about the ways in which things are done, and the teachers are often as unaware of conforming to these ways as their pupils are of being in the process of learning them—when to speak and when to remain silent; what is serious and what is playful; how to be friendly and how to show reserve; where "we" end and "they" begin; what can and cannot be said, and to whom and when; what is private and public; what is shameful and a matter of pride; what are the signs of authority, strangeness, danger, exclusion, and inclusion; how and where to dress, eat, eliminate, sleep, sit, lie down, and move; what is one's own and what belongs to others; what are the formulas for greeting, borrowing, thanking, asking, and expressing love, protest, indifference, pain, enjoyment. The acquisition of these and a multitude of similar tokens of practical knowledge is what constitutes initiation into a sensibility. Of course, the sensibility of a society is much richer than this description suggests. It also informs taste, style, work, play, aesthetics, religion, entertainment, sport, literature, and many other aspects of life. But for our purposes it is sufficient to bear in mind only these rather elementary constituents, for the aspect of character-morality concerned with avoiding evil is among them.

Part of the contribution of character-morality to sensibility is a set of prohibitions proscribing conduct that causes simple evil. Such prohibitions play an essential role in the sensibility of a society because if the prohibitions were not generally observed, people's lives and welfare would be at risk. The prohibitions are part of the minimum conditions in which people can endeavor to make good lives for themselves. If a society is morally healthy and so the prevailing sensibility reflects this desirable state, then, to most moral agents, the prohibitions do not represent obstacles to the satisfaction of their desires. They are not tempted to murder, torture, mutilate, or enslave people, and the prohibitions stop them, as a red light might stop drivers in a hurry. The prohibitions appear not as foreclosing options but as defining the domain of moral possibilities. Of course, to set limits is to put some things beyond them. The purpose of setting them, however, is not to make some tempting possibilities into taboos but rather to influence people to see some possibilities as real and others as unthinkable.

This attempt to influence people can indeed be, and has often been, cynically or idealistically, misused to inculcate some religious, political, or racial ideology. However, it need not be misused. The moral health of a society depends on the prohibitions embedded in the prevailing sensibility, putting beyond the pale conduct likely to cause simple evil. And what that is depends not on ideological considerations but on the physiological, psychological, and social truisms about human nature that establish the objectivity of part of character-morality.

The justifiability of this way of regarding the institutional dimension of character-morality depends on how the questions it raises are answered. Among the many questions, three seem to me to be crucial. The first is about knowledge of the relevant prohibitions. Moral agents are bombarded by countless prohibitions in their lives. How do they know which ones matter in the serious way I have attempted to describe? The second is about the justification of the prohibitions. What is the reason for observing them? The third is about the motivation reasonable moral agents may have for conducting themselves according to the prohibitions. This question arises because, although there are influences prompting reasonable people to observe the prohibitions, there are also influences prompting their violation. Why should reasonable people endeavor to avoid causing evil, when they are naturally motivated also in the opposite direction?

THE KNOWLEDGE OF PROHIBITIONS

We need to begin with a methodological difficulty. I am discussing the institutional dimension of character-morality, but in the course of doing so I have and will continue to appeal to the moral sensibility prevailing in our society. What is the relationship between the institutional dimension of morality as it is and that of character-morality? I cannot claim that they are identical, because part of my argument is that our existing morality is faulty because of its failure to face evil, which in turn is due to the influence of choice-morality. Nor can I regard them as radically different, because in that case my appeal to the disclosures of our moral sensibility could not support character-morality. The way out of this difficulty is to recognize that our existing morality is the context in which choice- and character-morality struggle for supremacy. Consequently, my remarks about our morality are partly descriptive and partly prescriptive. The point of the description is to show how, morally speaking, things stand with us. My view is that in some respects things are as they ought to be, but in some others we are in a deplorable state. The point of the prescription is to criticize what is deplorable and to suggest ways of improving it. So the institutional dimension of character-morality partly overlaps with our existing morality. In appealing to our moral sensibility, I draw on the overlapping parts.

In those parts, we find agreement among reasonable moral agents about what constitutes simple evil. The disagreements are not about whether or not some particular actions have or are likely to cause undeserved simple harm; rather, they concern the question of what our moral reaction should be toward the agents of these actions. It is here that the soft and hard reactions clash. But they can clash only because there is agreement about the facts to which the two reactions are incompatible responses. In discussing our knowledge of prohibitions, I intend to draw on the uncontroversial segment of our moral sensibility about simple evil.

Let us recall the sort of evil actions people dominated by the vices of insufficiency, expediency, and malevolence may do. There really can be no doubt in anybody's mind that, for instance, the mindless dogmatic persecution of innocent people is evil. Nor is it a contentious issue that it is evil also to cause simple harm to people who present obstacles to the achievement of one's goals. Similarly, reasonable people will not disagree that it is evil to vent one's hatred, resentment, or envy on people who have done nothing to deserve it. In each of these cases, prohibitions against simple evil are violated. We all know that these acts constitute violations, and we cannot but deplore the actions. How, then, do we know it? What kind of knowledge is it? How do we come to have it?

In all these cases, there occurs a point at which the facts jell into a pattern, and those who share our sensibility come to see them, then and there, in a certain light. The seeing of the facts in this immediate way is a sudden, but ususally unsurprising, realization that involves no conscious reflection. We simply know how matters stand. I shall call this kind of knowledge *moral intuition.*[1]

Reliance on moral intuitions was traditionally thought to involve unquestioning obedience to an authoritative inner voice requiring no justification. This is a dogmatic and obscurantist view, and it has done much to discredit old-style appeals to moral intuition. But the new-style appeal I propose to make here proceeds differently. At the dividing line between old and new styles stands W. D. Ross.[2] Before him, moral intuitions were generally regarded as involving self-evidence and unconditionality and as being the product of a moral sense. Self-evidence was supposed to yield infallible and incorrigible

---

[1] See Campbell, "Moral Intuitions and the Principle of Self-Realization"; Grice, "Moral Theories and Received Opinion"; Hampshire, *Two Theories of Morality* and *Morality and Conflict*; Platts, *Ways of Meaning*, chapter 10; Rorty, "Intuition"; Ross, *The Right and the Good* and *The Foundations of Ethics*; Sidgwick, *The Methods of Ethics*; Wiggins, "Truth, Invention, and the Meaning of Life."

[2] Ross, *The Right and the Good*, especially chapter 2.

knowledge, guaranteeing that intuitions could not be mistaken. Un-conditionality led to categorical moral judgments expressing intuitive knowledge. And the psychological apparatus making intuition possible was assumed to be an inborn human faculty whose proper functioning required only maturity and normality. This view was rightly criticized on the grounds that intuitions may conflict, that they are often incompatible with each other, that what a person or a society regards as an intuitive truth others frequently reject as dubious, and that there is to be found no trace of a faculty of moral sense. Ross jettisoned the idea that intuitions were produced by a moral sense, and for unconditional intuitions, he substituted prima facie ones. He gave a celebrated list of prima facie duties vouchsafed for by intuitions and claimed that all mature and normal human beings recognize their obligatoriness, provided they did not conflict with each other. In cases of conflict, we must put ourselves, actually or vicariously, in the concrete situation and try to intuit which prima facie duty has the stronger claim. We could err in such conflicts, but morality involves risks. Conflicts do not show that intuitions are unreliable, only that, in some cases, they are difficult.

Thus, the new-style defense of moral intuitions rejects their certainty and unconditionality and likens moral sense to a sense of humor or a sense of honor. As they do in other spheres, so intuitions also play an important role in morality. "There are vast areas of belief necessary for survival within which intuition is not discreditable, and in which the mind operates by a mechanism of causes and effects normally unknown to the thinking subject. . . . If it were possible to count beliefs, one could say that most of one's beliefs about the environment are of this character."[3] Examples are the recognition of pattern, color, size, persons, sounds, tastes, smells, and texture. But intuitions are also involved in logic, when we see, for instance, that a conclusion follows from the premises; in mathematics, when, if we understand a proof, we see that it is a proof; in remembering faces, estimating distance, getting the point of a joke, identifying a melody, and so on. It seems indisputable that we rely on intuitions in many areas of life, and I shall argue in the new style, we also do so in morality.

The object of moral intuition is a situation. It need not involve us personally, we need not be able to do anything about it, and it need not even be actual, for fictional situations may also be seen in this way. But there are many moral situations that would be intuitively recognized as being of a certain sort by the vast majority in a society. If

---

[3] Hampshire, *Two Theories of Morality*, 7.

some people in our society agreed about the facts but did not see the actions following from the three vices described above as involving evil, we would suspect them of immorality or of some sort of abnormality. On the other hand, there are situations whose intuitive apprehension is difficult. Only a few people are capable of seeing immediately and without reflection some patterns formed of publicly accessible facts. Othello cannot be faulted for not immediately recognizing Iago as the moral monster he was, and it is understandable that it took a long time for Anna Karenina to see her situation as hopeless. It appears, therefore, that moral intuitions are appropriate in some situations but not in others.

Intuitions are appropriate in simple moral situations and inappropriate in complex ones. We can distinguish between the two types of situation in terms of the Aristotelian scheme for practical reasoning. The scheme comprises two premises and a conclusion. In simple moral situations, the major premise is a moral prohibition known to all normal adults raised in a society. In our society, such prohibitions are, for instance, those of murder, torture, mutilation, and enslavement. The prohibitions are learned in the course of moral education. The minor premise involves the identification of a particular action as a possible or actual violation of the prohibition contained in the major premise. It is the most elementary form of moral knowledge in our society that certain actions would constitute murder, torture, mutilation, or enslavement, and as the jury system testifies to it, randomly selected members of our society need only to be clear about the facts to be able to identify particular actions as violating the prohibition. The conclusion is that the action ought not to be performed.

This scheme is not a psychological account of what goes on in the minds of typical agents in simple moral situations. It is rather a reconstruction of the logic implicit in the countless transactions among people sharing our sensibility. Most of the time, people are unaware of the steps I have articulated, precisely because they are well-trained moral agents. If the facts are clear, there is no room for hesitation; there is nothing to ponder, and doubt has no foothold. If insufficiency, expediency, and malevolence lead people to act as described, their actions are evil.

Moral situations cease to be simple if complications enter on the level either of the major or of the minor premise. There may be no prohibitions against some forms of simple evil, as there was not against murdering *Untermenschen* in Nazi Germany; or prohibitions and prescriptions may conflict, as in the case of mercy killing; or it may be unclear whether a particular action constitutes violation of a prohibition or conformity to a prescription, as capital punishment may be seen as institutional murder or as justice; or the moral sensibility of a society may be changing, so it becomes questionable whether old prohibitions should hold, as those against euthanasia or abortion, for instance, are questionable for us. These uncertainties create complex moral situations, and in them moral intuitions are inappropriate.

However, the fact of the matter is that in the normal course of events uncertainties about the prohibitions of simple evil are the exceptions, not the rule. For simple evil consists in undeservedly depriving people of the minimum requirements of their welfare. Knowledge of what these requirements are is not esoteric but part of the stock of information even illiterate and uneducated people normally possess. And whether the morality of one's society has an acceptable justification for the deprivation is also something that in normal circumstances all adults can be expected to know.

What, then, are the characteristics of moral intuition so that its possession could be so widespread and undemanding of skill or intelligence? To begin with, the intuitions are *moral*. They concern seeing situations primarily in terms of good and evil, although my interest here is only in seeing them as evil. Seeing in this way is *immediate*; there is no conscious inference, reflection, or thought involved in it. Our reaction is spontaneous, instant, automatic. As soon as the facts present themselves, they fall into a pattern for us. This is not to deny that there have been inferences in the past. The fact that our reaction is immediate now is no doubt explained by our having learned in the past to see similar situations in that way. But the lessons have been so thoroughly absorbed that we now have to struggle to evoke them no more than we have to remember how to walk or talk. The need to think occurs only in complex situations. Thus, we are led to recognize that intuitions occur *routinely*. They are not sudden revelations or striking discoveries but pedestrian, matter-of-course apprehensions of something being so. Therefore, the contexts of intuitions are not moral dilemmas and conflicts but the innumerable spontaneous occasions on which we refrain from jeopardizing the minimum conditions of other people's welfare.

Moral intuitions come to us as *imperatives*: they call for a response. The call may be resisted for many reasons, but unless something intervenes, we feel compelled to do something about the intuited situation. In this respect, moral intuitions differ from sensory intuitions, for we can intuit some empirical aspect of the world and be quite indifferent to it. Nor is it a sufficient explanation of the action-guiding force of moral intuitions to say that, unlike sensory intuitions, they are evaluative. Aesthetic intuitions are also evaluative, but they need not compel us to respond. Aesthetic intuitions are often passive; moral intuitions are typically active. We may be uplifted by beautiful objects and repelled by ugly ones without wanting or needing to do anything public about them. But moral situations call for a different response: we feel obliged to do something, at least to register public approval or disapproval. We typically want others to know where we stand, even if we do not participate in the situation.

Following Ross, we should recognize that intuitions are *presumptive*. Their occurrence establishes a prima facie case for the situation being as intuited. If there is no good reason to disbelieve them, it is reasonable to accept our intuitions. This initial presumption in favor of intuitions should be contrasted with the unconditionality old-style intuitionists attributed to them. The difference is that according to the old view, provided something really was an intuition, nothing could overrule it. By contrast, the new view allows for this possibility.

Moral intuitions are *interpretative*, rather than merely descriptive. They involve seeing *as*, not just seeing. They are perceptions of patterns formed by the relevant facts. But what we intuit is not a moral fact over and above nonmoral facts but an interpretation of nonmoral facts. In moral intuitions, we see nonmoral facts in a certain light. This involves the formation of a pattern of the nonmoral facts in which some facts are regarded as significant, while others are assigned no decisive influence. So, there are two components of an act of intuition, although they are separable only in thought. One is identifying the facts, and the other is recognizing their significance. Reasonable people often identify the same facts as relevant in a situation. And if they share a moral sensibility, then there will also be many situations in which they will attribute the same significance to the facts.

A further characteristic of moral intuitions is the agents' *ready acceptance* of them. In old-style intuitionism, this was identified as self-evidence. There is something right and something wrong with this idea. It is clearly true that if we have no doubts about the nonmoral facts of some situations, then their moral patterns may present themselves to us immediately and authoritatively, much as objects appear red, rectangular, or heavy. We are not aware of having made an inference, we are not entertaining a hypothesis, so we are not in need of evidence beyond what we already have. It is not unreasonable, therefore, to talk about self-evidence. But self-evidence carries with it a connotation of the impossibility of error, and this is not true of moral intuitions. Although we readily accept our intuitions, they may be mistaken, we may come to see that they are, and we may correct them.

Consequently, we should recognize that intuitions are *fallible*, and as we recognize it, so the appearance of self-evidence weakens. Old-style intuitionists thought that intuitions were infallible, thus strengthening their supposed self-evidence. According to them, if we get the facts of the case right, then since intuitions are the apprehensions of facts, we ipso facto get the intuition right, and so there is no room for error. Since I hold that intuitions are not merely of facts but also of the interpretations of facts, fallibility enters through possibly mistaken interpretations. We could get all the facts of the case right and still be mistaken, because in our interpretations of them we may have misjudged their significance.

Since the source of fallibility is misplaced significance and faulty interpretation, it is possible to knock out yet another pillar supporting self-evidence. Intuitions were supposed to be incorrigible because, if the facts were rightly apprehended, then the sources of error were eliminated, and so correction was neither needed nor could be provided. But if mistakes can happen in the way I have just described, then it becomes possible to correct them by putting right the misplaced emphasis. An essential step toward correcting intuitions is to understand what could produce faulty interpretations, a topic I shall take up in the next section.

In summary of the account I have been giving of our knowledge of prohibitions, then, the knowledge is in the form of moral intuition, and the prohibitions are against the undeserved violations of the minimum requirements of human welfare. Moral intuition is moral because it is concerned primarily with good and evil, and it is a form of intuition because it is immediate, routine, imperative, presumptive, interpretative, readily accepted, and yet fallible and corrigible. The minimum requirements of human welfare are established by physiological, psychological, and social facts that characterize all human beings, always, everywhere. Let us refer to prohibitions against violating these requirements as *deep prohibitions*. We can say, then, that we know by moral intuition that a particular action does or would involve the undeserved violation of a deep prohibition, and so its performance is or would be evil. We can also distinguish between prohibitions that morality requires us to take very seriously and prohibitions whose violation is a lesser matter. Deep prohibitions have the seriousness they have because their violation, involving simple evil, is the most damaging, while the violation of other prohibitions is less injurious.

The Justification of Deep Prohibitions

In one sense, the moral justification of deep prohibitions is perfectly straightforward. They are intended to minimize the amount of simple evil in our lives, and anyone committed to morality must accept that aim as a desirable goal. Moreover, deep prohibitions are also rationally justified because they are intended to protect all individuals in a society. Hence, it is in the interest of everyone so protected to observe the deep prohibitions. If the identity of deep prohibitions were always clear, this is all that would have to be said about justifying them. Unfortunately, this is not so, and we have to struggle with complications.

Complications arise for two reasons. First, the moral intuitions through which we normally know deep prohibitions are fallible, and they reflect the uncertainties of the prevailing morality. Second, moral intuitions are not restricted to deep prohibitions; as a result, less serious prohibitions may be confused with deep ones, and vice versa. I shall discuss these complications in turn.

It is important to be clear, however, that the complications do not call into question the simple and conclusive justification I offer above. They are occasioned rather by our mistakes in identifying the justified prohibitions. So, the complications may make us uncertain about a prohibition being deep, but not about a deep prohibition being justified. I say that it is important to be clear about this because if we are, then it becomes obvious that the way to remove the complication is to ascertain whether a prohibition is deep. And that, fortunately, is not difficult to do.

Let us then consider the first complication, that produced by the fallibility of moral intuitions. Take the position of typical moral agents who are called upon to act in what I have characterized as simple moral situations. They are familiar with the deep prohibitions of the morality prevailing in their society, the facts of the situation are not in doubt, and so they interpret the relevant facts immediately, noninferentially, often unconsciously as involving clear instances of evil possibilities. When the time comes to act, they are guided by their interpretations and spontaneously follow their guidance. For instance, pushing that nasty person off the cliff, keeping the teenager with the loud radio chained to the pipes of the basement, or using the Cuisinart to mangle the hands of the incompetent plumber or the chain saw to persuade one's spouse to take a more reasonable view would be murder, enslavement, mutilation, and torture—they know it, so they do not do it.

Suppose that we ask typical moral agents, when they conduct themselves in this manner, to justify the intuitions that guide them. Their perfectly proper reaction would be incomprehension—why should they need justification for the obvious? To do that sort of thing to that nasty person, thoughtless teenager, incompetent plumber, or infuriating spouse would be evil, and that is why they do not do it.

What more needs to be said? Indeed, whoever would need to say even that much? The very request for justification is a suspicious sign of gross stupidity or immorality.

Now of course, situations are not always as simple as these; there may be hidden facts, unrecognized complexities, or deeper conflicts. If so, the conditions for intuition are absent. When complications occur, reasonable people no longer respond immediately and spontaneously; intuition is appropriate only in routine simple moral situations. But the routine is what often happens, so in the morality of everyday life, intuition is often a reliable guide. If we regard a situation as simple, and yet it is complex, then our reliance on intuition is mistaken. If the demand for justification is based on some reason for thinking that such a mistake has been made, then it has a serious point and deserves an answer. But if there is no reason to doubt the obvious, then there is no need to advance arguments for justifying it either.

Furthermore, moral intuitions do not occur in a vacuum; people act on them, compare them, and they figure in each others' intuitions. Thus, there is a ready public test for them. If our intuitions are not shared by others in our morality, then, once again, there is ground for doubting them. But if what seems to us to be unquestionably so is reinforced by the concurrence of others, then there is no room for reasonable doubt of our intuitions in simple moral situations.

This justification for relying on moral intuitions and acting according to them appeals to our morality, from which the intuitions follow. Thus, the justification is internal. Of course, there remains the question of whether conformity to our morality is itself justified. The answer is that since morality is an essential ingredient of everyone's welfare in our society because it protects the conditions in which we can make good lives for ourselves, conformity to it is justified.

One sign of conformity is that deep prohibitions appear as intuitively binding. If these intuitive limits are widely shared, then they define simple moral situations and the proper sphere for moral intuitions. The deep prohibitions are then expressible as the major premise of the Aristotelian scheme. Ideally, it is in terms of these that well-trained moral agents react intuitively in the appropriate moral situations.

In this ideal state, society is cohesive and enduring partly because its members largely agree about how they must not treat each other. Their agreement rests on attachment to shared and strongly held deep prohibitions, and the prevailing morality embodies them. Many of the prohibitions have endured for generations, so they have been tested in practice and survived. Members of the society conduct themselves accordingly, and they expect others to do likewise. Their attempts to live good lives are made possible by the prevailing morality, so they value it, and they are rightly protective of it. One of the benefits of this ideal state is order, making it reasonable for people to have certain expectations about each others' conduct. These expectations rest on the justified assumption that members of a society are guided by the same moral sensibility developed through a shared moral education.

But it is not merely that the welfare of our society requires the existence of some moral prohibitions or another. There is good reason for holding that it requires the particular deep prohibitions our morality has, for they protect the fundamental requirements of human welfare, they guarantee the cohesion of the society by supporting order and the fulfillment of people's reasonable expectations about some limits that the conduct of others will not trespass, and so they constitute part of the framework in which individual endeavors to live good lives can proceed.

If we reflect on the moral life of our society, the first things that strike us are the conflicts, the turmoil, the violations, and the changes. This is the natural consequence of the disposition to notice the unusual and the unexpected, rather than the conformity to the deep prohibitions that most of us take for granted. In the vast majority of our impersonal interactions with other people, we simply—and correctly—assume that they, like we, will not, for instance, murder, mutilate, torture, or enslave others. It is only because these assumption normally hold that we become outraged by their violations or agonize over the exceptional situations in which the assumptions, for some reason, may not hold. Why else would we fight about euthanasia, abortion, capital punishment, and the like, if not because it is controversial whether they violate deep prohibitions? So, reflection on our conduct will lead to the recognition that behind the violations we argue about, there is the order and predictability we, as a matter of course, assume. And it is only because we are justified in holding this assumption that we can go on to live the lives we want to live. Our morality guarantees this possibility, and that is why it is reasonable to uphold its deep prohibitions, whatever may be true of other parts of it.

Nevertheless, it remains true that moral intuitions are fallible. But now we are able to diagnose the sources of their fallibility and, most important, recognize how mistaken intuitions could be corrected. Moral intuitions may fail either because the agents confuse complex moral situations with simple ones or because the morality from which they derive their intuitions is itself faulty. Both kinds of mistakes are easily corrigible.

Whether a moral situation is simple or complex depends on whether the prohibition contained in the major premise of its reconstruction in terms of the Aristotelian scheme is deep. The prohibition is deep if it concerns the undeserved violation of some minimum requirement of human welfare. What these requirements are is a plain question of fact, and answering it is within the competence of all normal moral agents. The same goes for the violation being undeserved; it is undeserved if there is no acceptable moral justification for it. A moral justification is acceptable in this context if, and only if, it licenses the violation of some deep prohibition on the ground that it prevents even greater simple evil than the violation itself would cause. And this too is a matter that typical moral agents can normally judge for themselves.

The other source of the fallibility of moral intuitions is the unreliability of the morality in the background. This can happen to a morality if it is disintegrating or undergoing fundamental revision. In such cases, the consensus about what prohibitions are deep is itself changing, and so moral situations can no longer be intuitively identified as simple. In a disintegrating morality, such as France during the Terror, Russia shortly after the fall of the czar, or Germany under Hitler, even the best-trained people had some reason to question their intuitions, for there were widespread disagreements about whether or not the old prohibitions should continue to be held. And even for those who continued to hold them, the ready test provided by the concurrence of other people became unavailable. In societies whose morality is undergoing fundamental revision, the situation is less dangerous because deep prohibitions and intuitive appeals to them may still be reliable in areas free of change. For instance, just because we, in our present circumstances, cannot trust our intuitions about sexual matters does not mean that we cannot trust them about murder, torture, mutilation, and enslavement. But once again, whether it is justifiable to revise or abandon deep prohibitions is an easily answerable question. Moral agents merely have to look around themselves to see whether people are being murdered, tortured, mutilated, or enslaved in their midst.

So, the way out of the first complication regarding the intuitive identification of deep prohibitions is to recognize the two main ways in which we can go wrong. If our moral intuitions are challenged on the ground that we have erred in one of these ways, then we can evaluate the challenge by reflecting on the intuition in the manner I have indicated above. If, however, the challenge is not grounded on the suspicion that this has happened, then we can respond to it by inviting the challenger, who may be ourselves, to provide some ground for the challenge. Failing this, we are justified in dismissing it, for if there is no ground for doubting the obvious, then there is no need to justify it either.

Let us turn then to the second complication about our knowledge of deep prohibitions through moral intuition. The complication occurs because our intuitive knowledge of moral situations includes, in addition to deep prohibitions, also prohibitions of a milder nature. A morality contains much more than deep prohibitions of simple evil. There is also complex evil, that is, undeserved harm that derives from violating the requirements of particular forms of good lives; and of course there are also various kinds of prescriptions about pursuing good lives. So, a morality will have prohibitions of complex evil and prohibitions against violating its various prescriptions. I have said little about these kinds of prohibitions, and I do not propose to discuss them now, since this book concentrates on simple evil. But this second complication forces us to recognize their existence because properly educated moral agents have a sensibility to which many prohibitions of both complex evil and violation of prescriptions will intuitively appear just as binding as deep prohibitions do. How, then, do they know which prohibitions are deep?

We cannot dismiss the question by smugly thinking that just as long as moral agents conform to the prohibitions of their morality, there is no need to worry about how deep the prohibitions are. For deep prohibitions are of simple evil, and they define simple moral situations. The objectivity of our moral judgments depends on our ability to identify such situations. If we could not do that, we could not tell which moral judgments apply to all people, always, everywhere, and which are the products of historically, culturally, or individually variable conditions. And then we could not distinguish between the violation of some minimum requirement of human welfare and the violation of some idiosyncratic rule. As a result, we could not criticize or justify moral conduct on the grounds that it advances or retards the cause of human welfare. Therefore, the alternative to answering the question is a pernicious relativism that regards all conduct as morally acceptable, provided it is part of the morality of a society.

The first step toward answering the question is to draw a sharp distinction between a prohibition's being deep and its being strongly held in a particular society. Whether a prohibition is deep depends solely on whether it protects a minimum requirement of human welfare. Thus, a prohibition could be deep, even if everyone in a society thinks otherwise. Whether or not a prohibition is strongly held in a society depends on the prevailing moral sensibility. That sensibility informs moral conduct and moral education, so there is a tendency to perpetuate strongly held prohibitions and to allow moral change in respect to weakly held ones.

Part of a society's being in a state of good moral health is that the set of deep prohibitions and the set of most strongly held prohibitions coincide. In that case, the prevailing moral sensibility is fundamentally opposed to the most serious kind of evil that could befall its members. Less serious evil is prohibited less strongly. So, there is a direct correlation between the depth of prohibitions and the strength with which they ought to be held.

This desirable correlation can be upset in two ways. There may be deep prohibitions that are unrecognized or merely weakly held. If that happens, the minimum requirements of human welfare, which the prohibitions ought to be protecting, will stand in jeopardy. As a result, in that society the endeavors of people to live good lives will be undermined. The natural reaction of people thus affected is to withdraw their allegiance from the prevailing morality. If the reaction is widespread, disintegration will follow. The other way the correlation can be upset is if the most strongly held prohibitions in a society are not deep. In such a society, at least part of morality will be ill founded. When reasonable people wonder about the moral justification of these most strongly held prohibitions, the good answer—that they protect the minimum requirements of everyone's welfare—will not be available. Ultimately, the prohibitions will rest on arbitrary authority maintained by threat, force, and deception. These can prevail for a long time, but it is unlikely that the allegiance thus extracted will be wholehearted or lasting. In any case, if deep prohibitions are not strongly held, the prevailing morality is too tolerant of evil; if the most strongly held prohibitions are not deep, the morality concentrates on the wrong things.

We can now deal with the complication produced by the possibility of confusion between deep and other prohibitions. The complication is due to the confusion of deep prohibitions with strongly held ones. If a society is in good moral health, the confusion does not occur, because deep prohibitions are held most strongly and the most strongly held prohibitions are deep. The intuitive knowledge of one would ipso facto be intuitive knowledge of the other. But since few, if any, societies are in good moral health, the confusion does occur. However, now that we know what causes it, we also know how the mistakes that follow may be corrected.

Moral intuitions are appropriate in simple moral situations. There is a deep prohibition, an action that clearly violates it, and the agent's recognition that the action therefore is not to be taken. If moral agents have reason to think that prohibitions that they regard as deep may only be strongly held, they have a ready test available to them to resolve their doubt. They need to ask whether or not what is prohibited is indeed simple evil. As we have seen, people can normally answer that question quite easily if the facts are available to them, for it is not hard to tell whether someone is being murdered, tortured, mutilated, or enslaved. If the facts are not available, then the conditions for intuition are lacking in any case, and then reflection should take the place of spontaneous response. On the other hand, if moral agents have reason to think that some action would cause simple evil, although there is no deep prohibition against it in their society, then the test, once again, is to get clear about whether what they suspect to be a case of simple evil is indeed so. In this manner, the mistaken intuitions caused by the confusion between deep and strongly held convictions may be corrected.

But to say that the mistakes may be corrected is not to say that they will be corrected, for correction requires questioning the morality from which intuitions follow. It requires moral agents not merely to conform to what their morality regards as deep prohibitions but to make sure that it is correct to regard them as such. It appears, therefore, that part of the motivation to conform to the deep prohibitions of a particular morality must be to reflect critically on that very morality. And this brings us to the third question raised earlier about the institutional dimension of character-morality: why should reasonable moral agents be motivated to conform to deep prohibitions?

THE MOTIVATION TO CONFORM TO DEEP PROHIBITIONS

At the beginning of this chapter, I distinguished between the institutional and personal dimensions of character-morality. The first is a set of external requirements among which, I have gone on to argue, deep prohibitions occupy pride of place. The second includes the impetus internal to moral agents to live in conformity to the external requirements. Part of the ideal of character-morality is that the external requirements and the internal impetus should coincide because moral agents justifiably see the external requirements as protecting the conditions in which they can endeavor to live good lives, and so they are naturally motivated to live in conformity to them.

The argument in this chapter concentrated on the institutional dimension of character-morality. My aim was to bring out the way in which the prevailing morality informs the sensibility of moral agents and influences their conduct. And this way, I argued, was largely intuitive. Normally, moral agents learn about their morality the same way as they learn about using their body or speaking their native language. And once they have learned it, they simply go on as they have learned unless something unusual interrupts them. Choice, deliberation, and commitment usually play no appreciable role in this process.

The significance of this process for the overall argument of the book is that the institutional dimension of character-morality is now identifiable as an influence upon moral agents, alongside the influence exerted by the essential conditions of life. But while the essential conditions of life tend to exert an evil influence, the ideal of character-morality is to exert a good influence.

The tragic view of life depicts our situation as a state of tension between the essential conditions of life and our aspirations to live good lives. I attempted to show in the first part of the book that if we want to live a good life, we must face the evil influences upon us. In the previous chapter and in this one, I have begun to consider what we can do after we have faced evil and in response to it. And so far, my answer has been that what we can do is to conform to the institutional dimension of character-morality in order to protect the conditions for living good lives.

Yet this answer provides no more than a necessary condition of good lives; as it stands, it is insufficient. Two intimately connected considerations show that this is so. The first is that even if everything I have argued for is accepted as true, the conclusion would merely permit us to recognize that the tragic view of life is correct, that there are indeed good and evil influences contending in us. The most that my argument could be said to have accomplished is that of showing how the good influences may be derived from the institutional dimension of character-morality. Tragedy amply shows the operation of evil influences, and so my argument, it may be granted, acts as a counterweight. But nothing I have said so far shows that we are justified in having any hope. Our situation, for all I have said, remains tragic, because we are not in control of the influences that shape our lives, and they may force us in directions we recognize as evil. Everything I have said about moral intuitions is true of Oedipus, Lear, and Kurtz, and it did not give them good lives, nor did it help them to avoid causing evil. And the very source of the evil caused by people who are ruled by the vices of insufficiency, expediency, and malevolence may be that they are understandable products of their morality. What is left out of my account is a way of resolving the tension between good and evil. We would have justifiable ground for hope if there were some way of achieving some control over the influences to which we are subject and if we could use that control to foster the good and to curb the evil in us. The possibility of such control rests within the personal dimension of character-morality.

The second consideration showing the insufficiency of the present state of my account follows from the complications moral agents were shown to encounter in resolving their doubts about whether strongly held prohibitions in their society are deep prohibitions. We have seen that to resolve such doubts they have to go beyond the deliverances of their moral sensibility and reflect critically on the morality from which their intuitions follow. This certainly can be done, because it has been done by countless people, but what we need to understand is why reasonable moral agents would be motivated to do it. Why would people with the vices of insufficiency, expediency, and malevolence question what seems obvious to them? The short answer is that they should question it to avoid the bad end to which they are likely to come as a result of their unreflective actions. But to have this short answer to the question of *why* reasonable moral agents would reflect critically on their morality is not yet to know *how* they could do so. If what they do is often influenced by forces beyond their control, whether forces for the good, such as morality ought to be, or forces for the evil, such as the essential conditions of life tend to be, then the very attempt to reflect critically on these forces is itself subject to their control. Thus, we are led, as before, to the question of how control is possible. And the answer to it, as we noted before, will come from the personal dimension of character-morality.

CHAPTER TEN

The Personal Dimension of Character-Morality: The Possibility of Control

UNDERSTANDING AND HOPE

If the tragic view of life is correct, we are not in control of our lives, because we are at the mercy of the essential conditions of life. I shall argue in this chapter that this is a half-truth. There are many aspects of our lives we cannot control, but there are also others whose control is possible, and it is also possible to enlarge our control. The tragic view portrays us as embodying a tension between good and evil, between our aspirations to live good lives and the vices of insufficiency, expediency, and malevolence through which the essential conditions of life often act to jeopardize our aspirations. Thus, our situation is seen as tragic.

My view is that what makes tragic situations tragic is partly our response to them. Tragedy is not intrinsic to the world; we collude in producing it. The tension between aspirations toward good lives and vices sabotaging their realization undoubtedly exists in us. But this, in itself, is not tragic. It is merely a fact, perhaps a sad one, of life. There are a lot of tensions between contrary forces that few regard as tragic; reason and passion, freedom and equality, science and religion, creativity and comfort, and breadth and depth are not usually thought of as standing in a tragic tension. We regard as tragic the tension between good and evil in us because it makes us frightened, outraged, disappointed, resigned, defiant, or defeated. We expect life to be otherwise, we find out that it is not, our feelings overflow, so we call it tragic. The first requirement of the possibility of control is to understand that this is so. My remarks are intended to describe in some detail the nature of this desirable understanding.

In going about the business of living our lives, we possess a limited amount of energy. Much of it is spent on perpetuating ourselves and on generating more energy. However, in this respect at least, we have been immensely successful. Our limited stock of energy is not exhausted by the need to satisfy our physical requirements. In civilized circumstances, we have enough left over to consider alternative courses of action, to reflect on how we should decide between them, and thus to some extent to control the manner in which we live our lives. We are not wholly driven by necessity: there is a gap between what we must and what we can do. Our recognition that this gap exists makes it possible for us to encourage or discourage some of the natural tendencies we find in ourselves.

One of the half-truths that lends force to choice-morality is its insistence on the importance of this gap. The gap *is* there, and it *is* important. But its importance is other than what defenders of choice-morality take it to be. It is not that morality lies on the side of the gap where choices are possible, while on the other side, where necessity rules, moral considerations have no foothold. The domain of morality includes both sides because human welfare is affected both by forces we can control and by those we cannot. The importance of the gap is that it reveals the possibility of control, the possibility of not being helpless in the face of the essential conditions of life. To be sure, control does not mean that in this limited area we can change the essential conditions of life. It means that we can shape our responses to these conditions. The control our choices make possible does not define the domain of morality; it defines one possible area of moral improvement.

I have accepted the diagnosis offered by the tragic view of life that the primary source of the secular problem of evil is that the tension within moral agents between the aspiration to live good lives and the essential conditions of life is resolved by the second subverting the first. But agreeing with the diagnosis does not commit me to the sense of hopelessness that follows from the tragic view. The possibility of control holds out the prospect of modest but true hope.

One aim of this chapter is to begin to answer the question of what should be our personal, as opposed to institutional, reaction toward the evil we cause as instruments of the essential conditions of life. If we reject the tragic view but acknowledge that contingency, indifference, and destructiveness may put our projects in jeopardy and that we are likely to come up against them because they are embedded in our makeup, what can we do then? My answer is that although we cannot avoid the adversity the essential conditions of life present, we can forge a reasonable response toward it. This is what may allow us modest hope.

The first requirement of this reasonable response is to enlarge our understanding of the essential conditions of life by taking a more generous view of what essential conditions can be inferred from nature. If humanity is part of the natural world, then what we are and do, what we experience, and what happens to us are also part of it. One of the things that happens to us is that our aspirations to live good lives are jeopardized by the contingency, indifference, and destructiveness we encounter. No matter how reasonable and decent our projects are, they may founder on the inhospitable essential conditions of life. The fact that they may founder in this way is the additional essential condition of life an enlarged understanding yields.

This understanding has both an individual and a general dimension. Individually, it is understanding that our personal aspirations are subject to the vicissitudes of contingency, indifference, and destructiveness, quite independently of our merits as agents or of the merits of our projects. Generally, it is understanding that what is true of ourselves is also true of humanity, that all human projects are in jeopardy because of the existence of evil.

The type of understanding I am describing is continuous with knowledge of other essential conditions. This will be apparent if we compare it with knowledge we may have of the essential conditions of life for nonhuman species. We may know what these conditions are for various kinds of living things. But in having this knowledge, we may or may not be engaged with it, and if we are engaged, our attitude may range anywhere from loving concern, through indifference, to hostility. Pandas and Great Danes are one thing; AIDS viruses, mosquitoes, and poisonous snakes are another.

Now, our understanding of the contingency, indifference, and destructiveness affecting *us* is like our knowledge of other species in that it has a descriptive component that would be the same for Martians and dolphins if they could describe the essential conditions of our lives. But it is also unlike it because it is not optional what attitude *we* have toward these conditions. Martians could remain uncommitted witnesses to our being buffeted by the essential conditions of our lives, but we cannot have that attitude. We care about the lives these conditions jeopardize, since they are our own.

So, although our understanding of the contingency, indifference, and destructiveness affecting our lives may start out as descriptive knowledge, it cannot remain so. For we are forced to realize that what we know has considerable significance for our aspirations, and so we are bound to care about it. Hence, the mere possession of this descriptive knowledge carries with it the motivation to acquire deeper understanding. Thus, actually, the enlargement of our understanding is not the imposition of an alien task but the cultivation of a pre-existing natural tendency. If this natural tendency becomes a significant force in our sensibility, we shall have ground for modest hope.

In support of this claim, consider why we find the situations of Oedipus, Lear, and Kurtz tragic. It cannot merely be because Oedipus was manipulated into doing what he regarded as immoral, Lear's suffering and improvement led only to more suffering, and Kurtz found himself succumbing to his own destructive impulses. After all, sad as it is, inflicting unwitting injury on those we love, disproportionate suffering, and self-loathing are common enough. Nor will it elevate them to the level of tragedy if we understand that their significance transcends the individual calamities depicted, because they reveal the essential conditions of life. What makes these figures emblematic for the tragic view of life is that their lives embody a conflict between the essential conditions of life and something else. Now, this something else is not just human aspirations; it is not even morally praiseworthy aspirations pursued reasonably and decently. What makes them emblematic is that the *expectation*—that if we pursue morally praiseworthy aspirations reasonably and decently we shall succeed—is shown by them to conflict with the essential conditions of life. Thus, the disappointed expectation is necessary for the tragic view of life. One benefit of possessing the enlarged understanding I am advocating is that it weakens the hold this expectation has on us.

Now, the expectation is *ours*, that is, of thoughtful readers of these stories. Oedipus, Lear, and Kurtz did not claim that their situations were tragic; they merely caused and suffered evil and were shown to do so. *We* see their situations as tragic because *we* have the expectation that contingency, indifference, and destructiveness will be overcome by reason and decency, and our expectation is disappointed. So, we respond to the signs of tragedy. We see the futility of human will and intellect, we watch the heroes discover their flaws, we see their fortunes reversed, we achieve a greater clarity of vision, and we see the motivating virtues and the vices. The result of our disappointed expectation is that we come to see human lives as tragic, and we are assailed by a sense of hopelessness. To see deeply, as the tragic view of life teaches us to do, is to see that there is no consolation, no hope.

But if we do not have this expectation, we shall not regard its disappointment as tragic. If we understand that reason and decency are insufficient for the successful pursuit of good lives because the essential conditions of life may frustrate even the noblest aspiration toward even the best lives, and that the lives may be our own, then the intrusion of evil will not come as a devastating surprise. The facts that produce tragic situations remain the same; what changes is that we have developed an enlarged understanding of them.

It may be objected that the possibility of achieving this understanding itself depends on the essential conditions of life and not on the agents' choices; hence, my advocacy of it is pointless. I think that the extent to which contingency, indifference, and destructiveness influence our conduct varies with people and circumstances. In some cases, their influence is decisive; we are powerless to resist it, and then my recommendation *is* pointless. It would be misplaced, if not obscene, to urge people on the way to the gas chamber to cultivate an enlarged understanding of the essential conditions of life. But not all situations are like this. In less extreme ones, it is possible to stand back and attempt to understand what is happening. Certainly Oedipus, Lear, and Kurtz could have done so before tragedy overtook their lives. So, my reply is that the cultivation of an enlarged understanding has a point for the vast majority of people whose lives are threatened, but not dominated, by the essential conditions.

But, it will be asked, why is it more desirable to pursue our projects with the understanding that they are vulnerable to evil no matter how hard and well we try to succeed at them than to have that understanding come to us as a result of failure? The answer is that having the understanding improves our lives. It equips us to cope with the evil we find in us and around us better than Oedipus, Lear, and Kurtz were able to do.

Consider Kurtz to begin with. Nothing he could have done would have removed destructiveness from his nature. But if he had had a better understanding, he would have known about its presence and motivating force. And then it would not have caused him a horrible shock to discover that he was moved by his own evil motives to act in ways that were at once natural and abhorrent to him. The point is not that the possession of better understanding would have freed Kurtz from his compulsion to do evil. We must assume with Conrad that the compulsion was irresistible, given the circumstances Kurtz created for himself. He removed himself from the familiar context where conventional constraints added their civilizing influence to internal constraints, and since his internal constraints were much too weak, he naturally acted on his evil impulses. The point is that if he had understood this about himself, he would not have selected of all the projects available to him one that was so likely to lead to his downfall. As Conrad shows us, Kurtz applied himself; he truly tried, and he failed. But to see him as tragic, and as emblematic of one type of human failure, is to overlook the fact that he got into trouble because he ignored the remedy readily available to mitigate his defect: the cultivation of the appropriate sort of understanding.

Thus, what caused Kurtz's downfall was not merely the inexorable force of destructiveness in his character. The cause was also his failure to develop his understanding of this force moving him. If he had had it, he would not have taken such great pains to create circumstances in which his destructiveness would have free rein. The understanding Kurtz lacked has an action-guiding force that can, in some cases, minimize, neutralize, or override the expression of destructiveness. Its success depends not on somehow eliminating destructiveness but on making itself felt at an earlier stage, before the destructive course of action is set in motion. At that stage it is still often possible to erect obstacles, to strengthen defenses, to remove the opportunities for and the temptations of destructiveness—provided, of course, that we understand the need for them. So, we are not totally hopeless in the face of destructiveness. The more understanding we possess, the less likely it is that we shall select projects conducive to the removal of the constraints on destructiveness.

Let us turn to Lear next. We must accept as given Lear's character defects, his suffering and moral improvement, Cordelia's unmerited death, and Lear's renewed and, this time, undeserved suffering. What can we learn from them about coping with the moral indifference of the world? The tragic view of life is correct in seeing that there is no cosmic justice assuring that at least in the long run we shall get what we deserve. What is missing from it is the recognition that we have constructed a system of human justice that stands as a mediating structure between us and our due. Of course, it is an imperfect system, riddled with inconsistencies, abuses, stupidity, and maladministration. But imperfect as it is, it stands as a bulwark between civilized life, in which at least lip service is being paid to giving people what they deserve, and barbarism, where there is no question of rewarding merit and punishing its opposite. And of course even if human justice functioned perfectly, it would still not be able to overcome the lack of cosmic justice. At best, human justice guides us in giving each other what is due, but we may be prevented from getting what we deserve by forces and circumstances over which we have no control. So, human justice is a fragile and inadequate device for coping with the moral indifference of nature.

At first, Lear does not understand either the lack of cosmic justice or the imperfection of human justice. As the play progresses and the consequences of his own injustice are visited upon Lear, he comes to understand the fickleness of human justice. But his belief in cosmic justice is still untouched. When Cordelia is killed, the illusion is killed with her, and we see the utter hopelessness Lear sees. This hopelessness, however, will not be ours if we do not have the illusory expectation of cosmic justice. The alternative is not false hope but understanding the essential conditions of life and our vulnerability to them, prompting us to respond to the unsurprising failure of human justice by trying to strengthen the stumbling system. This will not make it easier to bury our own Cordelias. However, if we have understood the nature and imperfections of the ideal of justice, we shall be less likely to respond to its failure by hopelessness, resulting in a further weakening of justice, and more likely to try to mitigate the adverse conditions that brought the calamity about. The alternative response will involve us in a collusion to produce the next calamity.

It is instructive to compare Socrates' response to the injustice done to him by Athens to Lear's desperation. Socrates saw the lessons he spent a lifetime teaching repudiated, he was falsely accused of a crime whose commission would have been a betrayal of his deepest conviction, and he was sentenced to death because most of the people he tried so hard to influence rejected what he stood for and blamed him for taking that stand. Yet his response was to support the system, no matter how unjust it was to him. He had the understanding Lear lacked, and when it came to the point, he was guided by it. Socrates may stand as an ideal for the rest of us. And the ideal in this case is that of character-morality: to maintain a system designed to give us our due, while recognizing its unavoidable imperfections. It is very difficult, and sometimes psychologically impossible, to be guided by this ideal when its imperfections cause the collapse of our own lives. Yet there is no reasonable alternative to upholding it, for without it, life would be even worse.

I turn to Oedipus last. His is the strongest case for hopelessness because the contingency it reveals is the least amenable to mitigation. But not even his case shows that life is hopeless; what it shows is how dangerous life is and how vulnerable we are. The circumstances in which we have to pursue our projects are often beyond our control. This may be so because we do not understand the forces that produce the circumstances or because, although we understand them, we do not know what to do about them. Arguably, science is our greatest achievement. It has done a very great deal to enlarge the area of our control. But much as that is, we have no difficulty in imagining countless situations in which we are as boxed in as Oedipus was in his. We must act, and whatever we do will be a serious violation of something we really value. What can we do?

We can, it seems to me, minimize the damage. The first step toward it is to understand the corrosive effects of contingency. The second is to judge the violations of others and of ourselves in the light of that understanding, as the extenuating version of the Principle ("ought implies can") prescribes. Blame and self-blame, shame and guilt, should be mitigated by the recognition that the evil contingency forces us to do, although undeniably evil, reflects less adversely on us, as its agents, than the evil we produce by choice. We see why Oedipus blinded himself. And we see also that another, less imperfect

Oedipus, who had the understanding he lacked, would have been gentler with himself than the actual Oedipus was.

The best I can say about minimizing the damage caused by contingency is that if we have the enlarged understanding I am recommending, we shall cultivate a morality more forgiving of violations due to contingency than the Greeks did. Nevertheless, it seems to me that it remains one of the essential conditions of life that contingency may not just make us act in evil ways but may make us evil.

I have been arguing that our sensibility is not without resources in contending with the adversity produced by the essential conditions of life. We are not doomed to a choice between false hope and living with the hopelessness bred by the tragic view of life. The alternative is to cultivate better understanding of the essential conditions of life and of how they may jeopardize our projects. Hopelessness is due to the unavoidable disappointment of the misguided expectation that reality is permeated by a prohuman order, that there is cosmic justice, and that destructiveness is under the control of our will and intellect. I have been arguing for enlarged understanding, one that acknowledges the pervasive forces of contingency, indifference, and destructiveness and motivates us to mitigate their consequences, while realizing that we may fail.

This enlarged understanding, leading to reduced expectations, is the ground for true hope. True hope is chastened hope; a hope purified and strengthened by having jettisoned the expectation of salvation. What is left is not much, but it is enough to fend off hopelessness. Although our projects may run afoul of the essential conditions of life, they need not suffer this fate. And even if they are damaged, they may not be destroyed. The enlarged understanding I am recommending permits true hope because it saves those who possess it from the futility of hounding the unresponsive heavens to relieve their misfortune and because it prepares the people who have grown to develop it to pick up the damaged pieces, if they can be picked up, and go on. True hope does not come from there being a guarantee that good projects reasonably conducted will succeed. It comes from the confidence that we have done what is in our power to make them succeed and that if they fail despite our merits and efforts, we need not be destroyed as a result. Thus, the possession of an enlarged understanding does not promise good lives; it promises to make lives as free from evil as the essential conditions permit.

The understanding I have been describing is a necessary condition of gaining greater control over our lives, but it is not sufficient for it. I shall proceed toward a fuller account of the possibility of control by examining three contemporary but flawed responses to the secular

problem of evil, responses that are based on the enlarged understanding I regard as important. I shall try to show in this chapter and
the next one why they are flawed and then use them as foils to help
complete my account of the possibility of control.

PRAGMATISM

I have argued that the enlarged understanding required for the possibility of control is, by its nature, action-guiding—reasonable people
will be moved to some response once they realize the fragility of their
efforts to make good lives for themselves. The question is what this
response should be so as to reduce the chances of failure, and Sidney
Hook proposes one answer.[1] Hook's statement of what I have called
the secular problem of evil and his explanation of its significance
leave nothing to be desired, so it seems clear that he possesses the
enlarged understanding I regard as a necessary condition of the development of a reasonable response. But then Hook combines this
understanding with a pragmatic response that, I shall argue, cannot
achieve its intended purpose.

Hook says that "the pragmatic approach to tragedy . . . does not
conceive of tragedy as a pre-ordained doom, but as one in which the
plot to some extent depends on us, so that we become creators of our
own tragic history. We cannot then palm off altogether the tragic outcome upon the universe in the same way as we can with a natural
disaster" (20). The aim of the pragmatic approach is "to make it possible for men to live in a world of inescapable tragedy . . . without
lamentation, defiance or make-believe. . . . [F]or even in the best of
human worlds there will be tragedy" (22). So far, of course, I strongly
agree. But Hook goes on, as he should, to explain how the pragmatic
approach is going to accomplish its desirable goal. And he says that it
does so by focusing "its analysis on problems of normative social in-
quiry in order to reduce the cost of tragedy" (22). What we should
get out of this analysis is "some method of negotiating conflicts of
value by intelligence. . . . But intelligence may not be enough . . . because of limitations of our knowledge, because of the limited reach of
our powers of control" (22–23). When we encounter these limitations, the remedy is to seek more knowledge and control. The trouble
with the scientific scheme of solving our problems is "not that it was
scientific, but that it wasn't scientific enough" (42). And how do we
become sufficiently scientific? By endeavoring to "find moral equiva-

---

[1] Hook, "Pragmatism and the Tragic Sense of Life" and "Intelligence and Evil in
Human History." References in the text are to the pages of the volume in which these
essays appeared.

lents for the expression of natural impulses which threaten the structure of our values" (25) through devoting "greater attention to *methods of action* by which political and institutional programs are carried out" (41). So the diagnosis is that if our schemes of problem solving fail, the fault lies with insufficient knowledge and control. And this suggests that the cure is greater knowledge and control.

In all this, Hook has provided an eloquent reaffirmation of his faith in social-scientific engineering and progress, but the fine rhetoric ignores the serious challenge posed by the tragic view of life. It is not, of course, that Hook is unaware of the challenge. He says, "The possibilities of human cruelty are ever present. The sudden rediscovery of its brutality by those who see the Nazi and Russian record of horror as signs of the crisis of our time adds nothing particularly enlightening. One wonders how they managed to escape learning the facts of political life so long. . . . [T]hese are characteristics which are pervasive. Almost every aspect of modern culture is marked by them" (29), and he adds that he is not "denying the demonic elements in human beings, that some human beings enjoy the spectacle of others' suffering, and that others suffer from compulsions to destroy the things or persons they love" (29). But how can he suppose that if we endeavor to correct our past failures at social-scientific engineering by increasing our knowledge and control, this new effort will be free from the "demonic element" that marks "almost every aspect of modern culture"? What has intervened between his understanding the significance of the secular problem of evil and his response to it that is given as if knowledge and control were free of evil? How can Hook both understand the problem so clearly and favor a "solution" that ignores what he has understood?

Of course, I do not know what went on in Hook's mind, nor am I interested in offering a psychological conjecture. My concern, rather, is with describing a line of thought that is sufficiently plausible to account for the gap between the clear understanding of the problem and the misguided pragmatic solution. It goes something like this. Humanity lives in an inhospitable world. We must cope with the adversity we encounter; otherwise we perish. We cannot count on outside help; we must rely on our own resources. It is true that our resources are tainted, but we have no acceptable alternative to using them. So, let us accentuate the positive and do our best to avoid calamity. Let reason and decency guide us, and if we fail, we should try to make amends by being more reasonable and decent, since there is nothing better we can do. Concentrating on the dark side of our life and fearing failure do not do us any good; on the contrary, they weaken our resolve. So, reasonable people avert their gaze; they focus on the task at hand and keep out of deep waters. Thus, we slide from understanding to a policy that ignores what we have understood. The lubricant is a carefully cultivated blindness.

Making ourselves blind in this way is wrong because it produces a self-defeating policy. If one main source of evil is in us, then it will do us no good whatever to pursue a policy for avoiding evil that ignores the possibility that the policy itself may propagate evil. People dominated by the vices of insufficiency, expediency, and malevolence could, as we have seen, sincerely and wholeheartedly embrace the pragmatic response. The trouble with this kind of self-imposed blindness is that it blocks the progression from understanding to a reasonable response. Whether we are entitled to modest hope depends on going on from understanding to a reasonable response. The question, of course, is how we can have even modest hope once we have faced evil in us and around us.

IRONY

The pragmatic response to the deeper understanding required for greater control propels us in the direction of misguided but energetic activity. The ironic response I shall now consider leads in the opposite direction, toward disengagement. It shifts our attitude from that of actors toward the attitude of spectators. It removes us from a wholehearted participation in our projects because, having understood the real possibility of failure in spite of the best efforts we can make, it encourages holding ourselves back.

The most thoughtful contemporary expression of this view is Thomas Nagel's.[2] He begins by attempting to understand what is meant by the claim that life is absurd. "In ordinary life a situation is absurd when it includes a conspicuous discrepancy between pretension or aspiration and reality: someone gives a complicated speech in support of a motion that has already been passed; a notorious criminal is made president of a major philanthropic foundation; you declare your love over the telephone to a recorded announcement" (13). The philosophical sense of absurdity is an extension of this ordinary sense. "The sense that life as a whole is absurd arises when we perceive, perhaps dimly, an inflated pretension or aspiration which is inseparable from the continuation of human life and which makes its absurdity inescapable, short of escape from life itself" (13). This sense "must arise from the perception of something universal—some

---

[2] Nagel, "The Absurd." References in the text are to the pages of the volume in which this essay appeared.

respect in which pretension and reality inevitably clash for us all. This condition is supplied . . . by the collision between the seriousness with which we take our lives and the perpetual possibility of regarding everything about which we are serious as arbitrary, or open to doubt" (13).

"Think," Nagel says, "of how an ordinary individual sweats over his appearance, his health, his sex life, his emotional honesty, his social utility, his self-knowledge, the quality of his ties with family, colleagues, and friends, how well he does his job, whether he understands the world and what is going on in it" (15). But, Nagel goes on, "Humans have the special capacity to step back and survey themselves and the lives to which they are committed with that detached amazement which comes from watching an ant struggle up a heap of sand. Without developing the illusion that they are able to escape from their highly specific and idiosyncratic position, they can view it *sub specie aeternitatis*—and the view is at once sobering and comical" (15).

What we find when we step back is "that the whole system of justification and criticism, which controls our choices and supports our claims to rationality, rests on responses and habits we never question, that we would not know how to defend without circularity, and to which we shall continue to adhere even after they are called into question" (15). "Yet when we take this view and recognize what we do as arbitrary, it does not disengage us from life, and there lies our absurdity: not in the fact that such an external view can be taken of us, but in the fact that we ourselves can take it, without ceasing to be the persons whose ultimate concerns are so coolly regarded" (15).

Nagel's diagnosis is that the absurdity of life is due to a tension in us between our projects and our recognition that even though the projects are in the last analysis arbitrary, we nevertheless continue to remain attached to them. And he suggests that irony may be the appropriate response to absurdity: "If a sense of the absurd is a way of perceiving our true situation . . . then what reason can we have to resent or escape it? . . . If *sub specie aeternitatis* there is no reason to believe that anything matters, then that does not matter either, and we can approach our absurd lives with irony" (23).

The ironic attitude Nagel recommends is cool, collected, civilized. It is especially appealing to thoughtful people who live in peace, security, and comfort and thus enjoy the luxury of being able to cultivate the sub specie aeternitatis perspective in tranquility. There is much to be said for viewing our own ambitions and petty quarrels and the ups and downs of our career, prestige, bank account, and sexual performance with the sort of disengagement irony makes possible. For if we so view them, we shall care less about them, we shall live at a more even keel, life will be made calmer by the sense of proportion that distancing ourselves from our projects is likely to provide.

We may begin to suspect, however, that something is askew with this attitude if we see the incongruity of recommending it to Oedipus, Lear, or Kurtz. How could people be ironic if they discover that they have violated their own fundamental moral commitments and irretrievably harmed innocent people whose welfare they intended to protect? How could irony be appropriate in response to being shamed by our own moral failure, to witnessing serious evil, to beholding the spectacle of great and undeserved suffering? We might learn to view with irony our own efforts to climb to the next rung of whatever ladder we happen to be on, but should we learn to view torture, concentration camps, slave labor, and similar horrors "with that detached amazement which comes from watching an ant struggle up a heap of sand" (15)?

Nagel certainly does not recommend irony in the face of evil. His view is that we have the commitments we have, but in addition to them, we also have the capacity to view our commitments from an external nonanthropocentric vantage point. And when we exercise this capacity, then "we can approach our absurd lives with irony instead of heroism or despair" (23). The trouble with this is that, although Nagel does not advocate irony as a response to evil, the result is the same as if he did just that.

To see why this is so, let us inquire why we should exercise the capacity to view our lives and projects sub specie aeternitatis? The answer, I suppose, is that this perspective acts as a corrective to our biases. It moves us in the direction of greater objectivity and impersonality by relegating to the sidelines our hopes, fears, and petty concerns. It helps us to see how things are, rather than how they appear through the distorting lens of anthropocentrism. It is to acquire, as Nagel paradoxically puts it in the title of his most recent book, the view from nowhere.

It is clearly true that in many areas of life this corrective is at once necessary and important. We may think of the physical and perhaps biological sciences as attempts to institutionalize the objectivity and impersonality of the sub specie aeternitatis perspective. They aim to discover how some segment of the world is independent of our stake in its being hospitable to our interests. But Nagel's remarks are intended to apply across the board: not just to science, but also to morality. Is it necessary and important to correct anthropocentrism in morality?

Well, what would the correction be? Morality is centrally concerned with good and evil as they affect human beings. To correct the anthropocentrism of morality would be to view good and evil independently of how they affect human beings. But good and evil are benefit and harm—deserved and undeserved—affecting *something* in the world. If we applied this corrective and removed the centrality of our concerns with good and evil for humanity, whose good and evil would we be concerned with then? As Nagel himself says, "If we take the recommended backward step we will land in thin air, without any basis for judgment about the natural responses we are supposed to be surveying" (17). But, Nagel argues, "this objection misconceives the nature of the backward step. It is not supposed to give us understanding of what is *really* important. . . . We never, in the course of these reflections, abandon the ordinary standards that guide our lives. We merely observe them in operation, and recognize that if they are called into question we can justify them only by reference to themselves, uselessly. We adhere to them because of the way we are put together; what seems to us important or serious or valuable would not seem so if we were differently constituted" (17–18).

This is true in a trivial sense, but false in the sense that matters. If we were incapable of feeling pain, then we would not think of torture as a great evil. But surely, however we as moral agents are constituted, we are subject to good and evil, we may or may not deserve what happens to us, we have some conception of our welfare, and we care about it. Morality is a system designed to make the world as hospitable to our interests as possible. It is intended as an embodiment of many of the values that seem to us to be important and serious. It is supposed to protect the conditions in which we can make good lives for ourselves. Why should we "take the recommended backward step" from morality? And is it not obvious that if we were to take it, the result would be our disengagement from good and evil?

Nagel may accept this but goes on to point out that we can justify our concern with good and evil only by reference to our interests. And that, he says, is useless. But what is useless about it? What sort of justification would be required for caring reasonably about what matters to us? And what force does it have to say, truly and trivially, that if we adopted a point of view independent of our interests, then from that new point of view our interests would not matter?

In sum, we certainly have the capacity to take the sub specie aeternitatis perspective in any area of our lives. In some areas, the perspective is a desirable corrective, and it should be cultivated. In morality, however, it is not, because it weakens our already poor chances of avoiding evil.

ROMANTICISM

The most recent defender of the romantic response is Martha Nussbaum. Her book *The Fragility of Goodness: Luck and Ethics in Greek Tragedy and Philosophy*, is a deeply serious and provocative approach to many of the problems I have been discussing.[3] Indeed, my formulation of the secular problem of evil is in several ways indebted to Nussbaum's work, as I have noted at the appropriate places. However, although I agree with her about the problem and also about its importance, I disagree about the reasonable response to it.

Nussbaum celebrates our vulnerability to the essential conditions of life. She regards the obstacles they present as catalysts calling forth virtues that we otherwise would not have. She sees the inhospitability of the world to human welfare as an opportunity for cultivating the best of our potentialities. She acknowledges the influence of contingency, indifference, and destructiveness on human lives; she recognizes the dangers they present and the risks we face because of them, but she interprets them as spurs to human greatness. She concentrates on nobility, not on baseness; on prevailing, not on being crushed; on the exaltation of heroism, not on the humiliation of defeat. She sees the possibilities of life in Promethean terms. Her attitude is captured by Knox: "The hero offered the ancient Greeks the assurance that in some chosen vessels humanity is capable of superhuman greatness, that there are some human beings who can imperiously deny the imperatives which others obey in order to live. . . . [The hero] is a reminder that a human being may at times magnificently defy the limits imposed on our will . . . [and] may refuse to accept humiliation and indifference and impose his will no matter the consequences to others and himself."[4] This is a romantic and, as I believe, a flawed response.

Early in the book, Nussbaum poses the question: "To what extent *can* we distinguish between what is up to the world and what is up to us, when assessing human life? To what extent *must* we insist on finding these distinctions, if we are to go on praising as we praise? And how can we improve this situation, making progress by placing the most important things, things such as personal achievement, politics, and love, under our control?" (2). She goes on: "In general, to eliminate luck from human life will be to put that life, or the most important things in it, under the control of the agent . . . [by] removing the element of reliance upon the external and undependable" (3–4). But

---

[3] Nussbaum, *The Fragility of Goodness*. References in the text are to the pages of the book.
[4] Knox, *The Heroic Temper*, 57.

we cannot eliminate luck. Our situation is "that much that I did not make goes towards making me whatever I shall be praised or blamed for being; . . . that circumstances may force me to a position in which I cannot help being false to something or doing something wrong; that an event that simply happens to me may, without my consent, alter my life; that it is equally problematic to entrust one's good to friends, lovers, or country and to try to have a good life without them—all these I take to be not just the material of tragedy, but everyday facts of lived practical reason" (5). With all of this, of course, I am in complete agreement. This is just the enlarged understanding that will get us beyond the tragic view of life, if anything does. However, the question is how we should go on from this understanding. It is here that Nussbaum, in my view, starts going wrong.

Commenting on Aristotle and agreeing with him, Nussbaum writes: "It is plain that these central human values [i.e. justice, courage, generosity, moderation] . . . cannot be found in a life without shortage, risk, need, and limitation. Their nature *and* their goodness are constituted by the fragile nature of human life. . . . What we find valuable depends essentially on what we need and how we are limited" (341–42). But how does it follow from this observation that "the peculiar beauty of *human* excellence just *is* its vulnerability" (2) or that "human excellence . . . could not be made invulnerable and keep its own peculiar fineness" (2)? It is true that "shortage, risk, need, and limitation," that is, the essential conditions of life, require human excellences if we are to cope with them. But surely this does not support Nussbaum's conclusion that what is good about human excellence just is its vulnerability to conditions that both call it forth and threaten to destroy it. Imagine someone arguing that since a robust constitution is required for coping with disease, therefore the peculiar beauty of a robust constitution just is its vulnerability to disease. Nussbaum illegitimately passes from the true claim that without the inhospitable essential conditions of life there would be no need for many human excellences to the false claim that human excellences are partly constituted by our vulnerability to these adverse conditions.

Vulnerability is an evil because it jeopardizes human welfare. Human excellences are good because they increase our chances of avoiding the evil of vulnerability. If we were not vulnerable, we would not need many of the excellences we do, as a matter of fact, need. Yet vulnerability is no more part of excellence than disease is part of the robust constitution needed to resist it.

Having begun with this mistake, Nussbaum goes on to spell out the implications of the flawed argument. If vulnerability is part of excellence, then vulnerability is, to that extent, excellent. So, what we normally regard as evil—"shortage, risk, need, and limitations"—are actually good. "There is a certain valuable quality in social virtue that is lost when social virtue is removed from the domain of uncontrolled happenings" (420). Thus, Nussbaum's argument implies, for instance, that justice and decency are lessened unless they are practiced in a context of anarchy. Or, as she generalizes the point, the "willingness to embrace something that *is* in the world and subject to its risks is, in fact, the virtue . . . of love . . . directed at the world itself, including its dangers" (42). Thus, if I love you, I must love cancer as well.

What is responsible for the progression from a clear-sighted and humane understanding of our vulnerability to evil to an attitude that embraces evil as good? What could make the victim celebrate the whip? The answer is romanticism, as Nussbaum herself acknowledges: "Not all devotion to the uncertain is foolish romanticism; or, rather, that something that might be called foolish romanticism . . . may actually be an essential ingredient in the best life for the human being, as our best account, arrived at by the best method we know, presents it" (420). At the root of this romanticism, foolish or otherwise, there is the unwillingness to face evil. I shall discuss it by considering Nussbaum's treatment of the death of Polyxena in Euripides' *Hecuba*.[5]

Polyxena is a young woman, the daughter of the king and queen of Troy and the sister of the leader of the Trojan forces. The Greeks have just conquered Troy, killed her father and brother, as well as most Trojan men; looted and burned her City; and enslaved the women and children, including Polyxena and her mother. Polyxena awaits being awarded as a prize to one of the Greeks. Her world has irretrievably collapsed, and she is undergoing the worst that can happen to her. Then news is brought that she has been given to Achilles' son, who is about to sacrifice her in his father's honor. Polyxena's situation is hopeless, and she sees it as such.

> I wish to die . . . why should I live? (351)

> . . . I see nothing in this life
> to give me hope, and nothing here at all
> worth living for. (369–71)

> . . . I am a novice
> to this life of shame, whose yoke I might endure,
> but with such pain that I prefer to die
> than go on living. (375–78)

---

[5] Euripides, *Hecuba*. References in the text are to the lines of the play.

Later we hear of her courage as she stands alone, exposed, bared to the waist, in front of the Greek army, waiting to have her throat cut. And then she dies.

Now, consider Nussbaum's commentary: "We see the nobility of her hope throughout, in her unsuspicious responses. Most touching of all, perhaps, is her final display of maidenly modesty. As she fell in death ... even at that ultimate moment she took thought to arrange her skirts so that her body would not be revealed in an immodest way" (405). And she goes on, "The simple splendor of this girl is ... largely constituted by this trusting openness concerning the conventions that structure her life" (405–6). This is an extraordinary reaction to the great evil Euripides shows us. Polyxena finds "nothing in this life to give me hope" (369–70), Nussbaum remarks on "the nobility of her hope" (405); Polyxena finds "this life of shame" too painful to endure (376), and Nussbaum wants us to see "her unsuspicious responses ... this trusting openness" (405–6); Polyxena has her throat cut, and Nussbaum finds "most touching ... her ... maidenly modesty" (405). What could lead a perceptive and sensitive reader to such a skewed judgment?

The attitude behind the judgment is a passionate love of life—a love that makes one open, vulnerable, and receptive; a love that is oblivious to risk and danger, disdains safety, and concentrates on its object with an intensity that relegates everything else to insignificance. The risk Nussbaum proposes to ignore is to oneself, but the risk I am worried about is to those who happen to stumble into the path of this passion. It is a dangerous passion, and it ought to be controlled. Although it burns with great purity, it is indifferent to good and evil. The passion carries with it the flaws of the person possessed by it. Thus, it may be the love of Medea, leading her to brutal murder of her family, children, and a few others as well, or it may be the love of Maggie Verver in *The Golden Bowl*, which makes her forge a chain of lies, deception, blackmail, and veiled ambiguous threats to keep her lukewarm husband in thrall. Nussbaum celebrates Medea and Maggie, not, of course, for the evil persons they became, but for their discovery and passionate affirmation of the love that matters to them more than anything.[6] She sees this process as moral growth. Given this attitude, it becomes understandable why she would go to such extreme lengths to find traces of hope, trust, openness, and affirmation in the dejection of that poor, innocent, half-formed child-woman, Polyxena. And we can see also why she concentrates on these

---

[6] For Maggie Verver, see Nussbaum, "Flawed Crystals"; see also the criticism of it by Olafson, "Moral Relationships." For Medea, see Nussbaum, "Serpents in the Soul."

traces at the expense of the glaring and overwhelming facts that Polyxena was being slaughtered and her family was either killed or enslaved.

The danger in passionate love is that it obscures the evil that may be caused in its name. The point is not that love causes evil but that it seriously weakens the control we have over our actions. Love is not alone in this—all passions do that. They possess us and divert our moral attention. Many of them, and especially love, shout yes to life, but life is full of evil, as well as of good. This is why the indiscriminate affirmation of life involves an unwillingness to face evil. It is clearly expressed by Lawrence: "Resolve to abide by your deepest prompting, and to sacrifice the smaller thing to the greater. Kill when you must, and be killed the same: the *must* coming from the gods inside you."[7] Now, of course, neither Lawrence nor Nussbaum recommends evil. Nonetheless, what they recommend does lead to evil because contingency, indifference, and destructiveness act through us, and we are likely to cause evil unless we control what we do. As we have seen, our control is tenuous at best, but we can still strengthen or weaken it. The romanticism of Nussbaum tends to weaken it, and that is why it is a flawed response to the secular problem of evil.

From Understanding toward Control

The purpose of this chapter has been to explore the possibility of increasing the extent to which we can control our lives. For the more control we have, the less we are at the mercy of the essential conditions of life. The great difficulty is that increasing our control cannot take the form of changing the essential conditions of life, for they are part of the basic structure of the world. Thus, we cannot reasonably suppose that the attempt to increase our control is unaffected by the conditions whose control we are attempting. I have argued that the first step toward achieving greater control is to enlarge our understanding of the essential conditions of life. This will yield the realization that our optimistic expectation is mistaken, that morally laudable projects pursued reasonably and decently need not succeed. Even our best efforts may founder on contingency, indifference, and destructiveness, and the instruments through which these conditions make themselves felt may be ourselves. If we understand that this is so, we shall be moved toward abandoning the optimistic expectation. However, without the expectation, we cannot be the victims of tragic situations. To be sure, we may suffer great evil, and we ourselves may

[7] Lawrence, *Selected Essays*, 235.

be instrumental in causing the evil from which we suffer. But without the contrary expectation, we shall find this merely sad, not tragic.

The significance of the shift is that it brings with it a new attitude. It allows us to see evil in a new way—not as being caused by the inscrutable acts of the gods, not as the effects of the malevolent designs of moral monsters, not as the results of our own great crimes or sins, but as the natural consequences of trying to make our lives as good as possible in a world that is inhospitable to our efforts. To see evil in this way is to demythologize it, it is to understand it realistically, and it is to free our experience of it, either in ourselves or in others, from the shock, horror, outrage, and devastation that was the reaction of tragic heroes. Yet to have this new attitude, in which unrealistic expectation is replaced by enlarged understanding, does not by itself give us a way of achieving greater control. Perhaps it gives us a more reasonable way of coping with the suffering evil causes, but it is not sufficient for reducing the amount of evil in the first place.

Character-morality aims to make our lives better, partly by reducing evil. It attempts to do so by setting certain external and internal requirements that reasonable moral agents will accept as binding on their conduct. In the previous chapter, I discussed the external requirements that constitute the institutional dimension of character-morality. In this chapter, I have begun to discuss the internal requirements, the personal dimension of character-morality. My strategy has been first to describe the type of understanding that is an internal requirement of character-morality and then to start to move beyond it toward a response to what has been understood, by considering and criticizing three flawed responses: the pragmatic, the ironic, and the romantic. The reason behind this strategy is that through understanding the defects of these responses, it will become possible to construct a better one. I shall try to do so in the next chapter.

CHAPTER ELEVEN

The Personal Dimension of Character-Morality: The Reflective Temper

THE REFLECTIVE TEMPER AND THE FLAWED RESPONSES

The reflective temper is an attitude to life. I call this attitude a temper to emphasize that it is not merely a cognitive stance but also an emotive and a motivational one. Those who possess it have the enlarged understanding I described in the previous chapter, but they also go beyond it in their emotive reactions to what they have understood and in being motivated by their understanding and emotions. But the temper is also reflective because it is a considered and calm attitude toward the activities we perform in the mundane conduct of our affairs, in pursuing our various projects, in doing what needs to be done to stay alive, in perpetuating ourselves, in achieving some comfort, and in having what we like and avoiding what we dislike. Thus, the reflective temper forms part, as it were, of our judicial powers, rather than of the executive ones. It is not a way of doing but a way of ordering what we do, not one project among others but an attitude toward the projects we have.

We need to have such an attitude because the goodness of our lives depends on the suitability and success of our projects. However, my concern in this book has been not with the construction of promising projects but with the prospect of their failure. And the most serious kind of failure is one that threatens all projects, regardless of their merits. That this threat exists and that it renders all projects vulnerable is the secular problem of evil. The reflective temper is an attitude to life that takes due account of evil.

Now, the objects of the enlarged understanding that is constitutive of the reflective temper are some enduring truths about the human condition. The discovery of such truths has been the dominant ambition of rationalist thought in our philosophical tradition. It has been supposed by its champions that there are timeless truths whose knowledge would reveal the ultimate nature of reality and that those who conduct themselves according to it have a key to making their lives good. Plato, Aquinas, Spinoza, and Hegel are some of the great thinkers moved by this ambition. The tragic view of life implies, however, that it is impossible to realize this ambition. The problem is not that timeless truths are unknowable but that knowledge of them cannot give us comfort. For what we come to know is that contingency, indifference, and destructiveness permeate the scheme of things, and they render our projects vulnerable. Thus, the truth does not make us free; on the contrary, it reveals that we are at the mercy of forces we cannot control, forces that shape our very attempts to control them. Underneath the shifting currents we may observe on the surface, there are deeper currents, equally shifting. And it is like that all the way, as it goes forever vertiginously down.

This is the deep and enduring truth about life, and about the evil besetting it, to which the reflective temper must respond. An enlarged understanding gives us the truth, but being passive, it does not constitute an adequate response. Hence, the reflective temper must go beyond it. One way of doing so is by discovering and learning from the deeper reason why the pragmatic, ironic, and romantic responses proved unsatisfactory. The reason is the unwillingness of their champions to take full account of what our enlarged understanding implies.

Consider first the pragmatic response. Why do its defenders ignore the obvious point that since the failure of our reasonable and decent projects is often not due to insufficient reasonableness or decency, doing more of the same will not help? The answer is that pragmatists are committed to a deeper belief whose truth is incompatible with the assumption upon which the criticism is based. This deeper belief is that if our projects are sufficiently reasonable and decent, then they will succeed. If this were true, it could not happen that truly reasonable and decent projects fail. Hence, it would be justified to ignore the criticism. But it is not true, as we know from tragic situations; moreover, it is inconsistent with the enlarged understanding to which pragmatism is a response. So, at the root of the pragmatic response there is a predominantly cognitive defect: commitment to a belief whose falsehood pragmatists cannot fail to realize, and yet they proceed as if it were true. Why?

Take irony next. The clash of perspectives supposedly makes commitment to our projects seem absurd. From a nonhuman perspective, our concerns lack the importance they have from the human perspective. Since we can adopt both perspectives, we are simultaneously committed to our projects and recognize their arbitrariness. But once again, what about the obvious objection that it is a mistake to suppose that human judgments of importance should be separated from the human perspective, since things are important for *us*? Why should we seek to judge our projects from an alien perspective? That we occasionally judge them so is true, but we can cultivate or resist our inclination in that direction. If we cultivate it, as advocates of the ironic response recommend, we shall disengage ourselves from our projects, undermine our commitments, teach ourselves to pursue our projects less wholeheartedly, and thus lessen even further our chances of living a good life. Thus, the ironic response leads to a primarily motivational defect. Why do its defenders ignore the obviously undesirable outcome of their recommendation?

We come last to the romantic response. It reacts to our vulnerability by embracing it as a catalyst of moral growth. It is a celebration of life, a passionate affirmation of its risks and possibilities and of our capacity to respond to defeats and victories with nobility. However, it ought naturally to occur to us to ask, before we allow ourselves to be carried by this wave of enthusiasm, whether we really wish to affirm everything in life, including the evil we cause and suffer. Much as we may applaud appetite for life, verve, the willingness to take risks, and a passionate wholeheartedness, we must be more discriminating and careful than romanticism is likely to permit. For our energy can be put to life-diminishing uses, and in celebrating all of life, we may well be engaged in making it mean, vicious, and brutish. And this is not just a remote logical possibility but a realistic and ever-present threat, since, as our enlarged understanding reveals, such nobility as we may be capable of coexists in us with a like capacity for baseness. The flaw in the romantic response is the largely emotive defect of encouraging a passionate response to life that easily leads to carelessness about evil. This danger is bound to be known to defenders of romanticism because the vulnerability that they celebrate is partly due to the human capacity to cause evil, a propensity from which they cannot reasonably suppose the romantic response to be free. But if this is so, why is the obvious difficulty ignored by them?

The answer is the same in each case. Advocates of pragmatism, irony, and romanticism ignore criticisms they cannot fail to be aware of, because they are unwilling to face the full implications of evil. The criticisms are different: the defect pragmatism is charged with is predominantly cognitive, irony is faulted chiefly for motivational shortcomings, and the objection to romanticism is that it allows too much scope to our emotions. But the reason for ignoring them is the same utter hopelessness that seems to loom in the wake of their acceptance. If reason and decency are not enough, what else can we put in the scale to tilt the balance in our favor? If irony weakens our commitments, is it not better to want less what it is so dubious that we shall get? If our love of life may nourish the flowers of evil, is not affirmation with a chance of success still preferable to the bleakness that its absence promises?

It is very difficult to hold steadily in front of our attention the tenuousness of the control we have over our lives. The difficulty is exacerbated by there being no obvious answer to the question of what good it does to concentrate on the truth. The temptation is to acknowledge the truth intellectually and then quickly pass on to other things before it can poison our feelings and motivation.

But the difficulty is not insuperable, and there are good reasons why we should try to overcome it. Facing the full implications of evil is likely to increase our control, save us from unrealistic expectations, and make failure, if it comes to us, easier to bear. The reflective temper brings us from the intellectual acknowledgment of the truth that an enlarged understanding provides to allowing this understanding to have an appropriate influence on our feelings and motivation. I shall give an account of the reflective temper by correcting the cognitive, motivational, and emotive defects whose presence makes the pragmatic, ironic, and romantic responses flawed.

REFLECTION AND INCREASED CONTROL

The background of the reflection involved in the reflective temper is the enlarged understanding of the essential conditions of life. The question is how we should go on if we have this understanding. I have criticized the pragmatic response to it for ignoring what we have understood and for carrying on as if we did not have the understanding. Why and how, then, does it improve our response if we reflect on the truths the pragmatic response ignored?

Our response is improved by reflection on the essential conditions of life because it increases our control.[1] To be sure, increased control does not change the essential conditions of life; rather, it changes the extent to which they threaten us with evil. Thus, increased control makes us less vulnerable. But it does so by changing *us*—in particular, by changing our attitude to evil. What we learn to control is ourselves, both as victims and as agents of evil.

If we are the victims of evil, increased control does not change the undeserved harm that befalls us, but it makes the harm easier to bear. If we make an effort to reflect on our vulnerability to contingency, indifference, and destructiveness, then we shall be better able to cope with the undeserved failure of our projects than we would be other-

---

[1] My account of reflection is indebted to Stuart Hampshire's writings. See his *Thought and Action, Freedom of the Individual*, "Freedom of Mind," and "Spinoza and the Idea of Freedom."

wise. Reflection on our vulnerability improves our ability to cope with evil in three ways.

First, it keeps our expectations realistic. It stands as a continuous reminder that the success of human projects depends on countless conditions over which we have no control, that the past success and the intrinsic merits of our projects imply no guarantees for the future. Thus, it saves us from what the Greeks called *hubris*. It is not, of course, that the gods will punish us if we become too uppity and pridefully pit ourselves against the scheme of things. Rather, projects formed on the basis of unrealistic expectations about success will be much more likely to fail, and their failure is the punishment we get. Realistic expectations will help us to avoid some failures. They will also help us to accommodate failures we could not avoid, by preparing us for them.

This preparation is the second way reflection on our vulnerability improves our capacity to cope with evil. The point is not that we should nurture in ourselves an anticipation of disaster. We should, rather, pursue our projects with the understanding that they may fail, so that if they do fail, the shock will not exacerbate the evil that is happening to us, because there will be no shock. Part of what makes evil so hard to bear is that we also have to bear the extremely unpleasant emotions its occurrence elicits in us. Outrage, panic, resentment, humiliation, thirst for revenge, the search for someone to blame, and the obsessive scrutiny of paltry details make matters worse. Knowing and reminding ourselves that things can go wrong, before they actually do go wrong, will tend to reduce the intensity with which we respond, if things do indeed go wrong. So, reflective understanding of the possibility of evil will help by keeping our emotional reactions from adding to the burden we already have to carry.

The third way reflection helps is by forcing us to face the implications evil has for us personally. The implication of the general proposition that all human projects are vulnerable is that the same is true of our own projects. It is easy to assent to the general proposition but exempt ourselves as being somehow special, protected, or immune. Reflection on our vulnerability makes us see ourselves as one among many, with the same liabilities as everyone else. So, we learn realism not only about the human condition but reflexively about our own conditions.

Thus, reflection on the possibility that we may become victims of evil benefits us by making our expectations fit our enlarged understanding of the world. The fit is achieved by keeping our expectations realistic, our emotional reactions to undeserved failure within control, and the appreciation of the risk we personally face in the focus of attention. Unrealistic expectations are more likely to be disappointed than realistic ones. And their disappointment is likely to be much more damaging for those who are unprepared for it than for those who understand their own vulnerability. So, one reason for cultivating reflection on evil is to avoid the unrealistic expectations that stand in our way of coping with evil when we are its victims.

But we are also agents of evil because we cause it. Contingency, indifference, and destructiveness exert their forces through us, through our vices, and through the actions that express our vices. And of course, the evil we cause may affect not only others but ourselves as well. We are often both the agents and the victims of the same evil acts. I have argued throughout the book that the evil we cause may or may not be within our control. The question we shall consider next is whether it is possible to extend our control by removing some of the incapacities that prevent us from exercising choice.

My answer is that it is possible to increase our control and enlarge the scope of our choices. The possibility rests with cultivating the very same kind of reflection on evil as we found to be required for the avoidance of unrealistic expectations. Increased control requires and is made possible by reflection on evil. It involves applying the enlarged understanding of the essential conditions of life to our own particular psychological states. The crux of the matter is to endeavor to concentrate our reflection on the process whereby contingency, indifference, and destructiveness claim us as their instruments. The result of this process, if all goes well, is greater clarity about our intentions, a growing impetus to develop capacities that enable us to choose, and a better understanding of our situation. The lack of clarity, of the required capacities, and of understanding are obstacles to control. The aim of reflection is to remove these obstacles. The more we reflect, the more we shall transform ourselves from being the instruments of the essential conditions of life toward being their controllers. I remarked earlier that knowledge of the world does not make us free; I propose to amend this by arguing that reflection on the part of the world that is our inner life tends to increase our control, consequently increase our choices, and so increase our freedom.

Let us begin with the idea of internal causation. A paradigmatic instance of it is wanting something. Causation is internal if it goes on inside or on the surface of the body. The boundary of internal causation is the skin. Pain, desire, fatigue, stupidity, and love may be internal causes. A gun being pointed, the sun shining, or the request of a friend may act as causes, but not as internal ones. Of course, if we act out of fear of the gun, feel hot because of the sun, or regard ourselves as indebted to a friend, then the causation is internal.

Internal causation, then, is not without external causes. Everything we do has causes; the causes also have causes, and some are internal, some external. The distinction between them is not ontological; they do not differ in their essential properties. I am not claiming that the skin or the brain marks a break in nature. The distinction between internal and external causes is on the level of explanation. Internal causal explanations can be reasonably terminated at certain familiar points, while external causal explanations have an entirely different terminus. If we ask, Why did she open the window? the answer, She felt hot, is a satisfactory internal causal explanation. Of course, she felt hot because the temperature was ninety degrees and because human beings have a certain physiology. But we do not need to talk about all that in order to explain her action.

Internal causes may be conscious or nonconscious. We may or may not know what prompts us to think, feel, decide, or act in a certain way. My interest here is exclusively in conscious internal causes, for increased control depends on our becoming aware, through reflection, of more and more of the internal causes that motivate us. Conscious internal causes may have external or internal effects. The object of a want may be to win the approval of the world or it may be to cease caring about the approval of the world. Thus, internal causes may lead to altering the world outside of the skin or to changing some aspect of ourselves.

The kind of conscious internal causation I shall concentrate on results in altering our own psychological states. I take it as noncontroversial that there are occasions on which we reflect on some belief, feeling, or want we have, and as result of our reflection, we succeed in changing it. I may cease to believe that you are my friend if I realize the pattern of hostility formed by your actions; I may stop envying you if I come to appreciate the paltriness of what you have; I may stop wanting to smoke if I convince myself that it is harmful.

Increased control depends on the kind of causation that is internal, conscious, and whose effect is the modification of some psychological state of ourselves. And the mechanism of increased control is the reflection involved in the reflective temper. Thus, the modification brought about in this manner has a special motive: to become aware of how and when the essential conditions of life express themselves, in the first instance, by forming our psychological states and then by motivating us to act on them. My central claim is that the possibility of achieving increased control over the essential conditions of life depends on the reflective understanding of how and when these conditions motivate us. For the very act of reflection alters the psychological states that are its objects, and hence it alters their motivational force.

Let us now consider a case of increased control and see what is involved in it. Take a pattern that characterizes the relationship of a married couple. The husband has enthusiasms, and the wife dampens them. This has been going on for years. One result is that the husband becomes dispirited, life depresses him, he feels defeated, stupid, unworthy. The wife loves him, and she is saddened by these changes in him. She wishes that he were his old excitable self. She does not understand that she had a major share in making him what he is. If she had been more attentive to what she was doing and to the effects her conduct had on him, she would not have been such a wet blanket. But she was what she was; she had only that much attention for him; there was her own career, the children, and the sad state of the world. Their marriage is an imperfect union, and part of what makes it so is her insufficient attention to him. She cares, but not enough. And given her character and circumstances, she just does not have more in her to give. The world is such that for him she is the instrument of one essential condition of life: indifference.

Suppose, then, that he has a nervous breakdown. The shock forces her to reflect on what could have caused it, on what could have gone wrong. And she realizes the truth. She understands the effect her indifference has had on him. He recovers, they pick up the pieces, and they soldier on. Now consider what happens when he next shows enthusiasm to her about some project. How she responds depends on many things. But however she responds, she can no longer be a mere instrument of indifference, for she has reflected and understood that that is what she has been. So, she may dampen his enthusiasm again because, upon reflection, she still thinks that it is childish; or she may encourage it as a therapeutic measure; or she may come to share it because she has reordered her priorities.

My interest is not in what she does but in the crucial fact that reflection has given her increased control over whatever she does. For having understood what she had been doing, she introduced a new element into the psychological state that is motivating her: understanding. And that changes her motivation, not necessarily its direction, but necessarily its content. Let us suppose that her actual decision is to encourage, therapeutically, her husband's enthusiasm. There are several points we need to discuss about this case of increased control.

To begin with, her decision is made against a vast background. It includes her character, beliefs, feelings, motivation, and the like.

These constitute the internal conditions of her decision. But the background also includes external conditions, such as his character and psychological states, what the children think, the psychiatrist's recommendation, the demands of her job, and so on. What has gone into her decision is the evaluation of the pattern of her habitual response to his enthusiasm, an evaluation conducted in the light of her reflection on the external and internal conditions of the decision.

The case I am describing is one of increased control because the decision resulted from her having changed the internal conditions that partly determine her decision. She came to the conclusion, having been forced to reflect by his breakdown, that she ought to be more attentive to him. She thus came to modify her previous indifference; her self-modification changed the internal conditions of the background of her decision; and the changed background altered the connection between the cause (her awareness of his enthusiasm) and the effect (her response to it). In the past the causal chain had connected her awareness of his enthusiasm to an expression of indifference; now the connection has the same beginning, but her reflection causes it to lead to an altered effect, to concern, encouragement, and sympathy. The decision could have gone the other way, for she could have concluded upon reflection that his enthusiasms were juvenile, the marriage is not worth her energy, and that her past unthinking reactions were correct after all. In that case, the internal conditions would still have been altered, although her increased control would have resulted in the old type of action.

Decisions of the sort I have just described are episodes in all normal human lives. There are countless such episodes. One of them rarely causes significant changes in us, but episodes have a cumulative force, and they make or break our dispositions. And that does alter us significantly. To a great extent, character depends on dispositions, and dispositions in turn are similarly fostered or thwarted by episodes. So, the significance of the reflective alteration of the internal conditions of a decision is not merely that it changes that particular decision. It also tends to change us through the pattern formed of accumulated episodes. If we have the reflective temper, we realize that this is so. We shall, then, endeavor to reflect not only on what we would want to do then and there but also on the effect of doing some particular thing on the shaping and forming of our characters. We shall ask ourselves not only, What shall I do? but also, Do I want to be the sort of person who does that sort of thing? Thus, increased control has a short-term significance and also a long-term character-building one.

In the context of our discussion of increased control, the significance of reflection is that it modifies the internal conditions of the causal process and thereby modifies the causal process itself through which the essential conditions of life influence our conduct. I do not, of course, mean that reflection can change the essential conditions of life. Reflection can change only the extent to which we are instrumental in expressing the essential conditions of life through our conduct. We can, to some extent, achieve control over the evil we may cause, because we can become aware, through reflection, of our various dispositions to cause evil and, as a result, change our conduct.

Yet this reflective self-modification is itself causally explicable. The important point the possibility of increased control establishes is that it is too simple to think of the causal chain linearly, proceeding in a more or less straight line from the past to the future. Cases of reflective self-modification are, as it were, loops in causal processes, where the progression involves the process turning back and changing its own direction. The possibility increased control establishes is not the suspension of the causal process but its alteration. And what makes the alteration possible is that we can sometimes reflect on our psychological states and thereby change the internal conditions upon which the direction of the causal process depends. This is the sense in which we can be said to be able to acquire increased control over our conduct through reflection.

It would be a great mistake, however, to exaggerate the significance of reflection. It makes increased control possible, but it does not free us from the essential conditions of life. For the extent to which we are capable of reflection and the extent to which our circumstances encourage or discourage reflection are themselves dependent on the essential conditions of life. Increased control is a matter of degree. Different people have it to a different extent, and the same people have it to a different extent during different periods of their lives. The reason for this is that the external and internal conditions of our lives vary. The more reflective we become about our psychological states, up to a self-stultifying neurotic level, the more we increase our control. But how much reflection is possible for particular people in particular situations depends both on how urgently the external conditions demand response and on their characters, capacities, and wants.

Thus, the possibility of increased control does not exist in all situations and for all people. As we go further back in the lives of people, so the balance between the external and internal causes of their conduct shifts toward the external ones. Correspondingly, the extent of control they have over their conduct diminishes. The reason for this is that reflection is learned slowly in the course of physiological and psychological maturation, and learning it requires favorable circumstances. Furthermore, there are fully mature people who have diminished capacity for control because they are insane or mentally defective and lack the required degree of cognitive, emotive, or motivational powers. And even people who have the powers may not be able to exercise them because they are in hostile circumstances that leave no room for reflection. In wars, serious illness, and disasters people may find themselves unable to exercise what is normal control for them. Life in extremis is dehumanizing, precisely because it deprives us of control. It is clear, however, that, whatever our situation is, the more control we have through reflection, the more likely it is that we can avoid causing evil. And the corollary is also true: the less control we have, the more likely it is that we shall cause evil as instruments of the essential conditions of life.

Reflection makes increased control possible, and increased control enlarges the area within which we can make choices. The particular way in which reflection may accomplish this is by improving our clarity about the decisions we make, motivating us to develop and exercise capacities that make control possible, and leading us to a better understanding of our circumstances. As these obstacles are overcome, so the area of choice grows; the more choices we have, the more likely it is that we can reduce the amount of evil we cause and suffer. But this possibility should not blind us to the fact that our capacity and opportunity for reflection are not themselves matters of choice. The chances of avoiding some of the evil that besets our lives depend on the prevailing success in protecting the institutional dimension of character-morality and on the conduct of people who may have the capacity and the opportunity for reflection.

We are in the process of developing an account of the reflective temper. As we have seen, its first requirement is an enlarged understanding that brings home to us our vulnerability and reduces our expectation that reasonable and decent projects will suffice for good lives. One aim of the reflective temper is to provide an appropriate response to what our enlarged understanding reveals. My strategy for formulating such a response is to correct the mistakes of flawed responses. And the first such correction has been to replace the pragmatic attempt to ignore what we have understood with the kind of reflection I just finished describing. The significance of this kind of reflection is that it increases our control over the extent to which the essential conditions of life can claim us as victims or agents; and it does so by changing us, rather than endeavoring to do the impossible and change the essential conditions of life. Thus, the reflective temper provides the beginning of a personal response toward overcoming the hopelessness created by a full consciousness of the secular problem of evil. It shows that in the normal course of life there *is* something we can do to control at least some of the evil we may cause or suffer.

THE MOTIVATION TO INCREASE CONTROL

Reflection is necessary but not sufficient for increased control over evil. To understand that there is something we can do, if we want to, is not yet to give us the motivation for wanting to do it. Consider the reaction of reasonable people to what I have been describing as their situation. They see themselves engaged in various projects whose ultimate justification is that they bring closer to realization some ideal of a good life. They recognize that the achievement of whatever happens to be the ideal is difficult and that there is no certainty that the ideal, if achieved, will indeed be found to be as good as they have assumed when they embarked on the quest for it. But then reflection teaches them that the obstacles in their way are far greater than they have hitherto supposed. The difficulty is not merely that they have to work very hard for uncertain rewards; it is also that no matter how hard they work, the serious risk of failure is ineliminable from their lives. They are in constant danger that contingency, indifference, and destructiveness will jeopardize their projects. And part of what reflection brings home to them is that they themselves are often the sources of their own failure and of the failure of others because the essential conditions of life at least partly rule the way they conduct themselves. They will also realize that through reflection they can, to some extent, increase their control and improve the chances that they may avoid causing and suffering evil. Yet not even the improved chances amount to much, because the extent to which they are capable of exercising control over themselves is itself beyond their control, and because whether or not the control they are capable of will prove sufficient to cope with the adversity they face depends, once again, on external factors that determine the severity of the adversity. Thus, reasonable people, reflecting on their situation, may justifiably ask themselves why they should engage in the difficult struggle required for translating the possibility of control into actuality.

This is a deeply serious question, and answering it requires considering what alternative there is to the struggle. One possibility, in current slang, is to go with the flow. We have wants and the capacity to satisfy them, and instinct and training dictate that we do so. We live as long as we can, as well as we can, and we do so because we are the kinds of organisms we are. It is nature, including our nature, that suggests the appropriate response. The view implicit in this alternative correctly depicts the past and present condition of the majority of people. They struggle because they are hungry, cold, and threatened, and they aim for comfort. One should have compassion for the multitudes whose lives are like this. However, not all of us face such unrelenting adversity. Hundreds of millions are able to enjoy the benefits of civilization. For them, the primitive struggle is over. They have gained the comforts for which the less fortunate billions yearn. The point of the struggle in primitive contexts is to overcome the obstacles to living. But why should we struggle for greater control once these obstacles are overcome?

The answer is that having a comfortable life does not mean that the struggle is over; it means only that it takes less deadly forms. The threat is loss of prestige, status, self-esteem; the dangers are psychological and social. Nonetheless, these we also want to avoid. Why should we not say, then, that in primitive conditions our purpose is to attain comfort, while in civilized conditions, it is to protect and enjoy the comforts we already have. We struggle to win such prizes as our society affords and to avoid being adversely judged by the prevailing standards.

But this is a superficial answer. No doubt, in civilized conditions many people are motivated in this way. However, in these contexts there is often the opportunity to stand back and reflect. Much of this reflection is concentrated on the strategy and tactics of the struggle. Yet there is some energy left over that enables many of us to ponder life and our own lives. If we are reflective, we shall ask why we should spend our lives in whatever happen to be the socially accredited ways. We know the standards by which success is judged; we know the rewards and the costs of failure. If we are honest, at least with ourselves, we shall admit that we care about success and want to avoid failure. Reflection may prompt us to ask, however, whether we should care.

It may seem to us that the whole business we are caught up in is bogus. We see that children are indoctrinated, adolescents are goaded and guided, and adults are rewarded and penalized by the vast, impersonal, ubiquitous mold into which civilized societies press their members. And we may ask why we should put up with it. Why should we care about the emblems of success and the stigma of failure? What does it matter to us in the dark hours of a sleepless night what our neighbors, acquaintances, or colleagues think about us? They employ standards and judge by them, but we have come to doubt the standards. The attempt to achieve greater control will seem pointless, if we reflect in this way.

This is the line of thought that supports the ironic response. For the detachment that the cultivation of a nonhuman perspective provides at least allows us a bit of dignity. We shall not cease to care about our all-too-human concerns, but we shall perhaps learn to care less. We shall not be able to disown our nature, but by understanding how it motivates us, we shall be able to reduce our ardor and hence tolerate failure better than if we were blindly impelled by our ununderstood aspirations. Thus, irony goes beyond the understanding reflection provides, but it moves us in the direction of quietism. If we think, as I do, that there is something wrong with the ironic response, then the question to which it gives one answer must be answered in a better way.

The fundamental defect of irony is that it makes matters worse. For if the attitude behind it were accepted, then the prospects of a good life for the people who accepted it, and for others affected by their conduct, would be endangered even more than the essential conditions of life make it. Irony undercuts our aspiration to seek good lives; it teaches us to care less, but what we care less about are the good and evil we cause and experience. Its response to the risk of failure is to withdraw from the venture that could fail. And since all of our ventures run this risk, the more we possess the ironic attitude, the less active we shall be in trying to avoid evil and to achieve what we think of as good.

Irony is an unsatisfactory attitude because, while it does not disengage itself from the ideal of a good life, it does tend to disengage itself from doing what is possible to achieve it. The failure of irony is a failure of nerve. It is daunted by the risk that after we have done all we can to succeed, we may still fail. The reasonable reaction is not to do less to succeed but to continue to do all we can and learn to cope with failure, if it comes to us. So, people who possess the reflective temper will also be motivated to do what they can to increase their control over their lives.

The alternative to irony is an engaged life. Reasonable people will go beyond the reflective understanding of their vulnerability and be engaged because they realize that doing so provides the best chance for a good life. And the best way in which they can attempt to achieve it is by translating the possibility of control into actuality. They will want to do this because they may gain thereby increased control over the good and evil in their lives. Of course, increased control is not anything like total control; increased control does not eliminate or overcome their vulnerability; it merely reduces it by making the risk of failure smaller. Reflection will lead reasonable people to understand that their option about living a good life is either to do what they can to try to achieve it or to give up the aspiration and thereby doom themselves to the likelihood of bad lives.

The encouraging fact is that the prospect of failure carries within it curative powers. The prospect of failure is that we shall not achieve what we regard as good lives. But the more we care about failing, the stronger must our attachment be to the threatened ideal; correspondingly, the weaker is our commitment to an ideal of a good life, the less we shall care about the possibility of being prevented from achieving it. So, we have a readily available motivational spur to overcome the temptation to disengage ourselves on account of our vulnerability. The spur is the attraction of the ideal of which we care about falling short.

The psychic economy of being concerned with failure and being attracted by some ideal of a good life is that they are directly proportional to each other; hence, they are intimately connected. Concern with failure motivates us to avoid it, and commitment to an ideal of a good life brings with it concern about the vulnerability of our attempts to achieve it. The remedy to being daunted is to remind ourselves of why we find being daunted so unpleasant. What threatens our ideals is threatening because we care about our ideals. If we remember that concern when we face the prospect of failure, the prospect itself will motivate us to seek increased control.

But what if we face failure itself, and not merely its prospect? What if Oedipus, Lear, and Kurtz do not represent dangerous possibilities only, and what if we find ourselves in positions much like theirs? Well, then there is very little we can do. The great question then is how well we have prepared ourselves to cope with tragedy before it strikes. As we have seen, the preparation of the three tragic figures was inadequate because they conspicuously lacked the enlarged understanding of the essential conditions of life and the reflective response to it. It is not, of course, that any preparation could be adequate to cope with the discovery that our characters are fundamentally flawed and that our characteristic actions caused what we regard as great evil. But if we have the reflective temper, we shall understand what is happening to us, the shock of it will be less surprising and devastating, it will be less destructive of our ideals, and we shall find it less impossible eventually to go on. In any case, the primary importance of the reflective temper is not that it enables us to cope with tragedy when it happens but that it helps us to increase our control over our lives by doing what we can to avoid causing and suffering evil.

INCREASED CONTROL AND EMOTIONAL REACTIONS

We have been discussing the cognitive and motivational components of the reflective temper, but we also have emotional reactions to what an enlarged understanding reveals about life. Hope and fear, anger and resignation, denial and acceptance, pity and vindictiveness, and desire for cosmic justice and frustration at its lack also shape our conduct. The reflective temper aims at a controlled emotional reaction. And control, in this case, consists in making our feelings appropriate to the understanding of the world and our situation in it that we gain from the reflective temper.

Generally speaking, the appropriateness of feelings depends, in the first instance, on their objects being as they are believed to be. Fear is an appropriate feeling about danger; pity is a fitting response to the spectacle of undeserved suffering; acceptance is reasonable in the face of situations we are powerless to alter. This suggests that the simplest way in which feelings can be inappropriate is that they are directed toward the wrong objects. And what makes the objects wrong for these feelings is that the agents hold false beliefs about them. If what is taken to be dangerous is not, then it is a mistake to fear it; if the injury someone suffers is the result of just punishment, then pity is misplaced; if we can and wish to change an unpleasant situation, then we should not accept it. This sort of inappropriateness is easy to control because, if the falsehood of the relevant beliefs is pointed out to the agents, they themselves will be motivated to rid themselves of the feeling. If, for instance, people feel hopeless about their lives because they believe that nothing they can do could make a difference, then if they accept my argument about the possibility of increased control, their feelings of hopelessness should, at the very least, weaken.

But feelings can be inappropriate in more complicated ways. The agents may be right in their beliefs about the objects toward which the feelings are directed, but their feelings may be excessive or insufficient. Hope, resignation, desire, or frustration can be too much or too little. It may be right for an object to elicit a particular emotional reaction, but the reaction may still be wrong on account of being disproportionate. Now there is an extent to which this aberration can also be corrected by a kind of cognitive therapy. It can be pointed out to the erring agents that it is in their interests not to get things out of proportion. The objects upon which the reflective temper concentrates are not passive targets of feelings; they are our lives, we are actively engaged in living them, and our feelings about them partly determine how we live. To feel too much or too little hope, fear, pity, or desire is likely to result in the wrong responses to the objects toward which they are directed. People given to emotional excess will tend to overestimate danger, nurture false hope, allow pity to deflect them from justice, or lose balance by inflating their desires. And similarly, people lacking in feelings of the appropriate strength will tend to belittle danger, be deprived of the much-needed motivational force of reasonable hope, fail to leaven justice with mercy, and lose the satisfactions that people with clear desires may enjoy. Thus, if people are brought to see that their feelings are too strong or too weak in particular situations, then self-interest may motivate them to assert the appropriate control.

The really troublesome cases, however, are those in which the agents' feelings are inappropriate, but they do not regard them as such. The source of this mistake is a mistaken judgment. The erring agents and their critics agree about the facts; what they disagree about is the significance of the facts. If the agents were right in their judgment about the significance of the facts, their emotional reactions would be appropriate. In fact, however, they are wrong, although they think otherwise. This is the kind of mistake that is at the root of romanticism.

In order to understand this mistake, we need to understand how people would be led to make it. The problem is not merely that of understanding how people can misappraise the significance of some set of facts but the deeper one of understanding their unwillingness to accept that they have made this sort of a mistake. One explanation of their unwillingness is sentimentality.[2]

Sentimentality is always a defective response, and it is always connected with an inappropriate emotive reaction. Furthermore, the emotive reaction always involves the falsification of the object toward which it is directed. By "falsification" I mean more than holding false beliefs; it also involves taking an active part in getting wrong the relevant beliefs. So, an emotive reaction is sentimental if it is based on the agents' cultivation of false beliefs about some objects and if the falsehood of these beliefs is such as to make their objects appropriate recipients of certain feelings when in fact they are not. As we have seen, the falsehood of the beliefs is of a special kind, namely, the misappraisal of the significance of the relevant facts. Thus, sentimentality is to react to a situation by contriving to inflate the significance of some unimportant feature of it at the expense of some truly significant feature, and to do so in order to make one's emotive reaction appropriate to the object. At the root of sentimentality, there is the mistake of trying to make the world fit our feelings, rather than the other way around.

Love of one's adult son is sentimental if it is based on the faint presence of some qualities one remembers him to have possessed as

---

[2] For this account of sentimentality, I draw on Savile's discussion in *The Test of Time*, 237–45.

a child; a film, play, novel, or a painting is sentimental if it emphasizes some comforting feature of an otherwise distressing situation, like focusing on instances of altruism in death camps at the expense of the horror that surrounds these heroic episodes, or on the fun kids have in collecting shrapnel fragments in their destroyed cities; our attitude to terrorists is sentimental if it is guided by their selflessness or loyalty. Or, to return to a case in point, sentimentality is to fasten onto Polyxena's maidenly modesty as she is having her throat cut.

But not all emotions lend themselves to sentimentality. Hatred, rage, the desire for revenge, cruelty, and greed may lead to the falsification of objects, and the falsification may have the aim of making the objects appear appropriate to our feelings when they are not, and yet the result would not be properly describable as sentimentality. If memory of Nazi mass murder makes me vindictive about the ruthlessness I perceive in all the Germans I encounter, whatever my mistake is, it is not that of sentimentality.

This gives us a clue to a further characteristic of sentimentality. The falsification involved in it always makes its object appear in a more favorable light than it should. The object is idealized in the eyes of the beholder. It makes the past better than it was, some people more lovable or deserving than they are; it finds hope in gross inhumanity, heroism in miserable victims, opportunity for growth in evil. What makes this sort of falsification so insidious and so recalcitrant to criticism is that it always contains an element of truth, for the feature of the situation it concentrates on is indeed there. It is just that its presence is insignificant in comparison to what else there is. What if Hitler loved dogs, a terrorist had polio as a child, or a mafioso looks after his mentally defective child? And so we are brought back to the question of why sentimentality involves an unwillingness to correct the idealization of its objects.

The answer is that through sentimentality the agents satisfy some desire that would otherwise be likely to remain frustrated. The object of this desire may be either to feel better about oneself or to feel better about the world. And the desire to feel better about the one or the other is likely to be felt, or felt especially strongly, if the agents lack the ground for its satisfaction. The temptation to sentimentalize one's past is likely to be strong if the past casts one in a poor light; we tend to idealize victims or their persecutors if we feel helpless about redressing the imbalance between merit and desert; and one frequent source of the romantic response to the essential conditions of life is that we cannot face the hopelessness created by the prevalence of evil. The reason why sentimentalizing agents are so unwilling to correct their falsifications is that they would be brought back to the frustration they were trying to avoid through the falsification. They do not want to feel badly about themselves or about the world, so they are strongly motivated not to see what they are doing as falsification.

Thus, the prospects of breaking through the sentimentality that nourishes romanticism are not encouraging. Unlike pragmatism and irony, romanticism is not open to the argument that the interests these attitudes were thought to serve would be better served by abandoning them. For the view of the world and of our situation in it to which romanticism responds with sentimentality is indeed bad enough, so the attempt at idealization is readily understandable. Once the attempt has become habitual and it comes to form a permanent component of the character of its agents, it is very hard to dislodge it. Arguments against it will be deflected, and contrary motives will be strong. Its agents may even agree that there is something wrong with romanticism. Nevertheless, they will be likely to go on to deny that what they are doing is an instance of it.

Understood in this way, romanticism is the most formidable obstacle to facing evil. It is one emotive source of the soft reaction to evil, for it nourishes the mistaken assumptions upon which the soft reaction rests. Belief in the essential goodness of human nature falsifies what we know about ourselves by emphasizing our virtues and underplaying our vices. Belief in equal human worth falsifies the readily available evidence that the lives and conduct of many people are dominated by insufficiency, expediency, malevolence, and other vices, and it leads to the absurd judgment that such people have the same worth as those who are generally strong, principled, and benevolent. Belief in choice being necessary for the appropriateness of moral judgments falsifies the extent to which we can control what we are and do by inflating the influence of our will and intellect at the expense of the causal forces of tradition, training, and inheritance. All these falsifications are idealizations. They make us appear in a better light than we should see ourselves; they mislead by making our situation seem more hopeful than it is. Thus, the falsifications of romanticism fuel false hope.

But false hope is not merely a harmless solace that people in difficult circumstances may cultivate and enjoy. False hope is harmful because it stands in the way of facing evil. It deceives us into believing that evil is not as formidable an obstacle to good lives as it is. And the harm that comes from that belief is that it undermines the motivation to increase, insofar as we can, our control over evil. The emotive component of the reflective temper aims at preventing that from happening.

This prevention has the best chance of succeeding at a particular period during moral growth. It should happen after we have acquired the enlarged understanding and the capacity and willingness to reflect on its implications, but before romanticism can set in. This is a period of life when we have understood both that our best chance of coping with evil is to increase the control we have and that not even increased control is sufficient to guarantee a good life. Yet we are motivated to seek increased control because we realize, at least intellectually, that doing so improves our chances, while not doing so diminishes them. But this intellectual motivation is not enough, because our feelings are also involved. And it is at this point, at the relation between our intellectual resolve to seek increased control and our feelings that are consonant or dissonant with that resolve, that the harm caused by romanticism can be best avoided. For here there is a possibility of avoiding dissonance between our reflective understanding and how we feel about what we have understood.

It is natural to feel frustration, anger, resentment, fear, disappointment, rebelliousness, sadness, or some mixture of these and other emotions when we understand our situation. It is appropriate to feel in these ways because the threat of evil is considerable and we cannot do as much as we would like to do about it. But this is also something that we can understand, and understanding it changes the situation. While we cannot control what feelings we have, we can control how large a role they play in motivating us. And the reasonable policy is to allow them to move us only when they are consonant with our understanding of evil and with our intellectual motivation to avoid it. These feelings may prove too strong, especially if evil is not merely a daunting prospect but something actually upon us, and then the reasonable policy fails. The most we can do is to try to avoid its failure by holding in the focus of our consciousness that our feelings cannot change the evil we face. Our best chance of avoiding evil is still to increase our control, including control over the feelings that falsify our situation. And this is what those who have the reflective temper can do better than those who lack it.

THE REFLECTIVE TEMPER: AN OVERVIEW

The account of the reflective temper is now complete. The benefit derivable from its possession is increased control over ourselves. And increased control is desirable because by exercising it we can reduce the amount of evil we cause and improve our capacity to cope with the evil we suffer.

The reflective temper is a combination of four components. The first is *an enlarged understanding of the essential conditions of life*. This embraces the understanding of how contingency, indifference, and destructiveness jeopardize human aspirations in general and our personal aspirations in particular. Furthermore, it makes us realize that the essential conditions of life often exert their influence through us, that we ourselves are often the agents who jeopardize human aspirations, including our own. The second component of the reflective temper is *a particular kind of reflection*. The aim of it is to modify our own psychological states and thereby control the actions that follow from them. It involves teaching ourselves to understand what motivates us. This understanding necessarily modifies the psychological state that is its object because the understanding changes the state from having a nonconscious to a conscious motivational force. Consciousness makes control possible, but it does not guarantee that control will be exerted. So, we come to the third component of the reflective temper, *the motivation to increase control over ourselves*. If we are reasonable, we understand that our aspiration to live a good life has a better chance of realization with increased control than without it. But we also understand that not even increased control removes our vulnerability because both the amount of control we can exercise and the chances of succeeding, given our control, depend on the essential conditions of life over which we have no control. We are bound to have emotional reactions to this. The fourth component of the reflective temper is *the capacity to restrain our emotional reactions* so that we shall not be led by them to falsify our situation and thus to respond to it inappropriately.

The reflective temper is the personal dimension of character-morality. But character-morality also has an institutional dimension. Both are necessary for good lives because the institutional prohibitions against evil cannot succeed unless people are personally motivated to abide by the prohibitions, and because the development of the reflective temper requires the institutional support of a hospitable moral tradition and education in it.

The basis of the modest hope to which I think we are entitled is that it is possible to develop character-morality in the directions I have been advocating. Its development requires, first, facing and avoiding evil, my chief concern in this book, and second, the approximation of good through doing what is possible to help people make good lives for themselves.

CHAPTER TWELVE

Character-Morality and Our Sensibility

CHARACTER-MORALITY AS A RESPONSE TO THE SECULAR PROBLEM OF EVIL

We began with the question of how our sensibility should respond to the secular problem of evil. It is fitting that we should come back to that question now that the answer I propose has been given. Our sensibility is decisively influenced by the Enlightenment. It rejects supernatural explanations in favor of scientific ones, it regards humanity as part of the natural world, and it holds that the goodness of our lives depends on the control we exercise over them.

The tragic view of life is a challenge to our sensibility, not because it calls into question its explicit beliefs, but because it casts doubt on the assumption implicit in it that our control is sufficient to make our lives good. The source of this doubt is that our attempts at exercising control are themselves influenced by the conditions we attempt to control. That this is so is a consequence of humanity being part of the natural world. We are vulnerable to the conditions that prevail. And our vulnerability is due not merely to inhospitable external conditions but to the presence of these conditions in our own makeup. This means that the extent to which we can control our lives is itself beyond our control and that the control we do have may not be exercised in order to make our lives good. The challenge presented by these ominous thoughts is the secular problem of evil, and it is a problem for our sensibility, much the same way as the traditional problem of evil is a problem for Christianity.

As a response to the secular problem of evil, I have proposed character-morality. The guiding ideal of character-morality is that people should get what they deserve. And what that is depends on the good and evil they have caused, or, in short, on their moral merit. But the achievement of this ideal is impossible because of the essential conditions of life, the scarcity of our resources, and the difficulty of establishing proportionality between merit and desert. These obstacles cannot be removed; they can only be made less formidable. Yet making them so is necessary for good lives; consequently, we have no reasonable alternative to doing what we can to approximate the ideal. Character-morality embodies not only this ideal and the reason for pursuing it but also prescriptions about how the pursuit should proceed.

The most fundamental of these prescriptions is that we should face evil. This involves the recognition that there are certain basic requirements of human welfare and that depriving people of them, without an acceptable moral justification, constitutes simple evil. Thus, simple evil is an objective fact of life. It follows from the objectivity of simple evil that what counts as such is independent of whether or not the agents causing it had a choice. And it is a further consequence of the objectivity of simple evil and of the irrelevance of choice to its status that if people habitually cause simple evil, then this must reflect adversely on their moral merit, even if their habitually evil-producing actions were unchosen. Facing evil requires reasonable people to regard patterns of evil-producing actions as evidence for vices in their agents and to regard agents dominated by vices as evil.

This requirement is rejected by choice-morality. The attitude of its defenders to evil results in the soft reaction. Underlying the soft reaction to evil, there are the three false assumptions that the appropriateness of moral judgments depends on the presence of choice, that all human beings have the same worth independently of their moral merits, and that human nature is basically good and evil is a corruption of it. If these assumptions were true, then it would be a mistake to allow unchosen actions to reflect on the moral standing of their agents or to suppose that evil actions could diminish human worth or to think that the capacity for evil is as fundamental to human nature as the capacity for good.

In fact, however, many of our morally relevant actions are the unexamined consequences of our characters, rather than the results of choices, and the choices themselves reflect the characters of the choosing agents. So, character is far more important to the assignment of appropriate moral judgments than choices. Moral agency does not uniquely depend on the choices we make, but on our capacity to perform both chosen and unchosen actions that cause good and evil. The role of moral judgment is to evaluate moral achievement by considering the actual good and evil we caused. Thus, what is central to moral judgment is the assignment of moral desert, and this may involve the distribution of both deserved benefits and deserved harms. Consequently, moral desert depends on moral merit, and since moral merit varies, it is justifiable to treat people with different moral merits differently. The justification of unequal treatment is strengthened by human nature embodying potentialities for both good and evil. Thus, our nature is mixed, and either potentiality may come to dominate the other. People dominated by their evil potentialities have less worth than those who are motivated by good potentialities. These theses give content to character-morality and form the justification of the hard reaction to evil.

Character-morality has an evil-avoiding and a good-producing aspect. The argument concentrated almost exclusively on the former, but of course a full account of the requirements of living a good life would have to include both. In its evil-avoiding aspect, character-morality stands as a bulwark between barbarism, where nothing is prohibited, and civilization, where we are guided by the imperfectly realizable ideal that the benefits and harms that come to people should be deserved. One indispensable element of civilization is the existence and enforcement of deep prohibitions that protect the minimum requirements of good lives. The reason why simple evil is such a serious threat is that it violates deep prohibitions and thereby not only causes undeserved harm to particular people but also undermines the general conditions required for all good lives. The hard reaction to evil requires us to face this fact, as well as the fact that the causes of evil are usually quite unexceptional people, often acting without much thought or effort, in ways that have become characteristic of them; more disturbing still, these people may include ourselves. Facing evil, as the hard reaction does, is necessary for avoiding it, and avoiding it requires tracing evil from the frequently unchosen actions that cause it to the vices of which the actions are the results, and from them to the characters in whom the vices achieved dominance. Given this account of the origin of much evil, the question is what we can do about it.

The answer of character-morality is that we can maintain and improve the institutions designed for avoiding evil and that we can increase our control over our conduct by developing the reflective temper. One main purpose of the institutional dimension of character-morality is to make conduct conforming to deep prohibitions intuitive. The desirable condition to aim at is that the vast majority of people living together in a society should unhesitatingly identify many specific actions as violations of deep prohibitions and therefore regard them as out of bounds. Such conduct is reasonable because deep prohibitions protect us from simple evil and thus establish the minimum requirements of good lives. But it is not necessary for people whose conduct is guided by moral intuitions to know that this is so or to be able to provide the justification, if challenged. The simple moral conduct involved in observing deep prohibitions is often unreflective, habitual, and unquestioningly accepted. Of course, not all moral situations are simple, intuitions are fallible, and changing conditions or internal defects may require the reinterpretation of deep prohibitions to protect us from new forms simple evil may take. And so we are led to the personal dimension of character-morality.

The institutional dimension of character-morality influences moral agents in one direction; the essential conditions of life exert their influence in the opposite direction. The first fosters our aspirations to live good lives; the second hinders them. The conflict between them gives rise to the secular problem of evil, and the aim of the personal dimension of character-morality is to develop in moral agents the reflective temper as a response to it. The reflective temper brings us to recognize that the control we have over our lives is limited and that the key to avoiding evil is to increase our control. We can do this by understanding that the essential conditions of life act through us and thus make us into agents of evil; by developing our capacity to reflect on and thus modify our psychological states, thereby gaining better control over the actions that follow from them; by motivating us to seek increased control because we understand that it gives us a better chance to make our lives good than any other policy; and by learning to control our emotional reactions to understanding that even if we do everything we can, our lives may still not be good.

We are not entitled to the hope nourished in their different ways by the Socratic ideal and the Enlightenment. Living and acting reasonably and decently are not sufficient for good lives, because the world is not made for us; it is not hospitable to our aspirations, and our control is insufficient to impose ourselves on it. Yet our situation is not as hopeless as the tragic view of life implies. We are not completely at the mercy of forces we cannot control. We have some control, and we can often increase the control we have. As we do that, so we improve the human prospect. This possibility is the ground for the modest hope that is reasonable to have.

CHARACTER-MORALITY AND CHANGES IN OUR SENSIBILITY

The relation between character-morality and our sensibility is complicated. Part of the reason for this is that while our sensibility is committed to favoring scientific explanation over supernatural beliefs, regarding humanity as part of the natural world, and to connecting good lives to the amount of control we have, this leaves room for much disagreement about the implications of these basic commitments. Indeed, this is illustrated by the conflict between character- and choice-morality, between the hard and the soft reactions to evil. Furthermore, while character-morality certainly accepts the basic commitments of our sensibility, it also conflicts with some of the less basic ones. So, there is no simple answer to the question I now propose to discuss of what changes in our sensibility does character-morality require.

Let us approach this question by recalling that the aim of character-morality is to enable people to make good lives for themselves. It is commonly supposed by many of those who share our sensibility that the best way to realize this aim is to remove impediments from the path of human endeavor. Thus, they suppose that the task of morality is to foster social arrangements in which poverty, crime, disease, exploitation, and injustice will be overcome. Their tacit assumption is that if external obstacles do not stand in the way, then people will conduct themselves reasonably and decently. Consequently, they regard freedom and equality as the most important social values. Freedom aims at overcoming the obstacles to doing what we want, and equality aims at a fair distribution of the remaining obstacles and of the resources needed to overcome them. Of course, disagreements remain even among those who regard freedom and equality as the most important social values, but their disagreements concern policies for achieving freedom and equality. The current controversies among and between utilitarians, Kantians, and contractarians largely concern such questions. Nevertheless, advocates of these theoretical positions undoubtedly articulate one interpretation of some of the implications of the basic commitments of our sensibility.

Character-morality regards this interpretation as mistaken. The trouble with it is not that freedom and equality are not important social values, nor is it that we should not do the best we can to overcome such external obstacles to good lives as poverty, crime, disease, and all the rest. The trouble is that this interpretation rests on the false assumption that if external obstacles are overcome, then people will act reasonably and decently. I have argued throughout the book that people often cause evil, not because they have been corrupted by external influences, but because they are motivated by such vices as insufficiency, expediency, and malevolence. The effort to guarantee freedom and equality generally, without regard to how individuals may conduct themselves in possession of these enabling values, will actually increase the amount of evil with which we have to cope and, consequently, undermine our aspirations to live good lives. Thus, if we abandon this false assumption, we must realize that the importance we assign to freedom and equality must take account of the evil that may be caused if they are enjoyed without restriction. But to recognize the need for curtailing freedom and equality is to recognize that they cannot be the sole important social values. The avoidance of evil is at least as important as they are. One main change that character-morality aims to produce in our sensibility, therefore, is to focus the general attention on evil and thereby on the need to curtail freedom and equality in order to avoid evil.

In trying to understand and describe this proposed change, the distinction between the evil-avoiding and the good-producing aspects of character-morality is crucial. The former is concerned with enforcing the deep prohibitions that enable people to make good lives for themselves; the latter aims at providing the external and internal goods and developing the character traits needed to achieve them. Freedom and equality are indeed among the most important values of the good-producing aspect of character-morality, for we need freedom to work for the goods and develop ourselves, and we also need equality to guarantee a fair distribution of burdens and resources. But freedom and equality are much less valuable in the context of the evil-avoiding aspect of character-morality, for there should be no freedom to violate deep prohibitions against murder, torture, enslavement, mutilation, and so on, and there should not be an equal distribution of burdens and resources between those who violate deep prohibitions and those who uphold them.

It is perhaps clear now that the origin of the misinterpretation that shapes our sensibility in the wrong way is the tendency to concentrate on the good-producing aspect of morality and to ignore or underemphasize the importance of the evil-avoiding aspect. This is an understandable tendency, because it is much more pleasant to concentrate on human potentialities for excellence than on the potentialities for baseness. But the optimism, exuberance, and affirmation of the sunny side of life that are the glories of the good-producing aspect of morality are made possible only by the pessimism, censoriousness, and control of the dark side of life that inform the evil-avoiding aspect of morality. Facing evil is the attempt to redirect our sensibility so that it recognizes and keeps in the focus of its attention the importance of the currently neglected evil-avoiding aspect.

RIGHTS AND MORAL MERIT

Let us now consider some of the ways in which this proposed redirection would affect our sensibility. One of the ways is that the appeal to rights would have to make room for the relevance of moral merit. Thus, the idea that rights are inalienable, indefeasible, or imprescriptible would have to be abandoned. It is not, of course, that anyone really believes that people should not be deprived of their rights under any circumstances, for the rights of soldiers, mental patients, criminals, and children are routinely and justifiably curtailed. The idea is rather that the rights of all individuals should be protected unless there are acceptable reasons for violating them. And so the debate about how to protect rights shifts to the question of what would justify violating them. The implications of this shift are considerable.

To begin with, it follows from this view that rights are not absolute, a conclusion that must be obvious to thoughtful people in any case. This ought to have an effect on the sometimes pious, sometimes shrill rhetoric that permeates so much of our public discourse. People can be, are, and ought to be forced to compromise their lives, liberty, property, and pursuit of happiness under certain circumstances. What, then, are these circumstances? Is there some general principle that could help in identifying them? I think there is. Rights aim to protect the minimum conditions of good lives. Their violation is justified if, and only if, it is required in order to protect the minimum conditions of good lives. Thus, killing enemy soldiers in a just war, imprisoning criminals, declaring the insane to be incompetent, paternalistically overruling the wishes of children are all justified in the same way: these violations of rights are required to protect the minimum conditions of good lives.

By and large, justifiable violations of rights fall into two classes. The first includes justifications based on the inability of people to use the protection afforded by rights to make good lives for themselves. Children and the insane are such people. The second class, however, is far more relevant to understanding how moral merit should curtail rights. This class includes people whose rights are violated because they themselves have or are about to violate the rights of others. The many forms of self-defense, both individual and social, are cases in point. Thus, the rights of terrorists, murderers, rapists, and the like are deservedly violated in order to protect the rights of their actual or unambiguously intended victims. In this way moral merit may become relevant to rights.

But there is more to this than the mere recognition that rights may be justifiably violated on the grounds of moral merit. There is also the question of where the burden of justification lies. Is it that rights should always be presumed to hold, and is it their violations that require justification? I think that the answer depends on the context in which the question arises. Clearly, in the context of the good-producing aspect of morality, where deep prohibitions are generally observed and the prevailing moral, political, and legal system is effective in enforcing them, the presumption is in favor of rights, and the burden of justification lies on their violators. But there is also the evil-avoiding context. When societies or individuals face evil enemies who have demonstrated their evil intentions in the past and are prepared to act on them in future, then the burden shifts. The question becomes: why should the rights of these evildoers be protected so that they can continue to undermine the conditions in which people in general can endeavor to make good lives for themselves? It is not unreasonable or morally suspect to pose the question thus about Hitler's Germany, Idi Amin's Uganda, Khomeini's Iran, or Qaddafi's Libya or about terrorists of various ideological coloring, wholesale drug dealers, or large criminal organizations. The fact is that in evil-avoiding contexts the protection of rights requires the violations of the rights of rights violators, and it is destructive of the rights whose protection is the goal not to do what is necessary to protect them.

Of course, to shift the burden of justification, as we concentrate on evil-avoiding contexts, does not mean that the violation of rights should be automatically justified. It means that the question should be posed differently and the issue of justification should be debated in a different way. In evil-avoiding contexts, the question should not be, How can we protect rights, including those of terrorists, drug dealers, and mass murderers? The question should rather be, Is this a justifiable violation of the rights of evildoers? Nor should the debate about justification focus on the good that protection of rights may produce; it should focus on the evil that violation of rights may prevent. The reason for these shifts is that avoiding evil is a precondition of good lives, and the rights required for making good lives must first be protected before they can be used. The present state of our sensibility, however, is opposed to these shifts. The assumption underlying the opposition is that people will use their rights reasonably and decently. That assumption, however, comes from the very unwillingness to face evil that character-morality aims to overcome.

In proposing this change in our sensibility, it has not been my intention to offer a social or a political program. Such a program would require a careful consideration of how existing institutions would have to be revised and what safeguards would be needed to prevent injustice. My intention has rather been to show the need for a program and to give some reasons why our sensibility should move in the direction of recognizing the need.

PSYCHOLOGIZING AND FACING EVIL

To "psychologize" is to bring in psychological considerations when they are irrelevant or to exaggerate the importance of psychological considerations and thereby respond inappropriately to some situation. Our sensibility is shot through with the tendency to psychologize about evil, and this is one of the obstacles to facing evil. The second way in which character-morality aims to redirect our sensibility is to reduce the amount of psychologizing we do about evil.

Let us begin by considering a disanalogy in the responses our sensibility prompts to good and evil. Suppose that we are the recipients of a great and unexpected act of kindness, generosity, conscientiousness, or self-sacrifice. We accept it; we benefit from it; we are surprised, grateful, and appreciative. We do not, however, make it part of our response to speculate about our benefactor's motives. It would be unseemly to do so, for the search for motives would testify to our suspicion that there was more to the good deed than meets the eye. The disinclination to psychologize about the motives of good private deeds also holds for our response to people who are widely regarded as secular saints. Few people probe the motives of Einstein, Schweitzer, Eleanor Roosevelt, Martin Luther King, or Mother Teresa, for to do so is to cast doubt on their moral achievements. However, we respond otherwise to evil deeds. If someone treats us in a particularly cruel, mean, unjust, or malicious way, our sensibility leads us to try to understand what motives led the person to injure us. The action offends us beyond the injury it causes, and we want to know why anyone would do such a thing. And the same goes for public figures. We want to understand very much indeed why Charles Manson or Adolf Eichmann did the horrible things they did. Our sensibility makes us feel that good deeds and people are to be cherished, but evil deeds and their agents cry out for an explanation. Why is this so?

The answer is that our sensibility regards evil as an anomaly. Conspicuous good deeds and people are unusual, but they do not require any special explanation, for, our sensibility suggests, they merely do better what the rest of us would do if we were not deterred from it. But evil is a disruption of the pattern and thus stands in need of explanation. And the explanation must be in terms of whatever it was that corrupted the agents and made them deviate from the pattern. Good deeds are evidence for human excellence, but we call evil deeds inhuman, and we wonder why their agents act contrary to human nature. Thus, we look at the motivation of evil-producing agents not merely to understand them but to remove the anomaly that threatens to undermine the assumption of our sensibility that the pattern of human conduct tends toward the good and that evil is a deviation from it.

One consequence of this assumption is the epidemic of specious speculation about human motivation that assails our systems of criminal justice, welfare, and education, as well as literature, soap operas, editorials, television commentaries, and the daily conversations of casual acquaintances. We domesticate evil; we make it acceptable and thus less threatening by attempting to understand it as a glitch. We tend to think that there is the usual, normally benign process of motivation, deliberation, and action, but then something intrudes, interferes with the process, and produces the defective result, much as dirt in the fuel tank may disrupt the operation of a car. So, we strive to understand what it was that intruded, and once we can tell an intelligible story, we feel better because we suppose ourselves to have understood what has gone wrong. And then we generalize. We say that it is understandable for that person to have acted in that way, and we mean that people in general would tend to act in that way in that sort of situation. The effect of seeing particular evil actions under the aspect of such generalizations is to weaken the link between the evil acts and their agents. The agents are seen merely as placeholders, the individuals who happened to be on the spot, and, we say, most of us would have acted that way had we been in that position.

I shall not dwell on the intellectual shoddiness of such speculations about motives. It will suffice to note that normally the facts appealed to are uncertain, the number and strength of influences that form a particular person are incalculable, the explanations offered are untestable, there are no control groups, there is no effort to consider people in similar circumstances who have acted differently, there is no search for alternative explanations, and if there happened to be several incompatible explanations, there is no way of deciding about their respective merits. The trouble is not just that psychologizing is based on disreputable thinking. After all, there is a lot of such thinking around, and few of us feel the need to inveigh against astrology, creationism, faith healing, or transcendental meditation. But psychologizing with the object of explaining evil is in a different class because it is an active force preventing our sensibility from facing evil.

The salient fact about evil actions is that they cause undeserved harm. They damage people, often grievously, and they jeopardize our aspirations to live good lives. That is why evil actions matter. The first thing we should do is to hold this firmly in our minds. The next step is to understand that evil actions are rarely exceptional episodes in otherwise benign lives. They are the predictable results of vices people have, and there are some people who are dominated by their vices. Evil people and vices are not anomalies but the commonplaces of moral life. That is why there are so many evil actions. Once we have taken these two steps, we can go on to the third and consider what we can do about evil actions, vices, and evil people. I have argued that the best we can do is to develop the institutional and personal dimensions of character-morality.

After we have done all this, we may, if we are inclined that way, consider the motivation of people who cause evil. But if our interest is in minimizing evil, this must be seen as a distinctly subordinate question. Understanding human motives cannot lead to a revised judgment about some action being evil or some character trait being a vice or some person ruled by vices being evil. For the judgment about something being evil depends on whether it causes undeserved harm and not on understanding the causes behind the causes of undeserved harm. Of course, there are such causes, and I see no reason why improved thinking, although not the present psychologizing, could not lead to discovering them. But the discovery cannot change the fact that some actions, character traits, and people cause undeserved harm and that, consequently, they are evil.

Thus, the second way character-morality would change our sensibility is to persuade us to abandon the assumptions that evil is an anomaly and that if we were to understand its source, then it would become somehow less harmful. In place of these false assumptions, by way of facing evil, character-morality would substitute, first, the recognition that evil is an unavoidable and standard feature of life and, second, the policy of developing institutions and ourselves so as to minimize evil as much as we can.

Relativism and the Objectivity of Evil

It is widely, but by no means unanimously, accepted by those who share our sensibility that there is no summum bonum, no such thing as a best life for human beings. Let us call this view *pluralism*. Pluralists believe that morality makes different types of claims on moral agents. These claims appeal to duties, rights, virtues, personal ideals, the general welfare, particular conceptions of good lives, and so on. Moral agents recognize the force of these claims because they regard their satisfactions as, in some sense, good. But the goods are qualitatively different; they support different types of moral claims; and they are not reducible to each other, because they are incommensurable. That is to say, there is no privileged type of good in terms of which all other types of goods are analyzable; there is no canonical ranking of various types of goods, so that one type would always take justifiable precedence over the others; and there is no neutral medium in terms of which different types of goods could be compared. The reason pluralists give against there being a summum bonum is that there are many ways of ordering and balancing various incommensurable goods in a single human life. As a result, human lives can be good in many different ways. The error of those who suppose that there is a summum bonum is to regard some particular arrangement of goods as superior. I think that pluralists are right, although I have not discussed the merits of their case here. The reason I broach the topic now is that there is a tendency in our sensibility to go on from pluralism to relativism, which constitutes another obstacle to facing evil.

Relativists suppose that one consequence of the incommensurability of goods is that the lives that aim to embody some particular arrangement of goods are also incommensurable. If this were so, it would be unjustifiable to direct moral criticism against any internally consistent way of life. There being no neutral medium, no canonical ranking, no privileged goods, the criticism of one way of life would have to come from the point of view of another way of life, and this would involve an unjustifiable appeal to standards that are rejected by those who are judged by them. Thus, according to relativists, there are different ways of life, different moral traditions, and different conceptions of good lives, and while moral criticism internal to them is possible and may even be important, external moral criticism is a sign of dogmatism, intolerance, and a noxious imperialism that attempts to impose alien standards on unwilling subjects. Following this line of thought, relativists see themselves as champions of alternative cultures, religions, and attitudes to life, sex, work, time, politics, and so on. I doubt that it is necessary to describe further this familiar component of our sensibility.

However, before we allow ourselves to be swamped by the rhetoric, we should remember that infanticide, child prostitution, suttee, female circumcision and footbinding, rampant disease, starvation and poverty, high rates of infant mortality and low life expectancy, tribal warfare, the caste system, the subhuman status of women, the prevalence of torture, the mutilation of criminals, wife and child beating, intolerance of other forms of life, financial corruption, and political instability are also parts of other forms of life. Is it really true that external moral criticism of these evils is always illegitimate? Should we, in the name of tolerance, tolerate obvious evil? Is it reasonable to suppose that if some practice or institution is an accepted and traditional part of a way of life, then outsiders cannot reasonably condemn them? Of course, many people, avowing the loftiest principles, suppose just that, and this is yet a third way in which our sensibility leads many of us to refuse to face evil and thereby encourage it.

The reason why the progression from pluralism to relativism is illegitimate is that it involves disregarding the objectivity of simple evil. Relativists are committed to holding that evil depends on what is so regarded in a particular form of life. If a society, culture, or individual genuinely does not think that something is evil, then it is not. But this is an untenable view. Evil is undeserved harm. There are some things that are harmful for all people, always, everywhere; as we have seen, human welfare has certain minimum physiological, psychological, and social requirements. Violations of these requirements are what I called simple harms. It makes no difference to something constituting a simple harm what moral views are held by its agent or by its victim. Furthermore, whether the simple harm people suffer is undeserved also has a context-independent answer: it is undeserved if there is no acceptable moral justification for inflicting it. And the only acceptable moral justification is that by inflicting some simple harm, greater simple harm is avoided. The ground of this moral justification is commitment to the fundamental goal of morality: promoting human welfare. If that goal is shared, then reasonable people cannot avoid the conclusion that some things count as undeserved simple harms, and thus they count as simple evils. Consequently, relativism about simple evil is mistaken.

Of course, not all evil is simple, and there are also goods. Complex evils and goods do vary with conceptions of good lives. If this were all relativists asserted, then their position would be indistinguishable from pluralism. But relativists go beyond pluralism, and at the heart of their case is the supposed illegitimacy of external moral criticism. Such criticism can be justified, however, if its target is simple evil. Societies, cultures, and individuals can be legitimately compared on the ground of their propensity to cause simple evil, or, to put it the other way, on the ground of their performance in protecting the minimum requirements of human welfare. Thus, we can say that some cultures, societies, or individuals are morally better or worse than others because they cause less or more simple evil. There is, therefore, no good reason for the prevalent reluctance manifested by many people who share our sensibility to criticize some tradition, institution, way of life, or practice on account of the simple evil it causes. And there is a very good reason to offer such criticisms, for if we are committed to promoting human welfare, then we must be opposed to simple evil. Moral criticism is an expression of this commitment.

The implication of the objectivity of simple evil extends beyond the falsehood of relativism. It provides the foundation for the rejection of psychologizing about evil and for the limitation of rights by moral merit. For it is the objectivity of simple evil that makes its occurrence independent of the motives of people who cause it. The questions of whether something is a part of the minimum requirements of human welfare, whether it has been violated, and whether its violation avoids greater harm can all be answered without knowing anything about the agents' beliefs, intention, or choices. Similarly, the question of whether it is justifiable to limit the rights of particular individuals is to be answered by considering the moral merits of the individuals in question. And their merits depend, in part, on the amount of simple evil they have caused in the past and are likely to cause in the future. It is in this way that commitments to rights, psychologizing, and relativism form an intricately connected, mutually reinforcing attitude that pervades our sensibility and stands as an obstacle to facing evil. The remedy is to juxtapose the objectivity of simple evil to these evasive stratagems. Thus, underlying the various ways in which character-morality would change our sensibility there lies its central concern with facing evil.

THE TRUE CENTER OF CHARACTER-MORALITY

Character-morality is a view about how to promote human welfare. Human welfare requires the maximization of good and minimization of evil. I have concentrated on the secular problem of evil, whose significance is that we ourselves are one of the most formidable obstacles to minimizing evil. This being so, we must accept the view that it is unreasonable to extend a blanket approval to all forms of human endeavor. Allegiance to the party of humanity requires that we should view human aspirations critically because some of them are evil.

If we so view them, we must conclude that moral inequality is part of the human condition. Our characters and circumstances are different, and they lead us to have lives of unequal moral merit. We differ in the amount of evil we cause. Our moral merit depends primarily on the amount, and only secondarily on how much we contributed to making our characters and circumstances such as they are.

Our sensibility has an equivocal reaction to the central fact of life that we may have no control over the evil we cause. It has been influenced by Christianity to hope for supernatural help, and it has also been influenced by the Enlightenment, the intended successor of Christianity, to repose hope in human reason and decency. The Enlightenment is correct in its view that we can depend only on ourselves, and Christianity is correct in its view that we are weak vessels. But the secular problem of evil brings home to us the groundlessness of the different kinds of hope each goes on to offer. If we turn back to the view of life the great Greek tragedians suggest, we are left without any hope at all, for they show the insignificance of the control we have over our lives. Our sensibility has an equivocal reaction to evil because it veers among these influences, as well as among the pragmatic, ironic, and romantic ones that, in their different ways, attempt to evade facing evil.

This is the background against which character-morality should be understood. Its central intention is to work out a response to the secular problem of evil that avoids both false hope and hopelessness, faces evil, and yet holds out the prospect of a reasonable and modest hope. The key to such a hope is to increase the limited control we have over our lives by developing the appropriate institutions in our society and the reflective temper in ourselves.

Works Cited

Adams, Robert M. "Involuntary Sins." *Philosophical Review* 94 (1985): 3–31.

Adkins, Arthur W. H. *Merit and Responsibility*. Oxford: Clarendon Press, 1960.

Aeschylus. *Oresteia: Agamemnon, The Libation Bearers, The Eumenides*. Translated by Richmond Lattimore. In *The Complete Greek Tragedies: Aeschylus I*, edited by David Grene and Richmond Lattimore. Chicago: University of Chicago Press, 1969.

———. *Prometheus Bound*. Translated by David Grene. In *The Complete Greek Tragedies: Aeschylus II*, edited by David Grene and Richmond Lattimore. Chicago: University of Chicago Press, 1969.

Annas, Julia. "Personal Love and Kantian Ethics in *Effi Briest*." *Philosophy and Literature* 8 (1984): 15–31.

Arendt, Hannah. *Eichmann in Jerusalem: A Report on the Banality of Evil*. New York: Viking Press, 1964.

Aristotle. *Nicomachean Ethics*. Translated by William David Ross and revised by John O. Urmson. In *The Complete Works of Aristotle*, edited by Jonathan Barnes. Princeton: Princeton University Press, 1984.

———. *Poetics*. Translated by I. Bywater. In *The Complete Works of Aristotle*, edited by Jonathan Barnes. Princeton: Princeton University Press, 1984.

———. *Politics*. Translated by Benjamin Jowett. In *The Complete Works of Aristotle*, edited by Jonathan Barnes. Princeton: Princeton University Press, 1984.

———. *Rhetoric*. Translated by W. Rhys Roberts. In *The Complete Works of Aristotle*, edited by Jonathan Barnes. Princeton: Princeton University Press, 1984.

Barry, Brian. *Political Argument*. London: Routledge, 1965.

Becker, Lawrence C. *Reciprocity*. New York: Routledge, 1986.

Beehler, Rodger. *Moral Life*. Oxford: Blackwell, 1978.

Benn, Stanley I. "Wickedness." *Ethics* 95 (1985): 795–810.

Bennett, Jonathan. "Accountability." In *Philosophical Subjects*, edited by Z. van Straaten. Oxford: Clarendon Press, 1980.

Bradley, A. C. "Hegel's Theory of Tragedy." In *Hegel on Tragedy*, edited by Anne Paolucci and Henry Paolucci. New York: Harper & Row, 1962.

Brandt, Richard B. "The Psychology of Benevolence and Its Implications for Philosophy." *Journal of Philosophy* 73 (1976): 429–53.

Brown, James. "Moral Theory and the Ought-Can Principle." *Mind* 86 (1977): 206–23.

Campbell, C. A. "Moral Intuitions and the Principle of Self-Realization." In C. A. Campbell's *In Defence of Free Will*. London: Allen & Unwin, 1967.

Cioffari, Vincenzo. "Fortune, Fate, and Chance." In *Dictionary of the History of Ideas*, edited by Philip P. Wiener. New York: Scribner's, 1973.

Conrad, Joseph. *Heart of Darkness.* In *Great Short Works of Joseph Conrad.* New York: Harper & Row, 1967.

Cooper, John M. "Aristotle on the Goods of Fortune." *Philosophical Review* 94 (1985): 173–96.

———. *Reason and the Human Good in Aristotle.* Cambridge: Harvard University Press, 1975.

Davis, Lawrence H. *Theory of Action.* Englewood Cliffs, N.J.: Prentice-Hall, 1979.

Dworkin, Ronald. *Taking Rights Seriously.* Cambridge: Harvard University Press, 1971.

Euripides. *Hecuba.* Translated by William Arrowsmith. In *The Complete Greek Tragedies: Euripides III,* edited by David Grene and Richmond Lattimore. Chicago: University of Chicago Press, 1969.

———. *Helen.* Translated by Richmond Lattimore. In *The Complete Greek Tragedies: Euripides II,* edited by David Grene and Richmond Lattimore. Chicago: University of Chicago Press, 1969.

———. *Hyppolitus.* Translated by David Grene. In *The Complete Greek Tragedies: Euripides I,* edited by David Grene and Richmond Lattimore. Chicago: University of Chicago Press, 1969.

———. *The Medea.* Translated by Rex Warner. In *The Complete Greek Tragedies: Euripides I,* edited by David Grene and Richmond Lattimore. Chicago: University of Chicago Press, 1969.

Falk, W. David. "Morality, Self, and Others." In *Ethics,* edited by Judith Jarvis Thomson and Gerald Dworkin. New York: Harper & Row, 1968.

Feinberg, Joel. "Justice and Personal Desert." In *Nomos VI: Justice,* edited by Carl J. Friedrich and John W. Chapman. New York: Atherton, 1963. Reprinted in Joel Feinberg's *Doing and Deserving.* Princeton: Princeton University Press, 1970.

Fischer, John M., ed. *Moral Responsibility.* Ithaca: Cornell University Press, 1986.

Flew, Anthony. "Tolstoi and the Meaning of Life." *Ethics* 74 (1963): 110–18.

Fontane, Theodor. *Effi Briest.* Translated by D. Parmee. Harmondsworth: Penguin, 1967.

Foot, Philippa. "Moral Beliefs." In Philippa Foot's *Virtues and Vices.* Berkeley: University of California Press, 1978.

Frankena, William. *Perspectives on Morality.* Edited by K. E. Goodpaster. Notre Dame: University of Notre Dame Press, 1976.

Frankfurt, Harry G. "Freedom of the Will and the Concept of a Person." In Harry G. Frankfurt's *The Importance of What We Care About.* Cambridge: Cambridge University Press, 1988.

———. *The Importance of What We Care About.* Cambridge: Cambridge University Press, 1988.

French, Peter, et al., eds. *Ethical Theory: Character and Virtue.* Midwest Studies in Philosophy, vol. 13. Notre Dame: University of Notre Dame Press, 1988.

Galston, William A. *Justice and the Human Good.* Chicago: University of Chicago Press, 1980.

Gert, Bernard. *The Moral Rules*. New York: Harper & Row, 1973.

Gewirth, Alan. *Reason and Morality*. Chicago: University of Chicago Press, 1978.

Gowans, Christopher W., ed. *Moral Dilemmas*. New York: Oxford University Press, 1987.

Grice, G. A. "Moral Theories and Received Opinion." *Proceedings of the Aristotelian Society*, supp. vol. 52 (1978): 1–12.

Hampshire, Stuart. "Freedom of Mind." In Stuart Hampshire's *Freedom of Mind*. Oxford: Clarendon Press, 1972.

———. *Freedom of the Individual*. New York: Harper & Row, 1965.

———. *Morality and Conflict*. Cambridge: Harvard University Press, 1983.

———. "Spinoza and the Idea of Freedom." In Stuart Hampshire's *Freedom of Mind*. Oxford: Clarendon Press, 1972.

———. *Thought and Action*. London: Chatto & Windus, 1960.

———. *Two Theories of Morality*. Oxford: Oxford University Press, 1977.

Hare, Richard M. "Nothing Matters." In Richard M. Hare's *Applications of Moral Philosophy*. London: Macmillan, 1972.

Hill, Thomas E., Jr. "Kant's Argument for the Rationality of Moral Conduct." *Pacific Philosophical Quarterly* 66 (1985): 3–23.

Hofstadter, Albert. *Reflections on Evil*. Lawrence: University Press of Kansas, 1973.

Hook, Sidney. "Intelligence and Evil in Human History." In Sidney Hook's *Pragmatism and the Tragic Sense of Life*. New York: Basic Books, 1974.

———. "Pragmatism and the Tragic Sense of Life." In Sidney Hook's *Pragmatism and the Tragic Sense of Life*. New York: Basic Books, 1974.

———. *Pragmatism and the Tragic Sense of Life*. New York: Basic Books, 1974.

Hume, David. *An Enquiry concerning the Principles of Morals*, edited by L. A. Selby-Bigge. Oxford: Clarendon Press, 1961.

———. *A Treatise of Human Nature*, edited by L. A. Selby-Bigge. Oxford: Clarendon Press, 1960.

Irwin, Terrence H. *Plato's Moral Theory*. Oxford: Clarendon Press, 1977.

———. "Reason and Responsibility in Aristotle." In *Essays on Aristotle's Ethics*, edited by Amelie Rorty. Berkeley: University of California Press, 1980.

Kalin, Jesse. "The Intent of Romanticism: Kant, Wordsworth, and Two Films." *Philosophy and Literature* 9 (1985): 121–38.

Kant, Immanuel. *Critique of Practical Reason*. Translated by Lewis White Beck. Chicago: University of Chicago Press, 1949.

———. *Critique of Pure Reason*. Translated by Norman Kemp Smith. London: Macmillan, 1953.

———. *Groundwork of the Metaphysics of Morals*. Translated by Herbert James Paton. New York: Harper & Row, 1964.

———. *The Metaphysical Principles of Virtue*. Translated by J. W. Ellington. Indianapolis: Hackett, 1983.

———. *Prolegomena to Any Future Metaphysics*. Translated and revised by Lewis White Beck. New York: Liberal Arts Press, 1950.

Kant, Immanuel. *Religion within the Limits of Reason Alone*. Translated by Theodore M. Greene and Hoyt H. Hudson. New York: Harper & Row, 1960.

Kavka, Gregory. *Hobbesian Moral and Political Theory*. Princeton: Princeton University Press, 1986.

Kekes, John. *The Examined Life*. Lewisburg, Pa.: Bucknell University Press, 1988.

―――. "Freedom." *Pacific Philosophical Quarterly* 61 (1980): 363–83.

―――. *Moral Tradition and Individuality*. Princeton: Princeton University Press, 1989.

Kenny, Anthony. *Aristotle's Theory of the Will*. New Haven: Yale University Press, 1979.

Kivy, Peter. "Melville's *Billy* and the Secular Problem of Evil: The Worm in the Bud." *Monist* 63 (1980): 480–93.

Knox, Bernard M. W. *The Heroic Temper: Studies in Sophoclean Tragedy*. Los Angeles: University of California Press, 1964.

Korsgaard, Christine M. "Kant's Formula of Universal Law." *Pacific Philosophical Quarterly* 66 (1986): 24–47.

―――. "The Right to Lie: Kant on Dealing with Evil." *Philosophy and Public Affairs* 15 (1986): 519–43.

Kruschwitz, Robert B., and Robert C. Roberts, eds. *The Virtues*. Belmont, Calif.: Wadsworth, 1987.

Kupperman, Joel. "Vulgar Consequentialism." *Mind* 89 (1980): 321–37.

Kurtz, Paul W. *Transcendental Temptation: A Critique of Religion and the Paranormal*. Buffalo, N.Y.: Prometheus Press, 1986.

Larmore, Charles E. *Patterns of Moral Complexity*. Cambridge: Cambridge University Press, 1987.

Lawrence, David Herbert. *Selected Essays*. Harmondsworth: Penguin, 1950.

Leavis, Frank R. *Lectures in America*. New York: Pantheon, 1969.

―――. "Tragedy and the 'Medium.' " In Frank R. Leavis's *The Common Pursuit*. London: Hogarth Press, 1984.

Louden, Robert B. "Can We Be Too Moral?" *Ethics* 98 (1988): 361–78.

Lovejoy, Arthur O. *The Great Chain of Being*. New York: Harper, 1960.

MacIntyre, Alasdair. *After Virtue*. Notre Dame: University of Notre Dame Press, 1981.

―――, ed. *Revisions*. Notre Dame: University of Notre Dame Press, 1983.

Mackie, John L. "Morality and the Retributive Emotions." *Criminal Justice Ethics* 3 (1982): 1–9.

Mason, H. A. *The Tragic Plane*. Oxford: Clarendon Press, 1985.

Matson, Wallace I. *Sentience*. Berkeley: University of California Press, 1976.

Midgley, Mary. *Wickedness*. London: Routledge, 1984.

Mill, John Stuart. *On Liberty*, edited by Elizabeth Rapaport. Indianapolis: Hackett, 1978.

Miller, David. *Social Justice*. Oxford: Clarendon Press, 1976.

Milo, Ronald D. *Immorality*. Princeton: Princeton University Press, 1984.

Mossman, Elliott, ed. *The Correspondence of Boris Pasternak and Olga Friedenberg, 1910–1954*. Translated by Elliott Mossman. New York: Harcourt Brace Jovanovich, 1982.

Nagel, Thomas. "The Absurd." In Thomas Nagel's *Mortal Questions*. Cambridge: Cambridge University Press, 1979.

———. "Moral Luck." *Aristotelian Society Proceedings*, supp. vol. 50 (1976): 115–35.

———. *The Possibility of Altruism*. Oxford: Clarendon Press, 1970.

———. *The View from Nowhere*. New York: Oxford University Press, 1986.

Nehamas, Alexander. *Nietzsche: Life as Literature*. Cambridge: Harvard University Press, 1985.

Nietzsche, Friedrich. *The Birth of Tragedy*. In *Basic Writings of Nietzsche*, translated and edited with commentaries by Walter Kaufmann. New York: Random House, 1968.

Norton, David L. *Personal Destinies*. Princeton: Princeton University Press, 1976.

Nozick, Robert. *Anarchy, State, and Utopia*. New York: Basic Books, 1974.

Nussbaum, Martha. "Consequences and Character in Sophocles' *Philoctetes*." *Philosophy and Literature* 1 (1976): 25–53.

———. "Flawed Crystals: James's *The Golden Bowl* and Literature as Moral Philosophy." *New Literary History* 15 (1983): 25–30.

———. *The Fragility of Goodness: Luck and Ethics in Greek Tragedy and Philosophy*. Cambridge: Cambridge University Press, 1986.

———. "Serpents in the Soul." Unpublished.

Olafson, Frederick A. "Moral Relationships in the Fiction of Henry James." *Ethics* 98 (1988): 294–312.

Paolucci, Anne, and Henry Paolucci, eds. *Hegel on Tragedy*. New York: Harper & Row, 1962.

Paton, Herbert James. *The Categorical Imperative*. London: Hutchinson, 1947.

Pincoffs, Edmund L. *Quandaries and Virtues*. Lawrence: University Press of Kansas, 1986.

Plato. *The Republic*. Vol. 1 in *The Dialogues of Plato*. Translated by Benjamin Jowett. New York: Random House, 1937.

Platts, Mark. *Ways of Meaning*. London: Routledge, 1979.

Quinton, Anthony. "Tragedy." *Aristotelian Society Proceedings*, supp. vol. 34 (1960): 145–65.

Rawls, John. "The Basic Structure as Subject." *American Philosophical Quarterly* 14 (1977): 159–65.

———. "The Independence of Moral Theory." *Proceedings and Addresses of the American Philosophical Association* 48 (1974–1975): 5–22.

———. *A Theory of Justice*. Cambridge: Harvard University Press, 1971.

Rescher, Nicholas. *Ethical Idealism*. Berkeley: University of California Press, 1987.

Richards, Ivor A. *The Principles of Literary Criticism*. New York: Harcourt, Brace & Jovanovich, 1961.

Rorty, Richard. "Intuition." In *The Encyclopedia of Philosophy*, 4:204–12, edited by Paul Edwards. New York: Macmillan, 1967.

Ross, William David. *The Foundations of Ethics*. Oxford: Clarendon Press, 1939.

———. *The Right and the Good*. Oxford: Clarendon Press, 1930.

Rousseau, Jean-Jacques. *Emile*. Translated by Barbara Foxley. London: Dent, 1986.

Sandel, Michael J. *Liberalism and the Limits of Justice*. Cambridge: Cambridge University Press, 1982.

Savile, Anthony. *The Test of Time*. Oxford: Clarendon Press, 1982.

Schopenhauer, Arthur. *The World as Will and Representation*. Translated by E.F.J. Payne. New York: Dover, 1969.

Shakespeare, William. *Coriolanus*. In *The Complete Works of William Shakespeare*, edited by W.J. Craig. London: Oxford University Press, 1954.

———. *King Lear*. In *The Complete Works of William Shakespeare*, edited by W. J. Craig. London: Oxford University Press, 1954.

———. *Macbeth*. In *The Complete Works of William Shakespeare*, edited by W. J. Craig. London: Oxford University Press, 1954.

———. *Othello, the Moor of Venice*. In *The Complete Works of William Shakespeare*, edited by W. J. Craig. London: Oxford University Press, 1954.

Sher, George. *Desert*. Princeton: Princeton University Press, 1987.

Shklar, Judith N. *Ordinary Vices*. Cambridge: Harvard University Press, 1984.

Sidgwick, Henry. *The Methods of Ethics*. 7th ed. Indianapolis: Hackett, 1981.

Silber, John R. "The Ethical Significance of Kant's *Religion*." In Immanuel Kant's *Religion within the Limits of Reason Alone*, translated by Theodore M. Greene and Hoyt H. Hudson. New York: Harper & Row, 1960.

Silk, Michael S., and Joseph P. Stern. *Nietzsche on Tragedy*. Cambridge: Cambridge University Press, 1981.

Smart, John J. C., and Bernard Williams. *Utilitarianism: For and Against*. Cambridge: Cambridge University Press, 1973.

Smith, Holly. "Culpable Ignorance." *Philosophical Review* 92 (1983): 543–71.

Sophocles. *Ajax*. Translated by John Moore. In *The Complete Greek Tragedies: Sophocles II*, edited by David Grene and Richmond Lattimore. Chicago: University of Chicago Press, 1969.

———. *Antigone*. In *The Three Theban Plays*. Translated by Robert Fagles. New York: Viking, 1982.

———. *Electra*. Translated by David Grene. In *The Complete Greek Tragedies: Sophocles II*, edited by David Grene and Richmond Lattimore. Chicago: University of Chicago Press, 1969.

———. *Oedipus the King*. In *The Three Theban Plays*. Translated by Robert Fagles. New York: Viking, 1982.

———. *Philoctetes*. Translated by David Grene. In *The Complete Greek Tragedies: Sophocles II*, edited by David Grene and Richmond Lattimore. Chicago: University of Chicago Press, 1969.

———. *The Women of Trachis*. Translated by Michael Jameson. In *The Complete Greek Tragedies: Sophocles II*, edited by David Grene and Richmond Lattimore. Chicago: University of Chicago Press, 1969.

Steinbock, Bonnie, ed. *Killing and Letting Die*. Englewood Cliffs, N.J.: Prentice-Hall, 1980.

Stephen, James Fitzjames. *Liberty, Equality, Fraternity*, edited by R. J. White. Cambridge: Cambridge University Press, 1967.

Strawson, Peter F. "Freedom and Resentment." In Peter F. Strawson's *Freedom and Resentment*. London: Methuen, 1974.

———. *Individuals*. London: Methuen, 1959.

Taylor, Charles. "Responsibility for Self." In *The Identities of Persons*, edited by Amelie Rorty. Berkeley: University of California Press, 1976.

Unamumo, Miguel de. *Tragic Sense of Life*. Translated by J. E. Crawford Flitch. New York: Dover, 1954.

Vlastos, Gregory. "Justice and Equality." In *Social Justice*, edited by Richard B. Brandt. Englewood Cliffs, N.J.: Prentice-Hall, 1962.

Wallace, James D. *Virtues and Vices*. Ithaca: Cornell University Press, 1978.

Walsh, Vivian Charles. *Scarcity and Evil*. Englewood Cliffs, N.J.: Prentice-Hall, 1961.

Warnock, Geoffrey J. *The Object of Morality*. London: Methuen, 1971.

Wasserman, Joseph. *The Maurizius Case*. Translated by C. Newton. New York: Carroll & Graf, 1985.

Watson, Gary. "Responsibility and the Limits of Evil." In *Responsibility, Character, and the Emotions*, edited by Ferdinand Schoeman. New York: Cambridge University Press, 1987.

———, ed. *Free Will*. New York: Oxford University Press, 1982.

Wiggins, David. "Truth, Invention, and the Meaning of Life." In David Wiggins's *Needs, Values, Truth*. Oxford: Blackwell, 1987.

Williams, Bernard. "Moral Luck." *Proceedings of the Aristotelian Society*, supp. vol. 50 (1976): 115–35.

Wolgast, Elizabeth. *The Grammar of Justice*. Ithaca: Cornell University Press, 1987.

———. "Intolerable Wrong and Punishment." *Philosophy* 60 (1985): 161–74.

Wollheim, Richard. *The Thread of Life*. Cambridge: Harvard University Press, 1984.

Wood, Allen W. *Kant's Moral Religion*. Ithaca: Cornell University Press, 1970.

Zaitchik, Alan. "On Deserving to Deserve." *Philosophy and Public Affairs* 6 (1977): 371–88.

Index

absurdity, 192–93
action, 91–92, 94–95, 99, 103
Adkins, Arthur W. H., 93n.13
Aeschylus, 37nn. 9 and 10, 41n.17
anthropocentrism, 194–95
Arendt, Hannah, 4n.3
Aristotle, 13, 32, 33, 34, 39, 91, 125, 151, 197
Aristotelian scheme, 169–70, 174, 176
autonomy, 128–40

Barry, Brian, 60n.11, 61n.14
Becker, Lawrence C., 63n.18
Beehler, Rodger, 143n.19
Benn, Stanley I., 86–87
Bennett, Jonathan, 71n.5
Brandt, Richard B., 60n.10
Brown, James, 92n.12

Campbell, C. A., 167n.1
catharsis, 39–40
character, 91–92, 93–94, 103, 104–5, 155, 164, 224
character-morality, 3, 9–10, 140–62, 223–37; versus choice-morality, 91–99, 166, 224; and deep prohibitions, 172–81, 225, 228; and desert, 55–65; and egalitarianism, 106–23; and emotional reactions, 216–21; and the essential conditions of life, 146–49, 205–22; and hard reaction, 122, 146–62, 225; and hope, 202–22; ideal of, 149–54, 163, 179, 188, 223; institutional deminsion of, 9, 10, 163–81, 226, 237; versus irony, 192–95, 203–5, 205–13; minimum content of, 55, 65–66, 103; and moral intuition, 167–79, 225; nine theses of, 9, 10, 154–56, 164; personal dimension of, 9, 10, 181, 182–222, 226; and pluralism, 233–34; and pragmatism, 190–92, 203–5, 205–13; and prohibitions, 165–81; and the reflective temper, 202–22, 225–26, 237; versus relativism, 233–36; versus romanticism, 196–200, 204–5, 218–21; and

the secular problem of evil, 4, 146–49, 223–26; versus sentimentality, 218–21; and simple evil, 50–55; versus the Socratic ideal, 27–30, 150–51; thesis of first, 53–54, 103, 155; thesis of second, 54, 103, 155; thesis of third, 54–55, 103, 155; thesis of fourth, 104, 155; thesis of fifth, 104–5, 155–56; thesis of sixth, 105, 156; thesis of seventh, 106, 156; thesis of eighth, 123, 156; thesis of ninth, 142–45, 156; versus the tragic view of life, 9, 182–83, 185–90, 202–3, 223; two aspects of, 157–61, 228–30
choice, 49–50, 54, 61, 67–71, 91–92, 93–94, 99, 103, 104, 106–8, 155, 180, 185–86, 212
choice-morality, 7, 183; assumption of first, 7–8, 88, 89–102, 124; assumption of second, 8, 88, 106–23, 124; assumption of third, 8–9, 88, 128–45; versus character-morality, 91–99, 166, 224; and soft reaction, 6–8, 85–105, 122, 147–49, 224
Christianity, 4, 27–28, 125, 143, 223, 236
Conrad, Joseph, 24, 25, 37, 47
contingency, 5, 11, 21–23, 29, 33, 36–37, 39, 42, 45, 64, 66, 69, 74–75, 107, 146, 149, 158, 183–90, 200, 203, 207, 222
control, 9, 83, 146–47, 151, 180–81, 182–222
Cooper, John M., 13n.5
corruption, 124–28, 144–45
cosmic justice, 23–24, 187–88

Davis, Lawrence H., 67n.1
deep prohibitions, 172–81, 225, 228
desert, 9, 10, 55–65, 96–105, 115–17, 147, 150–54, 156, 164, 223
destructiveness, 11, 24–25, 29, 33, 36–37, 39, 42, 45, 64, 66, 69, 82–83, 107, 146, 149, 158, 183–90, 200, 203, 207, 222
determinism, 70–71

Printed in the United States
46075LVS00005B/122